Art and Audacity

T. J. Honeyman

Art
and Audacity

Collins
St James's Place, London, 1971

William Collins Sons & Co Ltd
London · Glasgow · Sydney · Auckland
Toronto · Johannesburg

First published 1971
© T. J. Honeyman 1971

ISBN 0 00 211046 6

Set in Monotype Perpetua
Made and Printed in Great Britain by
William Collins Sons & Co Ltd Glasgow

For my wife

Contents

List of Illustrations

Preface

When I was privileged, in 1968, to give the first W. A. Cargill
Memorial Lecture at the University of Glasgow, with the title
'Patronage and Prejudice', some of my splendid audience said or
wrote 'What about making a book of Memoirs?' I was told also that
autobiography is a modern industry in which no one need be
unemployed.

I have known for a long time that the very heart of a conversation
is the man who talks. What he says may or may not be important.
Who or what he is cannot be withheld. Therefore, for rhetorical and
other reasons, I beg to intimate that for ten years I practised the Art
and Science of Medicine, for ten years I was a dealer in Works of
Art, and for fifteen years, for better or worse, in sickness and in
health, I was head of affairs at the Glasgow Art Gallery and Museum.

This is the story of the Fifteen Years. If it is difficult to read or
hopelessly dull, believe me, it was not easy to write. Indeed, I could
not get on with the job because of so many demanding interruptions.
So! I packed a suitcase with relevant 'raw material' and went off on
a voyage to the Pacific to make this book.

I invite you to go sailing with me.

Acknowledgments

I am grateful to a number of folks who are fond of doing good turns for people who have a job in hand. Among them are Mrs Jo Leggat, Miss Isobel Mackintosh, Messrs Harry McLean, Rupert Roddam and William Wells; and, especially, Robert and Colin Clark.

To the various Galleries and private collectors my thanks are due for authority to reproduce works in their possession.

A very kindly, tolerant and most helpful editor, who has given this production its elegant appearance, may, with his colleagues, elect to remain anonymous behind the publisher's imprint. They can never be that to me.

I

The Background

On 1st April 1939 the following advertisement appeared in a number of Scottish and English newspapers and journals:

CORPORATION OF GLASGOW

ART GALLERY AND MUSEUM DEPARTMENT

The Corporation invite applications for the position of Director of Art Galleries and Museums. The salary fixed for the position is £800 rising to £1,200 per annum by increments of £100 every two years with free house and coal.

Applicants must be over thirty and under fifty years of age, must possess a thorough knowledge and experience of art and must be prepared as one of the duties of the position to deliver lectures on various branches of art as the Corporation may require.

The appointment will be during the pleasure of the Corporation. Applicants must give details of qualifications, training and experience with three testimonials and references of three persons of position, and they may, if they please, send 24 copies of their application and testimonials.

Twenty-two people applied. Glasgow's advertisement, with the unusual 'must be prepared as one of the duties of the position to deliver lectures on various branches of art as the Corporation may require' had attracted some excellent candidates. They could not have been thinking of the emoluments. One later became Director of the National Gallery in London; another became Director of the National Gallery in Edinburgh, and a third went to the top post in Manchester. Some had Museum or Art Gallery experience. Others, like myself, thought we could fill the post through reliance on other qualifications. C. M. Grieve (Hugh McDiarmid) had a shot at it. We had been together on the staff of the 42nd General Hospital in Salonika in World War I. I often wondered how he would have tackled the job. Poetry in Scotland would have suffered, but as a dynamic personality he might have stirred things up. I remember on a special occasion attending a conference aimed at starting an Academy of Scottish Art and Letters. My contribution to the discussion was 'What's the use of having Christopher Grieve in anything like this? He always resigns.' 'It is a lie' came back the defiance. 'I get expelled.'

Eventually I was appointed – by the skin of my teeth. The recommendation of the Committee was reached by the casting vote of the Chairman, or Convener, as they say in Glasgow.

But it was not all as simple as that. A brief account of some of the events leading to my application is a necessary preface to what follows. Put in the form of questions these might be: What was the state of the climate in Glasgow Art circles? Why the unusual course of searching, by advertising, for someone not already in the service of the Corporation? What were my qualifications?

On the face of it a degree in Medicine is not precisely the kind of University preparation for directing a large and important civic enterprise. My interest in art and artists had its beginnings in 1909, the same year in which I matriculated as a student of medicine. Loyalties were apparently divided, for I also enrolled in an evening class for drawing in the Glasgow School of Art. Fra Newbery, the Director, welcomed me with great cordiality. I think he had visions of a course of classes in art being added to the medical curriculum. I let him down rather badly, not only by indifferent performances but by becoming conspicuous mainly through a weakness for discussing art instead of getting on with the job of trying to produce it. Then I met Duncan Macdonald, who was a very junior assistant in Davidson's, an active art dealing establishment in Sauchiehall Street. The premises were near Hope Street. W. B. Simpson, before he struck out on his own in St Vincent Street, was manager at Davidson's. Although he never showed any outward signs of it, he must often have cursed my tendency to haunt the place in order to persuade Macdonald that we were both in need of coffee and relaxation in Miss Cranston's elegant Charles Rennie Mackintosh-designed tea-room (now incorporated in Daly's, a leading Sauchiehall Street department store).

Macdonald and I were fellow-members of the choir in Cowcaddens Church to which our respective families had become attached through their devotion to the Rev. William Ross, a leading Scottish churchman of his day. Subsequent ministers included the Rev.

James Robertson, known as the singing minister. Sometimes he would treat us to sermons and Bible-readings in braid Scots. One of his sons was the kenspeckle, bearded Doctor Tom Robertson, who practised homoeopathy in the west-end of Glasgow and whose hobbies ranged from playing the fiddle to an authoritative publication, *Human Ecology*. Another son is the well-known TV commentator, J. Fyfe Robertson.

I must, of course, admit that my qualifications for choir member-ship were entirely imaginary. Macdonald may have been more decorative, but neither of us could do much more than keep in tune with the melodies of the popular psalms and hymns. When the organist was tempted to expand the repertoire or venture on an anthem, he regarded each of us as a menace.

As entertainers *qua* reciters we certainly thought we were the 'cat's pyjamas' or the 'snake's hips' – two phrases which, I think, had just come in as part of the currency of extravagant appreciation. Duncan favoured the Scottish comic stuff like *Mrs McLeerie* or *Wee Johnnie Paiterson*. He had one dramatic number, the title of which I forget, but the punch line, uttered in grim, sepulchral tones, was 'Take the lantern with you, child, and lead your father through the snow'. My party piece was a choice from *Gunga Din*, *Lasca* and *The Green Eye of the Little Yellow God*. Further recollections of the period, immediate pre-1914 World War, would seem to suggest that someone must have given the Romantic Movement a very powerful emetic.

In the midst of this varied and busy existence, we still maintained contact with each other, and after World War 1 collected the threads of our earlier friendship. By this time he had joined the Edinburgh firm of Aitken Dott and, like myself, was safely and happily married. It was at his wedding in St Giles Cathedral in Edinburgh that I met Patrick Geddes, although it was some time later, after a course of Lewis Mumford, when I became more fully aware of how great a man he was. If only he had been given a free hand to do with our cities what ought to have been done!

My education in art appreciation proceeded very slowly. I became a very humble patron and gradually passed from an interest in etchings to colour. To purchase some oil paintings, chiefly to furnish the walls of a larger house, seemed essential and Duncan helped me to achieve some bargains. In 1925 he joined McNeill Reid, whose grandfather had founded the business of dealers in works of art in the middle of last century. Actually the real founder of the firm, which became part of the art history of Glasgow, was McNeill's father. I had met him once or twice and exchanged smiles, but I never really knew him. Very occasionally when I saw something exciting in the window at West George Street I might go in, very nervously, for it was regarded as a place fit only for the rich. It was when Macdonald joined the firm that I became a more frequent visitor. By this time Alexander Reid had retired. He died in 1928 – at the age of seventy-three – one year before I left medicine for art.

Before he had completely retired from business, old Reid had reached the conclusion that art dealing in a big way was likely to peter out in Scotland. The family businesses which had produced fortunes for their owners were being turned into public companies, and in many cases the control was passing to London. The new generation of wealthy families was either not interested in art or was often in London with more leisure than it could find in Glasgow to look at pictures. Consequently, there came about a collaboration with the Lefevre Gallery in London and a new name for the firm, Alex. Reid & Lefevre. Macdonald moved to London and McNeill Reid continued to hold the fort in Glasgow. To maintain the physical well-being of himself and his family he took the risk of appointing me to the post of family physician. Indeed, my final obstetric engagement was to introduce his younger son into this exciting world.

I have never been able to discover if McNeill's private opinion of my medical accomplishments was in any way related to the invitation to abandon the profession and join Macdonald and him in the adventure of art dealing.

It was not an easy decision to make. I got a lot of advice. Two men, a surgeon and an artist, gave the best counsel. 'What does your wife say? You face an interesting adventure and you ought not to do it alone.' The artist was James McBey. He was in Scotland doing some portraits and when I said 'yes' to McNeill's invitation in the North British Hotel, McBey sketched the 'conspirators' from an adjoining table. He also offered to make my first 'show' an exhibition of his water-colours. That was in September 1929. It was a remarkable success. I was on the point of concluding that the art dealing business was an easy and pleasant way to make a living. Then, in October of the same year the economic slump hit the whole world.

Thereafter it was, for a few years, not at all easy but never un-interesting and frequently stimulating.

Having become an art dealer I had to become interested in the private and public patrons of Art. It was part of my job to find them or make them. Similarly, I thought it essential to know something about the history of my new profession. A number of people – collectors, critics and dealers in Scotland, London and Paris, in extending a welcome would say 'I knew old Reid. He was a great character. A man of personal taste, and with the courage to back it.'

I heard plenty of complimentary references but had the utmost difficulty in getting precise information. From time to time, aided by McNeill Reid and Sir William Burrell, I would pick up some fresh anecdote to help me to lend colour to newspaper articles on Whistler, Van Gogh or the Glasgow School, with whom it was possible to establish some links.

I waded through the firm's old books and files, hoping to find something of value. But it looked as if Alex Reid had done a lot of tidying up before his retiral. I knew that he had parted with his correspondence with Whistler. The fact is recorded by Neil Munro in *The Brave Days*. Like many another father, Reid senior was not very communicative in his replies to Reid junior's questioning about the early days in Paris, London and Glasgow. If he had left fuller records we should have had, among other things, an accurate account of his association with Whistler. The friendship, before the inevitable break, must have been close, for the McNeill in Reid junior's name derives from Whistler, who was his godfather.

I had dug out the references to Reid in the three volume edition of Vincent Van Gogh's letters to his brother Theo. I was also greatly helped in further research by D. S. MacColl, at one time Director of the Tate Gallery, who happened to be trying to extract information from McNeill Reid when I was engaged on the same enquiry. MacColl had first met Alex Reid in 1892, when, in conjunction with Arthur Collie, in a gallery in New Bond Street, he had an exhibition of paintings. Reid described himself as 'Directeur de la Société des Beaux Arts' (that was still the decorative title of the firm until 1926) and the exhibition was described as 'Pictures by the great French Impressionists'. No pictures were sold. Two years later, Reid took MacColl to Degas's studio in Paris. He was one of the few for whom the door was always open.

It is, however, the Van Gogh link with Alex Reid which I find most interesting. Unfortunately, there is no very full or direct record of their association, beyond the evidence that Van Gogh did two or three portraits of Reid.

When the *De la Faille* catalogue was published in 1928 McNeill Reid identified two of the numerous 'self-portraits' as portraits of his father. When compared with other portraits of Van Gogh the confusion is easy to understand. The likeness between the two men is quite remarkable. McNeill Reid was able to acquire his father's portrait from the artist's nephew, Theo's son, in whose possession it had remained throughout the intervening years.

There are over a dozen passages referring to Reid in the Van Gogh letters. Taken together – the critical, the suspicious, and the friendly – they show that the two men must have lived close to each other and shared experiences in more than one adventure.

It was through Theo that Reid met Vincent and, for reasons of economy, they decided to share rooms. Each of them had his special troubles. Vincent was constantly out of funds. Reid was out of favour with his sweetheart. One day, Reid unburdened himself to his room-mate who gallantly suggested a suicide pact. This appeared to Reid as altogether too drastic a solution and, as Vincent continued with the gruesome preparations, he decided to make himself scarce.

From the Vincent-Theo correspondence it is clear that Van Gogh does not place much reliance on the ways of dealers. He counsels Theo, who spent his entire adult life as an art dealer, to be on his guard and to keep a special eye on Reid. Vincent had apparently become irritated because Reid, as a partner in the enterprise to introduce the works of Monticelli and the Impressionists into Britain, had become over-cautious. The reaction of potential patrons was an unknown quantity and against Vincent's idea of direct purchase. Reid favoured business on a commission basis. One is able to gather that Vincent was greatly interested in all that was going on in the art dealing world. His earlier years at the Hague and in London and Paris had left him with definite theories about art dealing as well as about art, and he frequently expounded these with considerable violence. Later he writes:

'How often I think of Reid when I am reading Shakespeare, and how often I have thought of him while I was worse than I am now. Thinking that I was infinitely too hard on him and too discouraging when I claimed that it was better to care for the painters than for the pictures.'

Van Gogh and Reid had conflicting views on the question 'Is the artist more important than the picture?' It may be that they had an argument, although there is no record of it, when Reid nearly broke himself financially by purchasing Manet's 'Le Bon Bock' for £250. Everybody was talking about it, but nobody but Reid was prepared to buy it. Incidentally he had to keep it two years before he found a purchaser, and it appeared again in an exhibition in London in 1923. That was the year in which French painting, following on the Barbizon School, really began to be accepted in Britain. The Grafton Gallery exhibition and Roger Fry's enlightened propaganda had stirred up an amazing and bitter brew of opposition, but with a few exceptions, some in Scotland, collectors had been too timid. There were five exhibitions – three in London, one in Manchester and one in Glasgow.

It was round about this time I first began to be aware of the importance of these French paintings, but my knowledge of the history of the various artists and schools – the Impressionists and Post-Impressionists – was very sketchy. In London in 1912, my citadel of appreciation was the National Gallery. Anything outside of that was revolution, and in art I was a conformer. The first time I saw Wyndham Lewis's *Blast* was in an Edinburgh studio and I dismissed it and all associated with it as beneath contempt. As late as the early Twenties the work of Leslie Hunter and Peploe (two Scots artists now being highly valued) had meant nothing to me. I first met Hunter in 1924 and I think it was due more to him than to any other individual that I began to do my own thinking. He, and of course Peploe and Fergusson, were among the first of the enthusiasts, but I remember earlier conversations with Stuart Park. He was a popular painter of flower paintings and the last man, one would have thought, to have any sympathy for the 'moderns'. It was he who told me that Cézanne, Van Gogh, Gauguin were the greatest of the new 'Old Masters' and that Matisse, Picasso, Bonnard and Dufy were the greatest among the living. I thought he was pulling my leg.

The lease of the West George Street gallery in Glasgow expired, and, in accordance with previously arranged procedure, we moved to London. The Lefevre Gallery was then in King Street, St James's – a few doors from Christie's. Both places were devastated by war-time blitzes. Christie's came back to their original home, but the Reid & Lefevre firm, after a spell in Bond Street, is now in Bruton Street and under new management.

Our outfit was a source of surprise, not to say entertainment, to a number of people interested in the arts; especially to the dealers and writers who, in the thirties, had to make their escape from Hitler's Germany. Three Scotsmen, Reid, Macdonald and Honeyman, specialising in selling French paintings to the English-speaking world – not to mention our French partner, Etienne Bignou. Smallish and neat in build, Bignou oozed energy. His knowledge of European Art, artists and dealers was encyclopedic. The excitements incidental to a big deal were more important to him than the money involved. The acquisition of fine paintings intrigued him far more than their disposal to collectors. He dramatised his discoveries and the romantic tinges were so delightfully touched in that one completely forgot to stretch out for a pinch of salt. It was all part of the game, and if one dared an attempt to call his bluff nothing could prevail against his gentle smile and the expressive shrug of his fashionably clad shoulders.

I shall forever be grateful to Bignou for his particular contributions to my education. Through him especially I enjoyed the privilege of meeting several of the celebrated 'New Masters' of the School of Paris. I cannot claim to make it more than 'meeting'. Perhaps it could be said that I reached terms of friendship with Raoul Dufy, who was beginning to show signs of arthritis which, as in the case of Renoir, was to harass his declining years. Through the Reid & Lefevre association I met, either in Paris or London (when they would be visiting an exhibition of their work), Matisse, Braque, Bonnard and Dali. In Paul Rosenberg's gallery I met Picasso, and, thanks to Bignou, I once had a wonderful day at Josse Hessel's château, where I enjoyed a session with Vuillard. He had painted several portraits of Madame Hessel. Our host told me that Vuillard took three years to complete a portrait.

Whenever I study the catalogues of the important auction sales of French paintings, the *provenance* frequently reminds me of occasions when I was introduced to dealers whose names are part of French Art History. It was, at first, difficult to remember precisely who they had 'discovered' or 'exploited'. It was puzzling and disturbing to find some continental dealers masquerading as scholars. The scholarship may have been sound and reliable, just as their salesmanship was persistent and effective. One was sometimes amused, but more often exasperated by collectors and amateurs who would have been very angry if one regarded them as dealers in works of art; yet that was precisely what they were. Maybe it is natural to expect and receive a profit when parting with a well-loved object!

I retain happy memories of meetings with London dealers. We behaved like colleagues, not competitors, which was precisely what we were. I remember with affection and regard men like Dudley Tooth, Hugh Agnew, Ernest Brown and some others who are no longer active. They have died or retired. The London Scene has changed. The expansion has been fantastic, but reflecting, as it does, the fact that London has become the Art centre of the world. The Marlborough Gallery has become internationally important. I remember when it started with Harry Fischer, devoted more to Art books, and Miss Beston who has grown up with it. Mattieson Gallery is no more but Mrs Stefanie Maison continues the tradition, while her scholarly husband establishes a reputation as the authority on Daumier (a two-volumed catalogue raisonné bears witness). I cannot, of course, forget Roland, Browse & Delbanco – three musketeers who combined knowledge and enthusiasm in the making of a fine reputation. It was through them that I was persuaded to let our Derain *The Pool of London* go to the Tate Gallery. Blessings and curses upon them.

To recall all the artists whose works the Lefevre Gallery was privileged to show would be both difficult and outwith the range of my purpose. But I still summarise the pleasures of art dealing in two viewpoints. It is a thrill to bask in the reflected glory when viewing, or hearing about, items in a private or public collection which came through us. It is an even greater thrill to recollect that one was in a position to give young artists of promise their early opportunities to find the necessary patronage to aid their development. Among others I remember Ivon Hitchens and his wife, who continued to be known to the three of us as 'Evening Primrose'. She was the figure in a beautiful splash of colour in his first one man show. In keeping up the gentle title we retain the friendly remembrance of the struggling days.

One got to know the men and women who ran the Art magazines. William Gaunt was on *The Studio* complementing other writing enterprises. R. R. Tatlock was editor of *The Burlington*; but it seemed to me that Frank Davis was doing all the work. The life blood of most of these contemporary art journals derived from the advertisements, and, obviously, when times were bad they were the first to suffer. I have never ceased to admire and respect the productions of Frank Davis. His is the kind of knowledge – so extensive and reliable – which is of greater value than that of accepted experts who operate in the narrow grooves of specialisation.

The recollection of visits to Bignou's gallery in Rue la Boêtie, with its remarkable bar, decorated by Jean Lurçat and Dufy, makes me deplore many a missed opportunity. His library was unique, but one never seemed to have the time to investigate it thoroughly. The hospitality was overpowering and commanding. The visitors from America, especially the Chester Dales and Dr Barnes, had to be taken care of. There was so much to see, and one never saw it all. Bignou, anxious to enlarge my experience, took me to meet the great Ambroise Vollard. He was then (1930) living in the Rue de Martignac, and had become a legendary figure. To list the works of art acquired by Vollard and to trace their subsequent wanderings would be a colossal task. If it were ever done it would throw much light on the processes involved in the buying and selling of pictures, and on the impelling motives which stimulate or depress collectors – what makes them grow hot or cold in harmony with the vagaries of the art market?

Vollard has given us his recollections. His autobiography was first published in English – printed in Great Britain but issued from Boston, USA, in 1936. The French edition, through Albin Michel, came later and includes an account of his visits to London and New York. I remember him as a largely built man, anything but pre-possessing or handsome. His beard was scruffy, his left eye was hidden by a droop of the upper eyelid. He was untidy in appearance and his bald head was always covered by a black skull cap or a beret. He shuffled around. Now and then he might venture on a slow smile in reply to an observation or lift one shoulder as a silent but pleased acknowledgment of an appreciative comment on one of his treasures. Our first meeting was in what I took to be his dining-room, because of the rather grubby cloth which covered a large table in the centre of the room. It was in this room he generally displayed the paintings he 'might' be prepared to sell. On one wall was the celebrated portrait by Renoir of Vollard in the costume of a toreador. I saw it being sold at auction for £22,000. As a portrait it has always struck me as a poor thing. Two superb works by Degas were on the other walls. In a corner of the room was a large powerful-looking door, which suggested the entrance to a strong room. I was to discover that beyond this door was the Vollard collection. On a later visit I had the unique privilege of having a very rewarding hour turning over an amazing mixture of paintings. Vollard had forgotten all about me, having dozed off in a comfortable arm-chair.

I cannot go further back than 1923 in recalling the notable exhibitions Reid senior had brought to Glasgow. I remember a collection of Gauguin woodcuts at West George Street and an Exhibition in 1924 with Matisse, Picasso, Vuillard, Dufy, Rouault and others. What chances Reid gave to collectors. And what chances the continuing firm, Reid & Lefevre, continued to give after his death. In 1934 and 1937 I was responsible for two exhibitions in Glasgow. There were some notable items, especially *Le Paysan* by Van Gogh and *Les enfants en rose et blue* by Renoir. Either of them could have been got for around £10,000. The Van Gogh went to the Chester Beatty collection, and the Renoir is in São Paulo, Brazil. Present day values? I imagine somewhere near the half-million mark for each of them. The Hamilton Trustees, whose sole function is to buy paintings for the Glasgow Civic Collection, were tempted by the Van Gogh. They had the money but not the foresight.

These visits back home to Glasgow kept me in touch with the 'Art Climate'. It was anything but congenial. There was great public interest in the exhibitions which were very well attended; but at the higher levels there was a sad complacency and a depressing lack of interest.

It would seem that my average length of service in any post is ten years – Practice of Medicine (1919–1929); Reid & Lefevre (1929–1939). When we came to 1949 the family asked 'What next?' When I replied 'I was thinking of the Church', my wife – a daughter and grand-daughter of the manse – simply said 'That will be when I leave you'.

During the ten years in the Reid & Lefevre partnership I often had occasion to be at variance with Macdonald, but I have nevertheless admired his persistence, energy and capacity in overcoming a series of handicaps to achieve, eventually, a foremost place among art dealers in this country. Indeed, his reputation acquired international status.

I never met anyone who did not like McNeill Reid. The easiest of colleagues, approachable, constructive, calm, sympathetic, level-headed and, if he found himself in opposition to a suggestion, prepared to concede the value of a relevant discussion. He does not brush aside an idea or a proposal. He listens.

Etienne Bignou was, in most respects, a law unto himself. It was because I failed to view certain matters eye-to-eye with him and Macdonald that I decided to leave the Lefevre Gallery. The decision was actually made in October 1938; but I undertook to continue until April 1939. My wife, as always, shared the decision. Together we planned a long sea voyage with the promise of relaxation and quiet meditation. Invitations to visit Australia sounded attractive. We had accumulated enough funds and six months of spending – with or without augmentation – would still leave enough if it had to be a return to refresher courses and the practice of medicine.

Some of our friends – especially those with political contacts and interests – were deeply concerned over the gathering clouds of war. Notwithstanding the evidence of precautionary measures, we never seemed to be touched by it. I saw on television the news-reel of Neville Chamberlain returning from Munich, stepping off the plane waving the scrap of paper 'Peace with Honour'. We were in Broadcasting House in order primarily to view a programme of Modern versus Academic Art; Wyndham Lewis on the side of the moderns, with paintings borrowed from the Lefevre Gallery by John Piper (later to become famous in his own right as an artist). The lesson of the evening for me was to be careful on the choice of paintings for TV presentation. Abstract, or non-representational art, wins every time.

It became known that I was leaving the Lefevre Gallery and I began to receive suggestions about the future. One very well known Art firm asked if I would care to join their organisation in New York, London or Paris. Very flattering, but not what I thought I wanted. Tyrone Guthrie (Sir Tyrone now, but still Tony to his friends) revived an earlier invitation to consider the Administrative Director-ship at the Old Vic. I again refused because I was convinced I was not the man and that Tony should take it on himself.

I am told that in this kind of narrative one must be careful to include a pen picture of the people one is writing about, in case they are not as well known by sight as by achievement and reputation. There is, in some volume of memoirs, a reference to Sir Tyrone as a maypole of a man. This, to me, is misleading. A maypole suggests a long rigid tree with little people making rings round it. Guthrie, the most dynamic figure in the contemporary theatre! Nobody ever made rings round him. I think of him and his wife Judy, who could pass in height and looks for his sister, as experts in Thermos flasks and sandwiches. From the shadows in the stalls with the time-saving al fresco snacks, would come forth exciting and original first nights. Daddy Long-Legs, yes! Maypole, never.

Remembered and loved by many who knew him in his early days with the Scottish National Players and his association with James Bridie's contribution to the London Theatre, Tony has more than merited the distinctions which have followed his persistence and devotion in the world of Drama. From his exalted vantage point as Chancellor of Queen's University in Belfast, he once made a logical and persuasive appeal for a United Ireland. Unfortunately he made it to the wrong audience. That's the kind of man he is. A broth of a boy!

Bignou was incapable of carrying any ill-will from one argument to another. His displeasure evaporated quickly and he became very interested in our plans to visit Australia. He pressed me to consider taking some French paintings with me. It would be a good chance to develop a new market in the Commonwealth. He would guarantee substantial remuneration for what would be a part-time occupation. He was even more excited when I returned to Glasgow as Director of the Gallery and undertook to be of every possible help with exhibitions, catalogues and literature. It so turned out that I was able to do the first favour.

In 1940, just before Germany compelled France to surrender, I received an urgent request. Could we accept the custody of several cases of pictures? (Dufy's entire collection of works, early and recent.) The cases (seven in number) arrived and throughout the war were hidden in a branch museum in Tollcross Park. Not until the fighting was over did I become aware of having broken the law by not declaring these paintings as 'enemy property'. They were eventually returned, having survived the risks of war and innumerable temptations! Dufy was very grateful and said so. Unfortunately he died before giving effect to a promise to repay Glasgow's generous hospitality by presenting an important work. Louis Carré, a close friend of the Dufy family – he had succeeded Bignou as his agent – did his utmost. Maybe the generous gift (in 1960) to the Glasgow Gallery of a splendid example of Dufy's work by Mr & Mrs A. J. McNeill Reid can function as a consolation.

2

The Middle Distance

The Winter Exhibition – a comprehensive and retrospective display of Scottish Art – at the Royal Academy of Arts opened in January 1939. It brought to London a great number of our friends from Scotland. Among the lists of names on the various committees, honorary and executive, the Glasgow Art Gallery and Museum was not represented. Edinburgh was strongly featured through its eminently well qualified officials at the National Gallery and Royal Scottish Museum.

I was questioned about this state of affairs, especially by Glasgow's new Lord Provost, Patrick Dollan (later Sir Patrick). He was frequently in London and often looked in to see me at King Street. We had one or two meetings at the Café Royal, where we would be joined by some of the celebrated left-wing Glasgow MPs. At the time the Café Royal was still the haunt of celebrities in all the Arts. After-theatre suppers brought them in, and I basked in the glory of being able to point some of them out to my shy, modest companions. They were involved in an effort to have placed in the precincts of the House of Commons a bronze sculptured head, by Benno Schotz, of Keir Hardie, the first Labour Member of Parliament. I was of some service to the committee. The Chairman was James Maxton, the acknowledged leader of the 'Red Clyde' rebels. To mark the satisfactory conclusion of the project he gave a small dinner-party at the House. Most of the people to whom I was introduced appeared to suffer from an urge to tell me that my host was the best-loved man in the House of Commons.

One evening, to the Café Royal Pat Dollan brought David Kirkwood (later Lord Kirkwood). Both of us, like Keir Hardie and other pioneers of the political labour movement, did not indulge in alcoholic beverages. Someone in the party recalled one of H. M. Bateman's cartoons of 'the girl who asked for a glass of milk in the Café Royal'. I introduced Davie Kirkwood to my favourite thirst-quencher, a lime-juice and tonic; but for years Pat Dollan, if he spotted me in his audience, would stop in the middle of an inconsequential speech to say 'Look at him, the most persistent teetotaller I have ever known, and I always meet him in the two booziest places – the Café Royal in London or the Art Club in Glasgow.'

The Lord Provost first told me, on one of his London visits, that they were very anxious to get a good man to fill the vacant chief post at the Art Gallery. Was I likely to be in Glasgow soon? Some of his newspaper friends would like to see me – I think Sir Patrick was, at this time, the Scottish Editor of the *Daily Herald*.

I was in Glasgow for Christmas and New Year (1938–9). Among the festivities was a lunch at the Merchants Club. I had a great fondness for this snug little place, now no more, for it was there, through a well-known Glasgow Merchant, George Newton, that I was introduced to a lot of words new to me, e.g. *serendipity*. 'Pa' Newton antedated Ivor Brown in the operation of digging up unusual words, but he refused to put pen to paper. 'This is a club – not a class' was the measure of his resistance. James Willock, my host, a leading Glasgow journalist and editor of the *Evening Times*, who became managing editor in chief of the Outram Press, was a close friend of the Lord Provost. He seemed very anxious to have my views on what the Corporation should do about a man for Kelvingrove. I spread myself, urging them to go for an 'Art Man', and strongly advised Glasgow to try to get Philip Hendy, who was then in Leeds and not very happy. They should invite him to come, but they would have to do something about the totally inadequate salary. Willock asked me to let him have a summary of what I had said. This I did and a fairly close paraphrase by the Art Critic (Rosie by name) appeared in the *Glasgow Herald*, with a couple of complementary leading articles.

As part of the attractions to the Scottish Art exhibition a series of lectures was given in the rooms of the Royal Society. Among them was one by J. R. Richmond, Esq., CBE. His subject was The Glasgow School. Later he was to become Sir John. He was President of the Royal Glasgow Institute (founded over a hundred years ago as a kind of Royal Academy for the West of Scotland). He was also Chairman of Governors of the School of Art, and a prominent patron of the Arts.

At his invitation I spent some time with him. Our lunch engage-

ment lasted till 4.30 and I remember the date, 10th February 1939.
One reason leading me to expand on Sir John Richmond is a passage
from a book *The Scot in History*. It is written by a friendly, eager and
erudite American Professor of History, Wallace Notestein, of Yale.
In a chapter headed 'Decline of the Arts and Rise of Machinery' he
says, speaking of the Scottish manufacturer of last century:

> 'He was likely to be a narrow, hard-bitten man of little culture or
> breadth of view, passionate in his pursuit of his expanding schemes
> and with little time to spare for other things. He and his mind
> transformed Scotland within two generations. The talk of his
> friends was of machines and ships and markets. Scotland was on
> the up and up. Business ruled the roost.'

With due respect to Professor Notestein, I can only describe this
particular passage as inaccurate and misleading. We know that
businessmen are often depicted as hard, harsh, opinionated, unsympathetic men, hostile or indifferent to the arts and deaf to any
suggestions or appeals for enterprises devoted to the promotion of
the arts and the support of artists. A little more research might have
led the learned and distinguished professor to avoid the generalisation
and discover some very notable exceptions.

He could have started with Archibald McLellan, the Glasgow
coachbuilder and city magistrate, who literally founded Glasgow's
famous art collection. He ought to have known about the Reids of
Hydepark Locomotive Works, the Youngs of Paraffin Oil fame and a
host of other industrialists who, through their public benefactions,
revealed a great interest in the arts. And what about Sir William
Burrell, a ship-owner, who became excited about art in his 'teenage'
and eventually assembled and gave to Glasgow one of the greatest
collections to have been created by one individual?

I could go on with more examples, and I am thinking only of
Glasgow and the West of Scotland. In Sir John Richmond I can find
the more complete answer, for in him is the ideal combination.
Apart from his business he has always had two groups of interests.
Each of them has, at the appropriate time and occasion, demanded
and received the concentration without which nothing effective can
be achieved. The gentle art of dilettantism may be entertaining, but
it seldom leads to enjoyment. The distinction is important and one
does not have to dwell long in the privilege of Sir John's company
and conversation to appreciate the point.

In human affairs, most things happen by chance, but there are still a number of things which can be controlled. Here follows the proof.

In a little volume *The Poetical Works of Thomas Chatterton*, published in 1885, the 'Prefatory Notice, Biographical and Critical' is by John Richmond of Cambuslang, Glasgow. It is the same man, or should I say boy? He was then, at the age of sixteen, on the threshold of the University of Glasgow, where he became an undergraduate in the Arts Faculty. (Exactly sixty years later his Alma Mater conferred on him its highest honour – the LL.D. degree). It is more than likely that anyone interested in compiling a volume of Chatterton's poems must have attempted to create something of his own. The fact that this was so rests on the authority of Macaulay Stevenson, the grand old man of the Glasgow School of Painters. He remembered young Jack Richmond leaving with him some manuscripts for a critical opinion which Macaulay, in admiration, refused to give. For all I know, there may be, scattered through reviews, etc. a continuing evidence of the survival of an early urge. I certainly know that some years ago an attractive little painting exhibited in the annual exhibition of the Glasgow Institute of Fine Arts carried the signature R. H. Maund – a phonetic disguise which the 'know-alls' soon penetrated. An irrepressible inspiration is more easily concealed and kept to oneself in a poem than it is in a painting.

Gifted with a lively imagination, combined with the awakening in his mind of some intuitions of the beautiful things in life, the young Richmond was able, eventually, to merge the natural and the artificial into the atmosphere of their uses and associations. He had to grow up. He became an engineer, but although he felt bound to accept the station and prospects assigned to him by family tradition, his literary bent was not subdued. There was no call for him to live contrary to his inclinations.

The extraordinary range of interests and activities in peace and war is almost staggering. I remember the days when the name Weir, a Glasgow engineering firm founded in 1870, especially to men who go down to the sea in ships, was linked almost exclusively to the mysteries of marine pumps. On most ships there were two of them, and I think it was from my eldest brother, a marine engineer, that I first heard the legend that the feed pumps which came out of G. & J. Weir were affectionately known as 'Geordie' and 'Jamie'.

Obviously the Weir story belongs to another hand and occasion. Here I have to skirmish round a number of facts and treat them objectively. But when I begin to think and talk about Sir John

Richmond's contribution to the art life of Glasgow, most of my information is first-hand. Like a lot of other people, I have been at the receiving end of valuable advice and timely encouragement.

Among the many gifts of works he made to the civic collection is a fine late Pissarro (1900) which he bought from Alex Reid in 1911. Better perhaps to know now that his name is remembered in the first chair of its kind in the University of Glasgow – the Richmond Chair of Fine Art.

Our prolonged talk at the Arts Club in Dover Street was concerned mostly with the Art situation in Glasgow. Sir John had been informed by leading members of the Corporation that the gallery appointment was being very thoroughly discussed, that the University was being consulted and that they were determined to get an Art man. He had been consulted by the committee convener T. A. Kerr (he later became Lord Provost), to whom he intimated that if the Corporation did not make a good appointment on this occasion they would be subjected to very severe criticism and that he, John Richmond, would lead it.

I told Sir John that most of the Directors of Art Galleries throughout the country frequently visited the Lefevre Gallery. I knew them and some of their deputies. Moreover, I had collected a fair share of Museum gossip. 'Glasgow should try to get Philip Hendy' was a repeat of my previous counsel.

Hendy, still at Leeds, on a visit to London called to see me. He had heard rumours associating him with the Glasgow vacancy, and he had given it serious consideration. However, his friends were rallying round, his troubles were likely to be smoothed out and he was therefore not a candidate. Later on, almost on the last day for lodging applications, he changed his mind. Leeds had not kept to their promises. And I was already committed.

It was following a suggestion by W. O. Hutchison, then Director of the Glasgow School of Art, later to become President of the Royal Scottish Academy and achieve the honour of knighthood, that I began to give the Glasgow Art Gallery job serious consideration. I discovered later Sir John Richmond had first mentioned it – not to me, because he wanted to remain detached.

When I saw the result of the Corporation's long and serious 'deliberations' my disappointment was considerable. I thought I had better let it go. One of my Glasgow friends, Councillor Rosslyn Mitchell, said I should take a longer view and look upon this as a starting point. It was likely that the University would have something to say later – it would be possible to augment one's income through journalism, broadcasting and outside lecturing. That, somehow, seemed to me the wrong kind of way to approach a job of such importance. Obviously, one would have to concentrate on the principal reason for taking it on and not have to be tempted to accept outside remunerative work just to keep the wolf from the door.

Back I went into a domestic huddle. My average income over the previous five years had been five times the salary scale offered by Glasgow. We had a smallish cushion of capital, a collection of paintings and a lot of faith. The conclusion reached was to look upon Glasgow as a piece of missionary work and to remember that missionaries were not supposed to think in terms of money. It was Rosslyn Mitchell who had planted in my memory the notion that one of the curses of Scotland was 'too many people thinking of rewards and too few thinking of duty'. The curse is not peculiar to Scotland. On many occasions he inclined an ear when I became exasperated over what I thought were flagrant breaches of solemn undertakings. He was adept at smoothing ruffled feathers and tried to lead me into taking a calmer view of situations which were often as much comic as they were sad. With some reflection, I should have remembered that he – more than most men – has received much less in the way of thanks and appreciation, at civic and parliamentary levels, for what he set out to do. I must say more about him and how I came to know him.

My exercises in public speaking, following an erratic apprentice-ship in the University Dialectic Society, covered a number of themes and occasions. For many years Walter Freer, who had been Manager of the Glasgow Corporation Halls most of his active life, ran a series of 'Pleasant Sunday Evenings'. These were held in the St Andrews' Hall and the audience regularly numbered about 3,000. Admission was by 'silver collection', which led the promoter to put a curse on the 'threepenny bit'. However, they were so popular for a period that Freer extended them to the Coliseum Theatre on the South side.

The programme was in the nature of a popular concert with one or more 'up and coming' vocalists or instrumentalists and, occasion-ally, a once-renowned star on the way down. There was always a speaker and the subjects ranged over every conceivable theme, with a bias towards topical, non-controversial issues. It was at these

Sunday Evening meetings I gained valuable experience in addressing large audiences. And I often listened to men of mark in Politics (notably Walter Elliot), the Church, Literature and Music. I learned most from Rosslyn Mitchell, a prominent Glasgow lawyer who, in his prime – and it lasted a long time – was regarded as one of Scotland's great public orators. He has been described as the Pocket Rosebery. By no means tall in stature, he had a fine head, an infectious smile and a clear voice which he made into an effective instrument, never to be submitted to strain. He dressed with dapper elegance except when on holiday in his beloved Arran. A summer feature of this holiday Isle in the Clyde estuary was the spectacle of eminent Glasgow professional men in the garb of 'down and outs' – 'keelies' is the Scots word.

In parliamentary history R.M. will be remembered as the man who, through his superb gifts of speech and persuasion, won over the House in the debate on the Prayer Book. I remember too, when as a Labour candidate, he defeated H. H. Asquith at Paisley, the most memorable part of the campaign which pointed the end of Asquith's political career, was the victory speech of the new member, with its moving tribute to his defeated opponent.

Rosslyn and I were united in our views on a number of social problems and in our interests in Scottish traditions in art and literature. We have both been pamphleteers and 'memorial' lecturers on various aspects of the Alcohol Problem. Each of us inherited our interests from the pioneers of the labour movement, e.g. Keir Hardie, Arthur Henderson, Philip Snowden, David Kirkwood and, in my case, my parents. His most notable contribution was *Booze versus Brains* (a physiological and psychological argument). Mine are probably *Science Speaks* and an ethical tract *Make Up Your Mind*. Once or twice we did a 'double turn' at the St Andrew's Hall and were dubbed Moody and Sankey by someone with a long, but inaccurate, memory.

I was still harping on the theme in the course of a Rectorial Address (in 1954). True, nobody heard me, but it appeared in print:
'I take it for granted that you do not expect me to conceal my own opinions. There is no special virtue in the fact that a man chooses to dispense with artificial aids to help him to escape from the monotonies of life. It is just one way of living. I happen to think that human wit *au naturel* is not as poisonous or as feeble as some of our social customs appear to suggest. Besides, I am by

nature selfish. I hate to miss anything. Moreover, I have seen, too often for my liking, great hopes and prospects blasted and the promise of youth lamentably unfulfilled. And that is one reason why I counsel you to use your imagination. I know that

> *"To follow foolish precedents and wink,*
> *With both our eyes, is easier than to think."*

When Walter Freer was let down by his speaker I was one of his favourite stop-gaps. I did not mind, although preparation was often the source of some anxiety and apprehension. It was, for me, a great experience and I was always hoping to enjoy the thrill of feeling an audience as something in one's hands. I have had it about half-a-dozen times; most of them in St Andrew's Hall – one of them in the USA. A great hall, acoustically perfect – no microphone, 'just speak to the clock on the front of the back balcony' – it was burned down nine years ago and has not yet been replaced. At the Lincoln Centre in New York where they have had a load of problems on acoustics, they listed Glasgow's Hall as among the most perfect in the world.

I must add a little more about Walter Freer ('Wattie' to his cronies) because, as a city official, he had a pioneering mind and the determination to try out his ideas with imagination and persistence. He was a short, stout man, with neatly trimmed moustache and a goatee beard. He talked and walked as if to convey his importance in civic affairs. Almost totally bald, he wore a well-fitting wig. Only once did I see him without it. On a visit to his home, when he was in bed with a severe cold, his bald pate and piercing eyes keeking over the blanket reminded me of an ostrich egg which had suffered decoration by an irreverent small boy. His wig was hoisted on the knob of a solid brass bed-post, like a sad piece of discarded kitten.

Walter Freer was always interested in my career and welfare. This may have been linked to the fact that my wife's grandfather – one time Moderator of the United Free Church – the Rev. Dr Robert Howie of Govan, affectionately known as 'Hell-Fire and Brimstone Bob' – had married the Freers and was present at their Golden Wedding Reception.

I wonder what happened to his great collection of photographs of Scottish Variety Artists, like Sir Harry Lauder and W. F. Frame in their early days? I recall one of his great treasures – a photograph of himself with Chief Clear Sky of the Iroquois Indians, both of them in complete Redskin dress. 'Wattie' had been made a blood brother and sub-chief with the title of 'Sa-Go-Wee-Hay' meaning Chief Generous the Giver. It sums him up – even if somebody suggested it should mean 'Say-Go-Wee-Freer'.

The Corporation confirmed the committee's decision in June 1939 and I was asked to take up office as soon as possible. I did so in August. World War II started in September. I suppose I was lucky. We would probably have been on the other side of the world when war was declared. As it turned out our household goods were somewhere on the Great North Road that particular Sunday morning, remembered especially for the abrupt dismissal from a church service because German bombers were on their way to the Clydeside – a false alarm.

I had heard a lot about 'Committee Complex' in several galleries. And I knew all there was to be known on the 'audacity of the elected'. This reflected the view that, following a short introductory period, councillors fancied themselves as authorities on a wide range of subjects. How different was my experience! With one very notable exception, conveners and committees were kindness itself. Unanimity there might not have been, but ruling out the odd case of congenital idiocy I sensed a general climate of support. My trouble, as it turned out, was the 'Official Mind', not the city councillors. I shall have to return to this when I am able to illustrate the argument in the light of fifteen years' experience.

I got off to a bad start. Chief among the frustrations came the discovery that I was first of all a Corporation official, with some clear indications that to be a Director of a civic Art Gallery and Museum was, in a sense, coincidental. I think one has to begin in local government service when one is very young. My inability to reconcile the needs of a department with an indefinable thing labelled 'Party policy' and its application was liable to make me function as a 'pain in the neck' to colleagues for whom I acquired a high personal regard. The 'party policy' was a very elastic affair as it affected galleries and museums. The status quo was the rigid factor operating against bright ideas or anything new. The stumbling block I failed to overcome I have already defined as the 'Official Mind'. Another name for it, but with wider implications, is 'The Establishment'. Nothing seemed to prevail against it.

The Art Gallery and Museum Committee, not so long before my time, was a sub-committee of the Parks. Although it was now a separate department, officially, for the purpose of estimates of

Revenue and Expenditure, it came under the overall description *Parks, Burial Grounds and Art Galleries and Museums*. An American colleague cherishes a photostat of municipal accounts showing Art Galleries alongside Burial Grounds. The City Chamberlain could not see anything odd or funny about this! I thought, on commonsense grounds, that a first step towards destroying the idea that a Museum is a Mausoleum was to create the right atmosphere. I failed completely to get anyone in authority to support my efforts towards building a brave new art world from within the total corporation structure, working outwards. Prestige and psychology were just airy-fairy meanderings. 'Be patient and you will learn a lot' I was told, and certainly I had a lot to learn.

Tom Kerr was convener of the Committee when I was appointed. Tall, slim, sandy-haired in his younger days, he now had a good thatch of heather-mixture. He was a devotee of 'keep-fit' exercises, specialising on the bicycle. He crowned a civic service as a councillor extending over very many years when he became Lord Provost, in 1952. He did a very good job as the chief citizen and was the only one to instal a piano in his room, so that he could entertain his visitors with the songs of Scotland. Before I had moved to London I had got to know him, principally through his interest in music and painting.

There was an occasion when we exchanged some heated words, when I had to fight for a director's authority to run his own department, but neither ill-will nor enmity rose between us and I had good reason to be grateful for his support on several issues. The last time I saw him (he died in 1960) he was very feeble, but said with a smile 'I brought you back to Glasgow'.

I am writing this on board a freighter, somewhere off the Azores. The day before we sailed two of the best conveners a director could wish for died within hours of each other.

Alexander Burnett in his own gentle way exercised a fatherly guidance in my early years as a Corporation Official. Largely self-educated, he made it his business to read up all the books on Art he could find available as they were published. A heavily built man, he adapted himself to the severe handicap of an artificial leg. At times the pain in the amputation stump was more than he could bear and he had to rely on morphine hypodermics. He was, I think, a wood-carver to trade but had retired before being elected to the city council.

A.A.   C

We got on famously together and, unfailingly, when necessary he supported the department's viewpoint to the limit. I recall one example of his co-operation. At an exhibition of Painting and Sculpture by Jewish Artists there was a fine piece by Zadkine. Both of us thought it would be a good acquisition. The price, £100 (less 10% to us) seemed reasonable. Bailie Burnett feared it might be too modern to win the certain approval of the committee. 'Let's buy it,' said he, 'and I'll persuade my colleagues to "homologate our action".' He succeeded, and when I congratulated him he responded 'Aye, it came off, but it was a hell of a risk.' The work is still on view on the Art Gallery balcony, and its market value today is around £5,000.

We were not so successful with Henry Moore or Barbara Hepworth. I wasn't worried too much about this, relying on a 'certainty' which didn't come off. I thought we were in the line of some gifts or bequests. I have never ceased to deplore this and other omissions.

John Donald Kelly was a friend of long standing. Our first contacts were made through a shared interest in the amateur dramatic movement. He played a part in a James Bridie play *What it is to be Young*, directed by myself, in aid of some medical charity. I had to take on a part at short notice – an irascible, choleric, British Army General. I so terrified our daughter (aged seven) who had been allowed to attend a matinee, that she would scarcely speak to me for days thereafter. The show, supported as usual by coerced relatives and friends, did excellently financially and we had the honour to play before Mr & Mrs C. B. Cochran. The strain on them must have been considerable.

I lost touch with Jack Kelly for a bit during our spell in the South. He had become a city councillor and was in more or less direct succession to Sir John Richmond as President of the Fine Art Institute and Chairman of Art School Governors.

Throughout my fifteen years I often sought his counsel, and if he was not always certain about the value or wisdom of any suggestions he was prepared to listen. Very useful this, when one found it difficult to get a hearing. Jack Kelly was without question the most courteous, the most understanding, the most hospitable, the most entertaining Chairman of any committee I have had to deal with. A recent conversation comes to mind. In the Art Club, where we frequently met and chatted, he said, at the conclusion of a session devoted to criticism of several civic enterprises, 'You and I should go into partnership – Honeyman and Kelly, demolition contractors!' Appropriate enough when the Old Glasgow is being savagely destroyed to make way for the New Glasgow.

A great regret, shared by my family and many friends, is that Jack Kelly did not become the Lord Provost of Glasgow, as his father was when I first knew them both. The award of the St Mungo Prize was a consolation and maybe, some day, adequate acknowledgement will be made to his great services to many causes concerned in the spread of appreciation of all the Arts. A token of this service is the splendid gift he made of the Blythswood Gallery, where young artists, seeking a place in the sun, can exhibit their works for a nominal payment towards the total outlays.

I started on the job before the official date of my arrival. I wrote Convener T. A. Kerr on the 23rd June – some ten days after receiving the official letter of appointment from the Town Clerk – saying that the International Congress of the History of Art was due to meet in London. In fact I had applied for a personal membership. Did he think I could, in the light of my Glasgow appointment, be made an official delegate? I went on, 'I think this Congress is of such importance that one or more members of the Committee should be appointed to attend, because it would present an opportunity of meeting people who are alert in the world of art.' Nothing happened. Official sanction was not forthcoming. I went on my own. Among other things, I wanted to know how to pronounce Byzantine. Was it 'Bizz-antine' or 'Bizantine'? Both are right!

Following an interesting session – where I had asked a question – I was tackled by a formidable bearded gentleman with a pleasant American accent. He almost snapped at me, 'You are from Glasgow'. It was pointless for me to deny it. He told me that he had rushed north – up one night, down the next – just to have another look at the 'Greek' Thomson churches and terraces. Then he expanded on a description of Glasgow's perfect situation. No town in Europe had so many natural features for town planning – three rivers, seven hills – he named them all. His obvious enthusiasm thrilled me, and the original thought that I was being led up the garden path faded into a keen desire to prolong the conversation. Eventually, I knew I had been talking to Henry-Russell Hitchcock, previously known to me only by name. When I deplored the fact that we had lamentably wasted our inheritance he explained how it could all be won back –

in three generations – if the City was so-minded. All this was, for me, on the threshold of a new adventure, something to think about.

Whenever I got a chance I talked and wrote about what this distinguished American had said to me, until it seemed everybody got tired of listening, except the Architects, who knew that Henry-Russell Hitchcock was the President of the Society of Architectural Historians, and an authority of international standing. (In 1958 he wrote a large section of *The Pelican History of Art*, in which he devotes pages to Glasgow and its architecture.)

I started on an effort to get the River Kelvin cleaned up and found myself confronted with a strange complacency leading to opposition. In the corridors of the Municipal Chambers I was gently but firmly told to mind my own business. The Kelvin, which flows down to the Clyde through the Kelvingrove Park – between the University on Gilmorehill and the Art Gallery – was, in my student days, a reasonably pleasant river, and an added attraction to a walk in the Kelvingrove Park. In the International Exhibitions of 1901 and 1911 it served a great and noble purpose as a picturesque amenity. Now it was more or less constantly covered by an ugly scum due to the waste products from paper-mills higher up. The pollution had become excessive – but no one seemed to care very much. When, in collaboration with my friend and colleague George Garside, Director of the City's Parks, we arranged an exhibition of Open-Air Sculpture, on a site in the Kelvingrove Park half-encircled by the river, I thought of a final attempt to stimulate public interest and suggested, as part of our publicity, a series of vivid posters featuring the phrase *Scum and see the Sculpture*. The suggestion was not well received. It was lacking in dignity. When I remarked that the most dignified thing I had ever seen was a corpse and that we should aim at vitality, the disapproval was devastating.

3

Settling In

Chronologically, I could continue with a gaggle of girns (Scots for a number of complaints). And I have become aware of a digressive style of narrative, liable to disturb the sympathetic reader. Gauguin thought so in his *Intimate Journals*, 'There's gossip for you . . . but . . . this is not a book.' A systematic essay is beyond my powers of production. I never kept a reliable diary and I refuse to become the slave of a calendar. In any event I am not persuaded on any advantages over the kind of picture I am trying to paint.

John Fleming, who had been acting as interim director during the vacancy was, I think, quite pleased to be regarded as a character. If the occasion called for it he could play up to his own legend. While we were not unknown to each other, he knew more about me than I knew about him. The 'Building' was his name for the Art Gallery, and he was devoted to it. He went back to 'Paton's time' – his first chief was James Paton. To judge from the memoranda, catalogues, reports and other publications which I found on the book-shelves, James Paton was a very energetic and enterprising director, well-known and esteemed by press, public, artists and laymen. He was also highly regarded in the museum world and appears to have played a part in art gallery and museum affairs at a national level which none of his successors has achieved.

In 1896 he was President of the Museums Association and as such gave an address at the Annual General Meeting in Glasgow. This was five years before the present Gallery was opened. In the course of an admirable account, giving to Archibald McLellan the honour and credit of being the real founder of the Art Collection, he concludes by stating 'In this year of grace (1896) a prison is a more fundamental requirement of a great community than an Art Gallery . . . but it will be a happy day when the Police rates begin to fall, when our prisons become deserted and our Parks, Galleries and Libraries rates rise, and when these places swarm with instructed, happy and

appreciative citizens'. His outlook was certainly hopeful. Variations
on the same theme have marked a number of presidential addresses
down the years. Remember too, that the city bought the Whistler
Carlyle in 1891. What a row blew up over that! The adverse
criticism was worse than the turmoil over the Dali, sixty years later.

James A. McNeill Whistler died in 1903. At the Memorial
Exhibition held by the International Society in 1905, the honorary
committee included the names of Sir John Stirling Maxwell,
Principal Story of Glasgow University, Sir James Guthrie and J. L.
Paton. (On the small executive committee were Sir John Lavery and
E. A. Walton.) Glasgow's link with Whistler has still to be written
up. I did a pamphlet preamble in 1951 when we had on view the two
'Arrangements in Grey and Black', (1) the Artist's Mother, and
(2) Thomas Carlyle. The point here is that in J. L. Paton's time
Glasgow Art Gallery had a very high reputation.

Paton was John Fleming's hero to the extent, sometimes, of
becoming an exasperation. Frequently when I might suggest trying
out some ideas, designed to attract the public, I would be met with,
'I don't think it will be any use. We tried it in Paton's time'.
Nevertheless John Fleming went out of his way to be helpful to the
'new boy'. At one time he may have thought he ought to have
succeeded to my post. He was next in line, but when it became
evident that the Corporation were looking for an Art man he
became completely reconciled to the new set-up.

I had introduced myself to him and was, in turn, introduced by
him to other members of the staff some weeks before I was officially
due to begin. It was a very entertaining day. John had a fund of
reminiscences ranging from swimming and water-polo (in which he
had won many honours), to the cranks and 'culture vultures' who
made museum work exciting. He also treated me to the low-down
on all branches of Corporation activities from Lord Provosts,
Magistrates, Conveners, to permanent officials, Trade Unions, the
work-shy and the twisters. All this with a smile which lit up his face
and cancelled the menacing appearance of his deformed nose – sequel
no doubt to an earlier violent athletic combat. He had a slight
stammer which in no way prevented him from being a racy, if not
altogether reliable, guide to touring parties among the pictures.

There was one thing he would like me to do right away, even
before I took over. The Gallery had received a bequest and, because
of urgency, he had to take action. They were allowed to choose a

selection of paintings from the collection of Mr W. Y. Chrystal. He, Fleming, had already done so but wasn't very sure if he had chosen well. The transport was available and down we went to a mansion on the bonnie banks of Loch Lomond. Fleming had taken the purchase price from the valuation schedule as his guidance. Fortunately I could bring a knowledge of French Art to bear on the problem and suggested several changes in the original selection. These were gladly accepted and the only people who appeared to be annoyed at the intervention were the auctioneers who were instructed to sell the remainder. The values of the amended selection have risen very considerably, so that I can reflect that, before I arrived on the Corporation's pay-roll, I had been of service to them.

The Chrystal Bequest – ten paintings – were from a very mixed bunch. The collector had started with mid-nineteenth century Scottish genre painting mixed with overpowering landscapes and seascapes in the true Academic tradition. We got the cream of later developments in taste – Daubigny (2), Monticelli (2), Fantin-Latour (2), Corot and Ziem. I had never heard of Mr Chrystal, whose beautiful home at Auchendrennan is now a general purpose summer-school and youth hostel venue. I discovered he was a partner in a well-known Glasgow chemical manufacturing company. The top man was elevated to the peerage and, as Lord Overtoun, became well known as a philanthropist, devoted to every good evangelical Christian cause. He was not, however, universally popular, and in industrial disputes was regarded as a hard man.

His name recalls another, 'The Clincher'. He probably was the last of Glasgow's street characters, and has gone the way of the busker and the hurdy-gurdy. Very active in my undergraduate days, with his silk hat, frock-coat, longish grey hair, Rabelaisian wit bordering on obscenity, the Clincher was unpredictable. When Lord Overtoun died, the Clincher paraded up and down Buchanan Street in front of the *Herald* office, with its newspaper posters featuring the sad event. With a sandwichman's board back and front, he held up the traffic. On the front board was inscribed 'Consternation in Heaven' and on the back 'Non-arrival of Lord Overtoun'.

On the way back from Loch Lomond I asked Fleming, 'What about the house I am supposed to get?' He laughed, 'I'm in it.' Then he went on to tell me that months before, Convener Kerr had instructed him to move in to the previous director's house. 'A new house is being built for the new director. The plans are in existence.

It is to be alongside the "Palace of Art" in Bellahouston Park.'
Thus had spoken the all-powerful convener. I was advised to consult
the Town Clerk. This I did, taking with me the letter signed by him
in which the first paragraph of the 'terms and conditions of your
appointment' read:

> '(1) The salary to be £800 per annum, rising to £1,200 by
> instalments of £100 every two years with free house, coal and
> light.'

Following the exchange of compliments and courtesies in a very
friendly atmosphere I came to the point, 'Where is the free house?
I am due here in less than a month. My family is due to follow a
month later. Where do we go?' He replied, 'I haven't the foggiest
idea.'

'But,' I persisted, 'aren't you concerned? You signed the letter.'

'Yes, I signed the letter, but I didn't write it. There's the
reference (pointing to some initials). That's an assistant who looks
after the Art Gallery and Museum Department. Only things of
importance must come to me.'

'And don't you think this is important? Apparently the Corporation is going to break part of the contract.'

'What can I do?' said the Town Clerk. 'See the Convener.'

I tried another line. 'Look! As man to man, give me your counsel.
Where are we to go? Wouldn't it be better to ask me to find my
own house and adjust the salary accordingly? Tell me!' The only
reply I could get to this was the repeated observation, 'It's up to the
Committee – see the Convener.'

The pleasant interview was concluded by the invitation, 'Come
and have some lunch,' which was another way of saying 'Let's talk
about something else.'

At this point one thing must be made clear. When I talk of the
Town Clerk I am thinking more of a department than of particular
individuals. The Art Gallery business became the concern of a
Depute Town Clerk and we were very fortunate in having Mr
William Gordon in charge. His chief interest was Housing, on
which he had become an authority. But he had a special reason for
being interested in the Art Gallery. He had married a bright, good-
looking young lady called Elsie Brotchie, whose father was for a
time the Director. T. C. F. Brotchie had been a journalist and was
able to bring to the job a considerable ability in producing guides to
the city and environs, illustrated with his own sketches.

NORTH BRITISH STATION HOTEL, GLASGOW.

TOP. The Conspirators. A sketch by James McBey
Macdonald (left) and Reid (right) persuading Honeyman (centre) to join them in the
adventure of dealing in works of Art. The artist from a concealed vantage point recorded
the occasion

ABOVE LEFT. A Prophecy by James Bridie
A comment on T. J. Honeyman's future when he forsook Glasgow for London 'You are
heading straight for the Thames Embankment'

ABOVE RIGHT. The Critic. An etching by James McBey, dated 1924
The venue is the artist's studio in London. The figure is Duncan Macdonald, then with
Aitken Dott & Sons in Edinburgh before he joined Reid & Son, Glasgow, later to become
Reid & Lefevre, London

Ambroise Vollard and Dr A. C. Barnes in front of Cézanne's famous painting *The Card Players* in the Barnes Foundation. The corner of the painting above this is that of the large (79″× 99″) Seurat *Les Poseuses*. The smaller version (15½″× 19¾″) was sold (Christies 30th June, 1970) for £410,000. Barnes paid $85,000 and later refused an offer of $500,000 by the French Government. It is said that Dame Rebecca West remarked in front of the Barnes picture, 'My! I would give anything, anything at all, to own that painting.' Barnes immediately replied, 'All right, let me have your ability to write and the picture is yours.' The 'terrible-tempered' Dr Barnes had his moments

The Academic procession, led by the Chancellor Rt Hon Lord Boyd Orr followed by T. J. H. (Rector) and the Principal Sir Hector Hetherington; Dr James Cleland (Duke University, USA); Professor Mullo Weir (Glasgow) Rev. E. M. W. Neilson (New Deer); Canon Hodgson (Oxford) and Rev. Dr H. C. Whitley, minister of St Giles Cathedral, the High Kirk of Edinburgh

Head of a Young Girl
by Henri Matisse
Oil on canvas 16″× 13″ Signed
Presented in 1940 by William
McInnes to commemorate the
appointment of T. J. H. as
Director of the Art Gallery

The Pink Table-cloth by Henri Matisse
Oil on canvas 24″× 32″ Signed
McInnes Bequest 1944

Mrs T. J. Honeyman by Wyndham Lewis
Oil on canvas 30″× 20″ Signed
The chair appears in several portraits, e.g. T. S. Eliot and Stephen Spender

In his quiet incisive way of speaking Willie Gordon conveyed a sense of authority, and the general opinion in the corridors of power was that he was heading for the chief post in the department. He died too soon and the unfulfilled promise of his career was a civic loss of some magnitude. We were often on opposite sides of an argument. The wisdom or otherwise of maintaining the *status quo* was a frequent theme. His unfailing courtesy had a soothing effect if one's feelings of exasperation and frustration got out of hand.

Time passed. We – that is the family – arrived in Glasgow with no home to go to. Five months in a small hotel with our possessions in store – and very much the worse for it – while the housing problem was discussed and remitted *ad nauseam*. Eventually, and acting chiefly on friend Rosslyn Mitchell's private advice, we found a house in Kensington Gate. The Corporation approved the purchase for £1,200 – described by the City Engineer as a 'thief's bargain'. It required a good deal in the way of decoration. Again I consulted the Town Clerk to receive the magic spell, 'See the Convener; if he approves it will be all right.' There was no difficulty in getting the authority to go ahead and at a cost of another £500 we had a comfortable home, almost comparable to what we had left in London. Total expenditure therefore was £1,700 – less than it would have cost for the caretaker's house which was never proceeded with. However, the City was at least fulfilling its part of the contract. Or was it? The £500 had to be passed by the Committee, and then the Convener was told that he had exceeded his authority. They would only authorise £350 towards reconstruction and re-decoration. I was advised to bow to the peculiar workings and unpredictability of Corporation decisions. So, in order that Tom Kerr should be taught a lesson, I had to contribute £150. Later, when we gave up the house – it was sold for £3,500; but my contributions to the enhanced value were conveniently forgotten!

We are not supposed to write about our finances, in this kind of account. Modesty and refinement are expected of us. In my case it is self-defence.

I had also been informed, off the record, that at long last the Town Council had consulted the University and that it was certain that the new man, as in other places, would be offered some kind of lecturing appointment, carrying an honorarium to augment his civic salary. I called on the Principal, Sir Hector Hetherington, who put me wise to a number of things. Chief among these was the news that any approach from the Corporation to the University could properly be defined as 'eye-wash'. He didn't of course put it that way. Nevertheless Sir Hector was keen to see some kind of lectureship – in the History of Art perhaps – created at the University. We would discuss things once I got settled down.

From the window of the Principal's room at the University one can see the masts and funnels of the ships in the Clydeside Docks, and the Art Gallery down below in the Kelvingrove Park. I think he was relieved when we found an excuse (war risks) to remove the bronze angels precariously balanced on the spires. I liked our close-ness to the University. The only thing that separated us was the open sewer, already referred to as the River Kelvin. From the window of my office I could look up to the University, in more ways than one. When I heard the great bell chime out from the tower – striking the quarters in the day time, I recollected how it tortured me during examinations. Time then was fleeting. Now it helps me to sustain warmth in the glow of pride that my succeeding race of under-graduates thought me worthy to become their Rector.

I went about the task of getting to know the Gallery and Museum Staff with great deliberation. Some gave me a feeling, immediate and spontaneous like a reflex, that we were going to work together in harmony. Others would wait and see. A few made me sense that they looked upon me as an interloper. These I hoped to win over, but was not altogether successful. I had the great good fortune to inherit the most efficient secretary I have ever had in a long and varied experience of secretaries. Miss Isabel Mackintosh came to the Gallery from the Town Clerk's Department in 1935, and in her quiet way was capable of summing up a situation and the people concerned with penetration and humour. Apart from her ability to decipher my near illegible script – and I was constantly scribbling memoranda – she could drop a gentle hint which amounted to very useful guidance. Incidentally, I heard after I had left the Gallery that it was customary for the office staff to say that no one could read the chief's writing – they only recognised it.

A great advantage in having an efficient secretary, who has been on the premises for some time, is that one is kept on the right lines at the beginning. What one does later in making a new set of right lines is one's own affair. Isabel Mackintosh knew how the 'official mind' worked and she appeared to have no higher regard for it than I did. Following a suitable interval, when she was probably measuring what she had heard about me against what she was discovering, she was definitely and emphatically one of the supporters. More than anyone else in John Fleming's beloved 'building' did she convey to me – not in words but in the attitude of response to suggestions and proposals – that she was delighted something positive and progressive might be happening. In effect she seemed to say, 'This place could be doing with a lift and I am all out to help.' In the tidying up of good and sound procedures and practices, which had got a bit rusty, and in the trying out of new schemes and ideas, Isabel Mackintosh was admirable in support. If she thought I was in too big a hurry, very cleverly delaying tactics would be put in hand. Often – very often – I had reason to be grateful for the technique.

Before very long I became aware of what can only be described as a lack of discipline pervading the whole department. Maybe in some respects it would be more appropriate to say lack of enthusiasm. There was something wrong and it took a good deal of investigation before I reached the correct diagnosis. The general debility was due in the first instance to the failure of the Corporation to understand the significance and importance of an Art Gallery and Museum in the life of the City. The responsible committee was the Cinderella of committees. Very few of the councillors looked upon membership as more than a pleasant interruption of more important affairs.

In the light of such indifference how was it possible to make a fight for progressive action?

Some good men had been appointed as curators of departments. All of them had ideas, some perhaps adapted from what they had seen or read in museum publications. My desk was full of memoranda, submitted in response to instructions from my predecessor. He was probably acting on instructions from a Convener who in the first blush of a new-found authority wanted 'to do something active'. These recommendations from heads of departments must still be around. They were excellent in many respects and revealed an enthusiasm which I found had petered out. What can be more devastating than to be asked to submit ideas which one is convinced are reasonable, and not extravagant economically, to find that the effort leads nowhere? Nothing is done. The 'brush-off' is usually, 'Can't get the work included in the estimates.'

The department was well served by some excellent tradesmen who had adapted their skills to the kind of special work required in a Museum. The attendants, or guards as they are called in the USA, looked as smart as the rather drab uniforms would allow (we got permission to brighten them up at a later date). Then there were young technical assistants in the course of being trained. The bright boys went on to jobs in other cities.

Of course, World War 2 which, it will be remembered, was declared one month after my appearance on the scene, compelled us constantly to be adapting our staff situation to changing circumstances. The first war year – described as 'phoney' – did not produce much in the way of upset. We all had to take our turn at fire-watching duties. This meant sleeping on the premises one night in six or seven. I found it of great value, because apart from the chance of bringing delayed correspondence up to date, one got to know the men from a different angle. We were all, so to speak, off the chain for some hours – having frequently to stand to in groups until the alarm – real or false – had faded into the 'all-clear'.

At my first Museums Conference I was quizzed about staff in the course of a small friendly conference (within the bigger conference) of museum officials I had known for some years. 'What had I found in Glasgow?' I remember replying in something like these words, 'I consider myself, as a new man in this profession, very fortunate in the people with whom I have now to co-operate. There are some exceptions and I would sum it up thus: One third of the entire staff, whatever their duties, can be counted on in every respect. They are excellent, and it is a joy to work with them; another third, no less bright, more critical, but can be persuaded or chaffed or provoked into doing a good day's work; the remaining third are more or less complete passengers. I don't know why they were ever employed and I am stuck with them.' To my surprise and relief in a way, I found none of my friends was impressed by this conclusion. They appeared to be similarly situated.

The head attendant, John Campbell, whose black bristling moustache suggested authority, was the perfect aide. In addition to arranging duty hours for those under his direction he assumed the role of the Director's bodyguard. As a barrier against the known and unknown cranks and time-wasters, he was first-rate. Probably his army experience added to his uniform – and he looked well in it – had accustomed him to accept orders without argument. Anyhow, he was a great help in my early efforts to tighten things up. I discovered one reason for the early failures to establish, or should it be re-establish, the kind of *esprit de corps* I held to be indispensable for smooth and effective administration. It was a sense of insecurity.

Below stairs, so to speak, there was division. Attendants and cleaners were divided into two camps. The old hands were hostile to a number who had come in within recent years. And a very large proportion had been given jobs through the influence of my friend the Convener. Tom Kerr was a kind-hearted man and probably more than any other town councillor went out of his way to find jobs for those who sought his help. His protegés, however, were not all very easy to get on with, and they were very numerous – no less than eighteen. I was informed by John Fleming that a sullen feud had developed between the Kerrites and the anti-Kerrites. I was the last person to want to fall out with the man who had been so eager to bring me back to Glasgow, but I had to make some kind of move to establish the right kind of authority. I thought the centre of that must be the Director. In a friendly enough discussion Tom Kerr thought I was making heavy weather about trifles; but I had to point out that it was more than a matter of deciding who was running the show. I was trying to clear up a situation which was interfering with smooth working, and it was essential for us to achieve harmony among ourselves if we were to succeed in our service to the public.

I thought that was the end of a ticklish problem. A year later, however, when the blast of a land-mine so damaged the building that it had to be closed, the issue was re-opened. It was evident that there was going to be no work for those whose duty it was to clean the show-cases. There were no cases. The war effort everywhere was short of labour and following consultation with the Chief of the Welfare Department I arranged for the temporary transfer of some of our girls. They were also to receive more wages and work shorter hours for the period. To my surprise, instead of agreeing they phoned Councillor Kerr who told them to stay where they were. Nobody was going to shift them from the Art Gallery without his approval. The matter went before the Committee and I found myself confronted by a very unsympathetic group of people. They had been informed that I had chosen the occasion of a war catastrophe to dismiss Corporation employees of long standing without regard to their circumstances, and so on. When I was allowed to explain exactly what had happened, the tension disappeared. But I couldn't be stopped. I protested that I had discussed the matter with senior colleagues before deciding on a course of action in the interests of the Corporation as well as of the individuals concerned. And I concluded, 'Why doesn't the Committee ask who advised these employees to ignore the arrangements made by the Director and to stay on the job when there was no longer any job?' The Committee passed to the next business and Tom Kerr stamped out of the room with 'You haven't heard the end of this.' Somebody whispered to me 'Watch your step. He will never forgive you.' Utter nonsense. The very next day Tom Kerr was as friendly as ever, and throughout the rest of my service he supported me on many occasions. One sequel was a piece of advice I received from a leading member of the Labour Group. It was given in a friendly manner and intended to be helpful. 'You'll have to learn that, as an official, you are not supposed to argue with members at committee meetings. You are there to answer questions or give guidance when you are asked.' From this, and from other experiences, I became increasingly aware of the fact that I was not being very successful as a Local Government official.

4

Running the Show

I knew that for many years the Glasgow Art Gallery and Museum had not been playing any great part in the general life of the City, and I thought I knew where the fault lay. From time to time, and on special occasions, the Art Collection would be publicised as one of the finest in the kingdom. But the position had become something like this: 'We'll keep the door open and the place clean and tidy. If you behave yourself no one will interfere. We are not allowed much money but now and then we'll try to add to the collection, and at least appear to be up-to-date.' On the face of it there's nothing much wrong with that. A museum should be a Temple of the Muses and not primarily an Educational Institute. The visitor should be able to enjoy the works of man, without interruption, and in his own sweet way. But did he know how to enjoy them?

Something active and progressive was expected of me. The advertisement had featured ability to lecture, which meant that some form of an attack on the public had to come. I could not and did not lay claim to any high standard of scholarship – we would have to do something about that later when future appointments to the staff were under consideration. My chief job was to be a showman.

It was first of all necessary to become informed on what there was to be shown. But before we could do that the war made it more necessary to distribute the treasures to places of safety. The National Galleries had given a lead, but whereas they had plenty of money to spend – for example they converted a disused mine in Wales – we had to follow a more makeshift method.

In one way this immediate problem was a blessing. With the full assistance of the responsible curators I was able to do a quick survey of all our important possessions. So, before having to bother about the shop-window, I started behind the scenes. In other words I got my first chance to inspect the storage accommodation. It was a depressing experience.

Implicit in what I am about to report is a criticism of a preceding regime. This is unavoidable if I have to keep the record straight. At the same time it must be remembered that the malaise I imagined was responsible for the general discontent did not originate in the Gallery at Kelvingrove. It came from a lethargic Corporation, some of whose members were intellectually disreputable. No one need turn on me for saying such a thing. In effect I am quoting what the good men, in both parties, thought and said about some of their own associates. I suppose they couldn't do much about it. Democracy must be allowed to function. But they need not have been so complacent in the face of the occasional injustice and the wholesale indifference.

I have already indicated that my interest in civic and national collections of art, and in methods of their conservation and display goes back a few years. I had become a member of the Museums Association so that I might be kept up-to-date, whatever city I was able to visit, at home or abroad. I wanted to see and know how they operated. Often armed with introductions to the man in charge, it was easy to have a peep at those parts of the Gallery or Museum not open to the public view.

When I arrived in Glasgow therefore I said to myself, 'Maybe I'll have to introduce new methods of storage, picture conservation, and the keeping of records. I expect I'll have to see that the dossiers are looked over regularly and the gaps in information made good.' There wasn't a dossier in the place. Apart from the catalogue published in 1936 – not so long before – I could find neither files nor folders containing the history, records of exhibitions and collections of any of the paintings. There was a well-kept register in which was entered the source and date of every item presented, bought or loaned. I knew that a few years previously the famous *Man in Armour* by Rembrandt had been sent to Holland for cleaning. I came across the X-ray plates which were part of the preliminary investigation in a cupboard and eventually some relevant reports and letters in a general correspondence file. The second surprise was the method – or absence of method – in storing pictures. Without help from the gilder who was in charge of the store – and who relied on his memory – it was often an arduous business to find a particular painting. They were piled in deep rows against the wall – ten or more to a row – and of course if the required picture was the one nearest the wall all the others had to be moved to get at it.

The first step was to build racks. The second was to arrange paintings according to size, school and subject. With the help of the indefatigable Miss Mackintosh we devised a card index scheme and eventually were able to locate the exact position of any painting without having to move from the office. But we did not look upon this as more than a temporary measure.

The Committee became intrigued with some of the reconstruction plans we put before them and lent their support. On a visit to Edinburgh, taking in the annual exhibitions of the RSA and the National Gallery, my friend Stanley Cursiter, the Director, demonstrated their storage methods. They are now commonplace. One of our deputation said, 'Why can't we have this in Glasgow?' He got the obvious reply, 'Approve of it and authorise the expenditure.' This was done, with unfailing regularity, but every year when the estimates came up for consideration the item – estimated to cost £3,000 – was withdrawn. It seems that a 'credit squeeze' is a permanent feature in municipal gallery circles. At any rate the modern storage method was never installed in my time. It would cost a lot more now.

The museum stores were, if anything, worse than the picture store. There was a complete lack of system. The basement was divided into sections for each department, but when they overflowed a friendly argument, more or less, would develop over claims for more space. Nobody seemed anxious to put up shelves, and I had to point out something I thought was elementary. In any given room or store – the space could be so treated as to make the upper half as valuable as the floor area. Something had to be done with material which had never been put on exhibition within living memory. I was to find boxes, apparently unopened since the date of acceptance and registration, going back to last century. With memories of what I had seen in the British Museum I am not too critical of this. The new broom was simply confronted with the problem of space, common to most museums, but acute in Glasgow. Comparing myself to a broom helps to recall a discussion on the dustiness of the basement stores. I learned for the first time that dust was a 'natural preservative'. I am afraid for some time thereafter I over-worked the phrase 'Not so dusty'.

The space problem was not limited to storage. The staff accommodation and amenities were very inadequate. I thought it necessary for the head of each department to have a room of his own. And since the female staff was considerable, it seemed essential to have a comfortable rest-room, in place of the dump they had to put up with. My own room was palatial with a height of ceiling which seemed a waste of space. The general office was inadequate and it seemed wrong that my deputy, John Fleming, had to be content with a desk in the middle. He had often to interview members of the staff or the public, and the interruptions did not make for the right kind of efficiency. Of course he was chaffed into a smile on the suggestion that he probably liked to do the Sultan act with his harem of attractive lassies. In any event with his blessing – although he doubted if we would be allowed to go ahead – and with the co-operation of my senior colleagues – I was successful in winning the support of the committee. It was not an unqualified support. Some of my friends thought the changes might spoil the internal appearance of the building. On this they were reassured by the report of the City Engineer, without whose approval nothing could be done.

The late Robert Bruce was the Master of Works and City Engineer. He resigned from service with the Corporation a short time before I did, and for substantially the same reasons. He was one of the most obliging and most helpful of men. He established a private practice in Civil Engineering and his tragic death in a motor accident shortly afterwards was in every respect a sad event. Among other things he will be remembered as the creator of the Bruce Plan – the first heroic effort directed at replanning the City. I am not competent to say whether it was a good plan. It was much criticised at the time and is probably now forgotten. I shall remember him for many a friendly and understanding gesture of encouragement when I found myself at variance with some of our colleagues. With Bruce's reassurance that all our reconstruction plans would not alter the architectural features of the gallery, and that any changes could be restored as and when considered necessary, we were able to solve the immediate space problems.

In one thing however, Robert Bruce did not support me. Having settled the urgent requirements reference storage and staff accommodation I had the idea that we ought to increase the exhibition space within the existing building. It seemed to me that the East and West Courts could be adapted to give us two more picture galleries. I had seen a similar treatment of 'waste space' elsewhere and had been told by architect friends that it was quite a feasible proposal.

But friend Bruce insisted that this time the suggested course could not be looked upon as temporary. It would, in his view, make a profound and irrevocable alteration to the internal architectural features of an important public building. Besides, it would cost a lot of money. We agreed that the Art Gallery was at least fifty years out of date when it was built, that extensions outside would be a gross assault on whatever qualities it had as an architectural unit. He had heard, and I was able to confirm, that the Corporation in principle had agreed to a new Art Gallery, separate from the present building which would then become a Museum. This decision had been taken a few years before I arrived, so that my subsequent repetitions on the wisdom of separating Art from History, natural and otherwise, was in line with a policy already determined. It was because I knew that this 'agreed in principle' was liable to be interpreted as 'indefinitely postponed' I tried hard to push for this alternative. The additional gallery space would be so useful for short-term exhibitions and special features, without having to interfere so often with the permanent collection.

We failed to overcome Robert Bruce's objections, although good-naturedly he accepted my reply to his defence of architectural features. I had to point out the ceilings in the two courts; they had escaped his notice. For reasons of economy they had never been completed. They are still as they were seventy years ago – arches of steel girders without any final decoration as was done in the Central Hall. And what about facilities for lectures? Having seen in so many galleries a multi-purpose auditorium, I did what I could to get a corner somewhere as a lecture room. There was no luck with this idea. The adaptation has been done splendidly in the Royal Scottish Museum in Edinburgh.

In the course of all this rummaging round stores and in trying to re-capture space which could be made to function, I unearthed some old favourites among the paintings long ago consigned to the basement. War or no war we must begin to create special exhibitions and try out new methods of publicising them. What better than to start with the kind of picture most people find easy to look at, even if they are anathema to those who think they know something about Art. Such an exhibition would be inexpensive to organise. All the items were already there. The scattering of Old Masters to places of safety had left plenty of wall space.

So, with great deliberation and calculation I got started on my first exhibition. A descriptive title had to be found. Suggestions ranged from the facetious to the outworn, and we finally settled on 'Narrative Paintings'. The exhibition was opened in March 1940 by the President of the Royal Scottish Academy, Sir George Pirie, and ran until September. A list of the names will give some idea of the nature of the exhibition and at the same time reflect the standard of taste governing acquisitions by gift and purchase earlier in the century. Many of them were old favourites of my own and I was glad to see them again. Some of them, especially by our Scottish artists such as Sir David Wilkie, William McTaggart, Sam Bough and Sir W. O. Orchardson, were included from the general permanent display. The same applied to the Glasgow School – the early works before they had completely abandoned the picture which tells a story. We illustrated Josef Israel's 'The Frugal Meal', Sir John Millais' 'The Ornithologist', Ford Madox Brown's 'Wyckliffe on Trial', John Pettie's 'Two Strings to her Bow', Albert J. Moore's 'Reading Aloud' (I located this fine painting in the Council Chambers), Briton Riviere's 'The Last of the Crew', Robert Gibb's 'Alma – Forward the 42nd', Sir W. O. Orchardson's 'Peveril of the Peak'. We included a large painting by William Yeames 'Prisoners of War'. Once upon a time it raised a lump in my throat, as did the same artist's 'When did you last see your father?' which is now in Liverpool. Now, some of these paintings still had a compelling attraction for a great number of people, and I got some valuable lessons in trying to assess how spectators react to a work of art when left to their own volition.

Apart from the reaction of the general public, the exhibition was not well received by some of the artist members of the Art Club. The Art School staff – apart from the notable exception of the Director, had not been favourable to my appointment. I just had to accept a slightly morbid animosity. My interest in Modern Art did not appear to be a recommendation, and the idea of going right back to the Victorians was looked on with grave suspicion. Was I trying to be funny?

My motives were quite simple. I had to feel my way in planning a very large scale exhibition and in testing public response. For example, one question I have seldom been able to answer with complete satisfaction is, 'How many catalogues do you think should be printed?' I forget how many were printed, but in the first month we appeared to have recovered most of the production costs –

thanks to the warm-hearted support from my friends in the Art trade. To enable us to sell the catalogue (214 exhibits with 8 full-page illustrations) for the nominal sum of 3d, the Art Dealers allowed themselves to be cajoled into taking advertisement space. Of six Glasgow firms and two Edinburgh firms only two in Glasgow and one in Edinburgh are still in existence. The significance of this is tied up with the London pull and the lamentable centralisation of all the arts – a situation not peculiar to this country. But an illustrated catalogue for 3d – changed days!

In talking of dealers, of course I suffer from a bias; but surely the more the merrier is a contribution to an overall activity. We still have in Glasgow, in the person of John Annan, the fourth generation of photographers and art dealers stretching back to Octavius Hill – pioneer photographer and artist, whose work is now receiving a reassessment through the Arts Council.

But the only solid link with the Glasgow and West of Scotland Art collectors and their possessions of last century is through the energetic, widely informed Ian MacNicol. Independent to the last ditch – aided and supported only by his delightful wife and daughter, a real family concern – his contacts at home and overseas are infinitely greater than his London competitors are able to fathom. For a time he had the first call on the productions of A. J. Munnings and D. Y. Cameron, but his most remarkable achievements have been in unearthing forgotten treasures of the Barbizon School and their successors.

Somebody said or wrote a long time ago, 'There are as many kinds of Art as there are kinds of feeling.' The Narrative Paintings exhibition seemed to show that it would be better to put it the other way round, viz. 'There are as many kinds of feeling as there are kinds of Art.' I was beginning to find confirmation of this in the attitude of mind of some who, when they have a painting before them, link it to a desire to find something wrong with it.

A reputation as a lecturer of sorts had preceded me; but apart from secretaries of various guilds, church literary societies and the like – kind people rather desperate to get their syllabus completed – I couldn't get at the audiences I wanted. We had therefore to make a start in trying to get the audiences to come to us. At first I didn't get much encouragement from John Fleming. 'We tried lectures in old Paton's time – but it didn't work. Sometimes, on a special occasion, with a name, they would turn up. Besides, there's the

black-out – it's not worth opening the place up in the evening.'
I pointed out to him a feature of the advertisement for the post
which I held '. . . must be prepared as one of the duties of the
position to deliver lectures on various branches of art as the
Corporation may require.'

We decided to have a try with a series of afternoon lectures, and
to our surprise we were crowded out. The chief purpose of this very
tentative effort was to create an interest in Art by talking about it as
well as by displaying it. My experience in public speaking was varied
enough to know that the audience is half the speech, just as in my
University days I had discovered that the class is half the lecture.
It was evident that there was an audience – and a very friendly and
interested audience. The greatest compliment paid me was by Sir
James Caw, for many years the Director of the National Gallery in
Scotland. He had come over specially from Edinburgh to be present
at the first of the series. He said afterwards that he thought the
approach was original, persuasive and effective. Of course I had
spent a lot of time and thought in preparation. And it wasn't so very
original. I was trying to apply, with some degree of adaptation to the
immediate occasion, the approach to Art Appreciation which I had
picked up elsewhere – especially from the Barnes Foundation in
America.

I shall introduce Barnes in due course. In the meantime, it may
explain, or excuse, some later observations and judgments if I tell
you that my earliest education in Art appreciation came through
Roger Fry, Clive Bell and some others. In Glasgow we heard and
felt the rumblings of the Art-quake – as it was called – of 1910.
I mean the celebrated exhibition of the post-impressionists at the
Grafton Galleries in London. The sole begetter of that exhibition
was Roger Fry. That is on the authority of Desmond MacCarthy,
whom I also heard say that the label 'Post-Impressionists' was coined
by Fry.

I kept the menu card of a dinner in the Students Union also in
1910, when H. H. Asquith was the guest of honour (I think he came
north to receive the Freedom of Glasgow). Among other things he
said this, and it impressed me:

'I would rather see doubtful and even perilous experiments tried,
than the cynical and timorous lethargy, which prefers to leave
things alone.'

Clive Bell had a lot to do with the post-impressionist exhibition.

He bought a Vlaminck for £14. In 1956 I saw and heard it being sold
at auction for £5,400. It was when I began to read what the critics
had to say that I began to apprehend how appreciation might mean
one thing at the beginning and a different thing years later; but
always pleasurable and rewarding. Roger Fry was the most lucid and
inspiring of talkers. I think his successor is Sir Kenneth Clark (now
Lord Clark). I commend all the writings of Fry, Bell and Clark.
Each of them can bring the 'significant form' and content of a work
of art within the compass of the plain man's understanding. The
memorable 'significant form' was coined by Clive Bell. He was
never allowed to forget it, and indeed, enjoyed watching the
innumerable attempts at tearing it to pieces.

To sit in the company of Roger Fry in front of a newly discovered
masterpiece by Renoir and hear him say in his deep voice 'It's swell'
was an unforgettable experience. It seemed as if enough had been
said. From Fry I got a convenient definition of Romantic and
Classical Art, very helpful in the kind of Art Talks I was later called
upon to deliver.

'Romantic Art produces its effect by relying on the association of
ideas which it sets up in the mind of the Spectator. Classical Art
creates its emotional effect through its own formal and pictorial
organisation.'

I suppose we, who try to popularise Art, must have a theme song, or
is it a signature tune? Fry and Bell and Clark and, on occasion,
Herbert Read, composed one or two for me. The news of our
lectures got around and eventually reached the City Chambers. At
the third of them I was honoured by the presence of a number of
City Magistrates and Councillors including my friend Tom Kerr.
Later, when I was able to free myself from the usual post-lecture
anxious enquirers, and reached the Director's room where tea was
on tap for our distinguished visitors, Tom Kerr broke away from a
group and said, 'I was just telling them, Doctor, what I told them
long ago. You're the man who will bring art to the "Midden Heid".'
This compliment with its implied assurance that I was reaching to
the man in the street survived as a family joke for quite a long time.

One of my disappointments was my failure to be accepted by the
Art School – another of those 'Establishment' complexes perhaps.
I had several friends among members of the staff. Douglas Percy Bliss
the Director, I had known in Lefevre Gallery days when, among
other things, he was the London Art Critic for the *Scotsman*. I said of

him then, 'He has some very original views on contemporary art . . . when he approves he argues with conviction; when he disapproves he becomes satirical. The unique thing about Mr Bliss is his gift of being able to satirise with paint and brush as well as with pen and ink. One day he will have to decide which exercise is to be *the* vocation. When he does so, the world is going to hear a lot more about him.' I doubt if he was altogether happy as an administrator, although he passed out some young men and women who made their mark. Anyhow, a fine art historian and critic was, more or less, lost to Scottish Art and Letters.

Benno Schotz, RSA, who became head of the Department of Sculpture and is now Queen's Sculptor in Ordinary for Scotland (since 1963), and an honorary graduate of Strathclyde University, is among my oldest friends. He is one of the survivors of my medical practice days and we have never ceased to be willing to help each other when the occasion arises. For example, one of the most attractive and most successful of our efforts to pull in the public was Benno's lecture-demonstration. He modelled the head of a subject taken at random from a capacity audience, at the same time maintaining a light-hearted, witty and informative running commentary on the art of sculpture. It was great fun, reinforcing all we were trying to do in telling the public to cast off the cloak of solemnity generally associated with lectures on Art. Hugh Crawford, RSA, head of the School of Painting, performed a similar service, starting with a blank canvas and demonstrating step by step how a portrait in oils acquired the vitality which made it a work of Art. Hugh went on to be the head of the Art School in Aberdeen and then Dundee, exercising a considerable influence on the younger generation.

In spite of all this my appointment had not impressed the Art School staff as a whole. I know that my interest in Jankel Adler and Josef Herman, when the Poles were 'invading' Glasgow, was not regarded with favour. Indeed, I was taken to task for writing a foreword to Herman's first one man show in this country. I was told it was my duty as Director of the Gallery not to become mixed up with young painters 'who didn't know what they were talking about'. And when we bought the Dali painting (in 1952) the outside limit, to judge from the views coming out of the School of Art, had been over-reached.

I thought I was beginning to make some progress against those

who insisted that lectures and talks on art are just a waste of time –
they lead nowhere. I had to become an advocate for the case that a
systematic method in cultivating an appreciation of Art is likely to
be more fruitful than the haphazard untrained approach which I
found is common among the overwhelming majority of visitors to
art exhibitions. I had to test the inference. This I did frequently, by
wandering round the gallery, and exhibitions elsewhere, trying to
look like an ordinary visitor. Through engaging others in conversation I had no difficulty in reaching a conclusion from which I felt
justified in making a start. Nothing I had in mind would interfere
with anybody who wished to be left alone to enjoy works of art in
their own particular way, even if others thought it was peculiar.
On the other hand I thought we had a duty to perform for those who
were puzzled or who experienced a sense of frustration in that they
were unable to appreciate the 'beauties in' and the 'greatness of'
works which appeal to people whose delight and understanding are
unmistakably sincere.

I had collected some of the epigrams used in opposition, 'Taste
cannot be taught – it just happens'; 'If a work of art has to be
explained the author of it isn't an artist'; 'Analysis destroys the
appreciation of Beauty'; 'Beauty is something we apprehend without
reflection'; 'When the people undertake to reason all is lost'.
Against all these and others I suggested that our approach was worth
trying because if it fails no harm is done. Above all, in any kind of
analysis nothing is added or taken from any work under consideration.
We should probably discover that we are really analysing ourselves.
On the matter of taste, I acknowledged that I was always prepared to
be helped towards developing my own, through guidance from
those whose opinions I respect. My most valuable guides have been
artists who, in addition to their gifts and powers as creators, were
lucid and competent in exposition.

For further authoritative support I could stay in Scotland, turning
to two professors – one, W. Macneile Dixon, the greatly loved and
respected Professor of English at Glasgow University from 1902 to
1935, who told me to help myself to anything he had ever said or
written; the other was his opposite number in Edinburgh, Sir
Herbert Grierson, who, after his retiral, was elected Rector of
Edinburgh University. Grierson said,

'Some of you say, can we be taught to enjoy? We either do so or
we do not. That is a great mistake. In nothing does one need more

careful and prolonged discipline than in learning to discriminate between the good and the inferior in every line of experience, from art and literature to, shall I say, wines and cigars. Joy is the final test and reward of achievement in every activity.'

I got help from another hero of mine, the late Professor Gilbert Murray, who practically began his distinguished professorial career in Glasgow. He was professor of Greek from 1889–99. Shortly before he died, Edinburgh University did me the great honour of inviting me to act as his substitute with a lecture on 'The Universities and the Arts' at the opening of the Edinburgh Festival in 1955. Some years before that, to help me to make a case for my special brand of public relationship at the Art Gallery I was allowed to quote him on Socrates. To justify talking as against writing I turned to this,

'Socrates himself wrote nothing. Why not? The reason he gives is very characteristic. A book is such a dead thing. If you ask it a question it will not answer. If it makes a mistake it goes on forever making the same mistake. Socrates wanted to learn and he could only learn by talking to live people, questioning them, making them think, and thinking with them.'

About the same time I heard Gilbert Murray discuss, in a broadcast, the present state of Society. He had been told it was terribly corrupt and wicked and materialist, hence the wars etc. He didn't quite believe this because people have always talked like that. He recollected that in the British Museum there is an ancient Babylonian Tablet from about 3,000 BC which starts 'Alas! Alas! Alas! this modern world is very wicked'. I have failed to find the tablet in the British Museum but I do not therefore conclude that museum people are careless. Following a delightful correspondence and several lines of enquiry I am satisfied that ancient Babylonian and Egyptian savants often believed their times were more wicked and more disastrous than any other period.

Although we publicised them as lectures, I preferred to think and speak of them as talks. I had picked up somewhere the definition of a lecture as 'A process whereby the notes of the lecturer become the notes of the student without passing through the mind of either'. Hence the escape into 'Talks'.

We had plenty of them. I was told that the only kind of Art Talk likely to be effective was for the speaker to communicate his own personal enthusiasm. This would be infectious and the hearer would soon apprehend greatness when he saw it. I heard the same kind of argument the other day when the discussion was centred on television programmes. One teacher said to me, 'We do not require to analyse a poem in order to convey its beauty to our pupils.' But is that not precisely what a teacher is doing if he reads or recites a poem in a manner which expresses poetic values? i.e. the rhythms, the flow of thought, the music of the words, the right words in the right places, and so on. Analysis does not mean paraphrasing the context into work-a-day language. (I got something of this kind to do in my school days.)

In another argument I was informed by one who was well-known in art circles that I was just an amiable blether. (For the benefit of those who are unacquainted with the Scots expression, a blether has been defined as 'a man who starts his mouth talking and then goes away and leaves it'.) He laid down the law to me in this fashion, 'When I say that I like a work of art I can't tell anybody why I like it. It just happens! It's like falling in love!'

Now that kind of confession is generally accepted as something beyond discussion. But is it? It is true that appreciation of a work of art appears to come to one as something in the nature of a discovery. Nevertheless a little consideration will lead to several factors contributing to the discovery. A very mild cross-examination in front of a painting of his choice revealed that my friend liked the colour. Then the design pleased him. He thought the light was very happily manipulated. He 'imagined' that the general scheme of the painting was beautifully reinforced by minor passages complementing the main idea. These are, substantially, his phrases and finally his further reactions were too vague to be put into words. I suggested that the overall indefinable quality might be described as 'vitality'. He agreed. I don't know yet when he reached the point of falling in love. As in human relations 'love at first sight' does not always lead to enduring convictions.

Is this 'falling in love' business solely a matter of intuitive apprehension? Ibsen does not make Peer Gynt act accordingly. As his gaze follows Solveig he says, 'How fair she is. Was there ever a fairer? Eyes glancing down at her shoes and white apron – and the way she held on to her mother's skirt too – and carried her prayer book wrapped in a kerchief! I must have a look at her!'

By the way, I was to hear this illustration from *Peer Gynt* come back to me once or twice. It happens frequently with our pe-

discoveries. As I had borrowed freely from other men's gardens I regarded anything of this nature as a compliment. I tend to become exasperated, however, when I hear so many people grow agitated about infringement of copyright. How seldom are any of us original! Artists have certain rights and these should be protected, but in many cases if they were honest about it they should be searching out the dependents of those whose work they have rather slavishly relied on. The question of reproduction fees and royalties was constantly a problem with us, and we never seemed to be able to arrive at the right answer. I still think public galleries, national and civic, are far too rigid and unreasonable. They ought to encourage anyone who, in one way or another, helps to make their treasures known. Does it matter so very much if they make some money in the process?

To return for a summing up of the case we tried to make out for more methodical methods in talking about art, we adumbrated these points. It is necessary to acquire the habit of seeing in pictures something more than (a) the subject represented; (b) the technical skill by which it is represented, and (c) a conformity to preconceived standards made by oneself or borrowed from somebody else. It all seems so elementary now, but I was frequently criticised for 'ramming theories down people's throats'. I always insisted that if visitors to the Art Gallery preferred to come and go as they pleased their visits were not necessarily unrewarding. There were lots of *entertainment*, e.g. in recognising a favourite scene skilfully re-produced – in coveting a lovely lady or a beautiful child – in being reminded of something totally irrelevant to the picture – in 'spotting' style or mannerisms or influences – in comparisons which need not necessarily be odious. But with all that we shall still be missing the pleasures to be found in the *enjoyment* of an artist's creation. The distinction between entertainment and enjoyment has to be made. The former is practically effortless. A tired mind and body can take part in the game. Enjoyment demands active participation. One has to be alert, attentive and prepared to be thoughtful. What you are to 'see' is your own affair, and if you should happen to 'see' something the artist never dreamt of putting into his picture, what of it? T. S. Eliot came to my aid on this point.

'A poem may appear to mean very different things, to different readers, and all of these meanings may be different from what the author thought he meant. . . . The reader's interpretation may differ from the author's and be equally valid – it may even be better.'

Another angle to 'aesthetic' appreciation came through John Fleming. Although his speciality was Shipbuilding and Engineering, his long and varied experience made him competent to converse on topics or items in every department. I encouraged all the museum officers to acquire some kind of information apropos other departments in the building. This for the obvious reason that often, at week-ends especially, they were in sole charge and might have to conduct distinguished visitors, with catholic interests. Better to have a smattering of knowledge about the important items and be able to say something about their history. Indeed, I was so keen on the idea that I instituted a voluntary morning class for senior attendants, with the same purpose in view.

John Fleming's method in the art section was to tell any group he might be conducting round the interesting facts about our well-known possessions. For example a very popular picture was Pettie's 'Two Strings to her Bow' – an early favourite of mine in my student days. This depicted a bright young girl with a shy young male on either arm. John would tell who the men were, one of them was the son of the artist, and then he would leave them guessing as to which was the successful suitor and if they lived happily ever afterwards. One day he had a group of young ladies from a Church society in one of our less prosperous city areas. Eventually John brought them to Rembrandt's 'Man in Armour' and addressed the ladies thus: 'Now, we come to one of the most valuable paintings in the collection. It is worth – what? Ten thousand pounds? Twenty thousand? Fifty thousand? – right up the scale until dramatically he said, 'Ladies. This picture is worth one hundred thousand pounds!' The impressive silence was broken by a voice from a tall bright-looking figure in the back row, ejaculating with the requisite note of spontaneous surprise, 'God Almighty!'

I never had a success like that.

Some kind of reputation must have been building up for I began to receive a great number of invitations to speak at a variety of associations and societies – Rotary clubs – Publicity clubs – and all the rest of it. I accepted as many as I could because, apart from the pleasant company and free lunches, they provided excellent opportunities for publicising our activities. The press was wonderfully co-operative, so much so that my friends would remark, 'You are never out of the newspapers'. For many years back the gossip writers had been warned off the Art Gallery. There had been an indiscretion or a premature leak of committee information. In due course we won them back and laid ourselves out to be as informative as we could, even to the extent of inventing stories which, when there wasn't much news about, could make a paragraph in some columnist's diary. To our critics we were fortunate in being able to point at the great energy and imagination Sir Kenneth Clark was demonstrating at the National Gallery in London. His war-time efforts were splendid and did much to help others, including me, to break away from the rigid or inelastic procedures which suffocated so many of our galleries and museums.

I was criticised for publicising myself. Of course I was, but I couldn't succeed in anything of the kind without publicising the gallery. I had taken a lot of trouble and done a lot of hard work to make myself an acceptable public speaker. In my time I must have spoken at most of the annual dinners of City Incorporations, St Andrew's Nights, Burns' Suppers and all types of Societies. At every one of them I was identified as the Director of the Art Gallery and Museum and, by hook or by crook, I got in some mention of this civic service with a hint – seldom concealed – that my audience weren't living a full life if they had no place for the arts.

Moreover, as a Corporation official – paid by the City – I thought it was a duty to render assistance where and when I could to the various organisations devoted to public welfare. I knew that whenever I might reach the stage of being regarded as a bore I would be dropped. Meanwhile, in the first blush of novelty and enthusiasm I was kept uncommonly busy. When I began to investigate the criticisms I found some of them came from councillors and colleagues who were either unwilling or unable to take the same view on the usefulness of this 'extra-mural' activity. There was a danger that I might become puffed up by my own conceit. I was saved from that by a number of friends – many of them old associates from my medical days – ready to debunk me. And there were as many laughs against me as there were with me.

I had to consider other things besides painting and sculpture. The city had inherited an outstanding collection of Arms and Armour. This had been bequeathed by Robert Lyons Scott, head of an old-established family business, Scotts Shipbuilding & Engineering Company of Greenock. It was quite outside my range and that of everyone else on the staff, but I had, of course, to consider and advise on how it could be displayed. We had the great good fortune to be able to call in Mr James Mann – he became Sir James – Master of the Armouries, HM Tower of London, and keeper of the Wallace Collection. Accepted as the leading authority on the subject, and very well acquainted with the collection, he had frequently advised Mr Scott on pieces which were internationally known.

The size and importance of the collection, which I was informed is the most valuable thing of its kind outside London, made it clear that we had to do some rearranging of the Museum Section to provide space for this feature. I think we acted wisely in clearing what was called the Glasgow Room by removing the contents to the People's Palace, a Branch Museum located in Glasgow Green at the East end of the City.

We were then able to construct a unit with up-to-date show cases for the display of the Scott Armour, in accordance with Sir James Mann's guidance. Not many changes have been found necessary in the original plan and, with the addition of some special Scottish items from the Whitelaw Collection, the Armour Section, on the left as one enters the building, remains very much as it was arranged then.

Making space for the Scott Collection led to what I still think were more steps in the right direction. Later I thought of another but was instructed to mark time. I ought to confess in the first place, that I have never thought much of Branch Museums unless they have a specific and unique character. Too often they are little more than a nondescript collection of items, surplus to the displays at the central institutions or, for a period, on loan to brighten things up. The contents of the People's Palace were a queer mixture. A large room was given over to the Sir Thomas Lipton Collection. Most of these were the yachting trophies assembled in the course of the amazing career of this great Glasgow merchant and sportsman. Historically important perhaps, and there were some fascinating stories linked to most of them. Among the drawings and cartoons, illustrating his popularity, is an illuminated address from the 'Mutual Welfare League of Sing Sing Prison' inscribed 'To a good loser from some good losers'.

There was also a fine, if incomplete, collection of Regimental Uniforms, badges and accoutrements associated with the history of Glasgow's military achievements. And for safe keeping there was the mess-plate of some of the Battalions. The Curator, Captain Philippe Durand, was an authority on the subject and, indeed, the major part of the collection was his own property. His enthusiasm was embarrassing, for some of the Committee took a dim view of the Curator's hobby becoming mixed up with a civic collection. The dilemma was eventually cleared up and gradually we succeeded in establishing what is now called the Old Glasgow Museum. When Captain Durand retired (and I am glad to say he continued to be of service to enquirers seeking information on old Glasgow) he was succeeded by Mr James D. Boyd, who is now the energetic Director of the Art Gallery and Museum in Dundee.

Then, in the face of some doubts and murmurs of a 'dangerous precedent' the Corporation appointed Miss Elspeth Gallie. In my view, this was one of the best appointments they ever made. Miss Gallie, prominent as a leader among the undergraduates of her time, specialising in Scottish History, brought to her new job the right kind of precise and thorough research we needed. In an incredibly short space of time she introduced changes which combined imaginative display and effective publicity, and at the same time became a reliable source of relevant information. Alas! marriage plus Corporation rules were responsible for her departure.

Although on occasion the public might be attracted by special exhibitions, and the evening group visits were very successful, I still clung to the view that a Museum concentrating on 'The History of Glasgow' ought to be more centrally situated. A chance to have this came and was missed. Perhaps it would be more accurate to say it was rejected without adequate consideration.

The idea was planted in my mind by the late Mr Gray Buchanan, Director of the well-known firm of William Jack & Sons. They had strong Glasgow associations, especially through one-time Prime Minister Bonar Law, whose career in business was in Jacks' before he went in for politics.

Gray Buchanan's business headquarters were in London but he spent a lot of his time in Rothesay. I met him there, and one evening he said to me, 'You must get hold of the Glasgow Royal Exchange building. It is a Museum piece and I have good reason for knowing that a big commercial firm has its eye on it.' He went on to point out that the old Exchange methods of doing business had faded out, and that in some cities the central site and the building itself might be of civic importance.

Together we planned out the best use to be made of the Royal Exchange Building if the City got hold of the property – a fine island site, architecturally important as a period piece dating back to the 18th century and the Tobacco Lords. Certainly something that must be preserved.

I was all for it for two purposes (a) History of Glasgow, and (b) Gallery space for regular exhibitions, with provision for small lunch-hour concerts, or something of the kind. Gray Buchanan wasn't much interested in details. 'Save the building from the speculators and maintain the amenities of the area' was his chief consideration. When I expanded on the idea of art shows, where the business community could drop in as the spirit or occasion moved them, instead of having to face the deliberate journey to Kelvingrove, he was all in favour. Moreover, we thought it possible that the Exchange Square would become the centre for trading in antiques, rare books, paintings and sculpture and the like – a kind of Glasgow's Bond Street, Rue la Boètie, or 57th Street. I expanded my vision with a newspaper article and tried to work up some interest in the project.

It all came to nothing. Maybe – and this is very likely – I talked too much, without enough discrimination. A year later, and out of the blue, came the information that the Libraries Committee had its eye on the Royal Exchange to accommodate the Stirling Reference Library. We – the Art Gallery Committee – didn't have a chance. The possibility of an Old Glasgow Museum, as an alternative, was raised. I was informed that it was stated at a meeting that our Committee had been consulted, but the Director (me) was against the idea on the grounds of unsuitability. I discovered later the source of such misleading information to be met with 'I remember now. It wasn't you who said it. It was somebody else. However it doesn't matter very much. Besides, the Library Committee has more pull with the Corporation.'

Apart altogether from the strange workings in local government I still think that the wrong decision was made. A central reference library is an excellent and very necessary piece of public service. But the Royal Exchange – even now only partly occupied – comes into the category of a Glasgow landmark, and could be better operated as an architectural feature of the city's history, apart altogether from a down-town centre for art exhibitions.

A.A.   E

5

University Interlude

I got a note from the Principal of the University, Sir Hector Hetherington, asking me to look in one day. What about a series of lectures in the University? Not a class – not academic – nothing to do with aesthetics or art history, except incidentally. He wanted to create an interest in art among the undergraduate body, and members of the staff who might be inclined to come. It was something worth trying and he thought I could do it. I spent a lot of time preparing material and collecting illustrations. I had diagrams and charts made and, with some anxiety, looked forward to doing something different. I was flattered by the size and range of the audience, but when the novelty wore off and examinations drew near the staff on occasions appeared to outnumber the students. In some respects it was rather a thrill to appear in the Zoology lecture room (Professor Hindle, who later became Director of the London Zoo, was most hospitable and a regular attender) and to recollect that in turn I had tried to teach Physiology and Clinical Medicine under the authority of the University.

There is no doubt about the seriousness with which I approached this new experience. As usual Isabel Mackintosh co-operated from a seat in the back row in order to make a verbatim record of my solemn, or not so solemn, utterances. As I spoke off the cuff from notes which varied from profuse to scanty and the lights were often lowered to show slides or to use an epidiascope, the results were better than I had expected. Sir Hector did me the honour of slipping in to my second lecture. When it was over I was very anxious to discover if he thought my performance was in accordance with his instructions. He used one word and a smile – 'Admirable'.

Thus fortified and encouraged we continued for another year or two and I found my name on the staff list in the University Diary as an Honorary Lecturer in the History of Art. It was dawning on me, however, as it must have dawned on others, that I was getting nowhere.

This must have occurred to my friend and neighbour, Professor Peter Alexander. He was interested in what I was trying to do, and he suggested that the weakness of the effort lay in the fact that it was not linked to any specific department of study. Constantly willing to try anything, and of course with authoritative backing and blessing, I switched to a series of four lectures on 'John Constable and his Times' to the Class in English. The series was to be complementary to the prescribed book for study, C. R. Leslie's *Memoirs of the Life of John Constable*. This was right up my street, for my interest in the field of Art Study began with Constable, leading on to French Painting of the Nineteenth Century. More preparation and a wonderful class. By the time I had done the course three times these lectures on Constable were the most polished productions I had ever achieved on any Art Theme.

The popularity of the lectures preceded me to Australia. In 1963, at a luncheon at the University of New South Wales, I heard that the University Archivist, David MacMillan by name, had used them as a build-up for our visit. He was relying on a memory of his undergraduate days in Glasgow. Professor Alexander heard them at least twice and we continued to be, to the day of his death, on friendly terms! He is an authority on Shakespeare, and when, not so long ago, I was glancing through his *Shakespeare's Life and Art* I came across a reference to W. G. Riddell. I remember bringing these two friends of mine together. Peter Alexander, to support his argument 'we need no Socrates to remind us that a man's very virtues may provoke the envy and slander of the multitude', quoted from Riddell's book *Memoirs of an Obscure Victorian*. Here is the quotation:

'Mr Rankin of the Indus was by far the best engineer I ever sailed with, and he taught me more about my business than all the others put together. I thought he would one day fill a great position but he never did. I have known many men his inferiors in every way who easily outstripped him. I think his hatred of deceit and humbug hindered him more than anything. He was not a prig, and he rarely expressed his dislike for trickery, but mean men felt uncomfortable in his presence, and I was often surprised to find how much he was hated by humbugs who hardly knew him.'

Tall, lean, with bright eyes and a smile which drew back the corners of his mouth, slightly hesitant in speech, W.G. was grand company. His book was actually an autobiography dating from his days as an apprentice in engineering on the Clyde. He was, when I knew him, doing important work for the Admiralty. We had got to know each other through his interest in painting and his friendship with Scottish artists. From a fund of reminiscences he could keep a company going for hours without appearing to monopolise the conversation. He told me that from a bunch of favourable reviews on his book the one that pleased him most was that which described it, through a printer's error, as 'Memories of an Obscene Victorian'.

The obvious time to retire from University lecturing came with the creation of a department of the History of Fine Art, and the appointment of Andrew McLaren Young as lecturer. He was working at the Tate Gallery when I came back to Glasgow and at one time it looked as if he might come our way. As things turned out he went to Birmingham, working at the Barber Institute until he came to the University to build up, from zero, an additional course in the Arts Faculty. I then bowed myself out of University lecturing but continued to address student societies when invited.

Under the new lecturer's direction more attention was drawn towards the significance of old and recent bequests and other acquisitions. For too long Glasgow University has been hiding its light and I rejoiced to see signs of the University resuming the leadership in cultural interests which it held so prominently in the eighteenth century.

How I used to weary University friends by constantly harping back to Francis Hutcheson, the Foulis Academy, and all the rest of it! To keep faith with other things I have said, I must add the hope that some day the University will rescue the department of Art from being something more than a Department of History. The philosophy of Art should not be a foreign language to a student of Art, and what about practising the arts as well as theorising about them? With what I have seen in the course of travel I hope one day to see the link up with the School of Art which has already been established become more effective. I am well aware of the fact that there are other opinions on the matter; but, having in mind the procedures followed in the departments of music and drama, I am not willing to abandon my own opinion.

In deploring the gaps in my own schooling I have thought it right to say that in the educational structure (I know the pedants will say that a structure cannot be educational), a start must be made at

University level. We have to face up to the fact that we turn out all kinds of graduates with their degrees stamped upon them and they take into the great wide world an almost complete lack of interest in, or knowledge of, any of the Fine Arts. I've said all this already in *The Universities and the Arts* published by Edinburgh University. Others have said it better, before and since. One fine day somebody will do something about it.

In thinking of the University and my small part in the move towards a new Department of Art I am bound to suffer from recollections of the earlier days. Some of the friendships then formed were sustained and I had reason to be grateful for them in my 'settling in' efforts at the Art Gallery.

When I returned from war service in 1919 to become a very diffident, rusty assistant to the Professor of Physiology I found myself in very pleasant and stimulating company. Concentrated efforts rubbed off the rust and my chief, Professor D. Noël Paton, made me into a competent enough teacher. He was the son of the celebrated Scots artist Sir Joseph Noël Paton, who was appointed Queen's Limner for Scotland in 1866. Fame and fortune attended him for a long spell, but his paintings are now little more than an item in Scottish art history. It was rumoured that Artist Noël Paton in his religious paintings used his son, Physiologist Noël Paton, as the model for the figure of Christ. As a teacher he scared the wits out of me. As a chief he was the kindest of men and, somehow, he created an atmosphere which led most of us to behave and talk as if we were his disciples.

In and out of the staff-room in Physiology there came and went E. P. Cathcart, who should have been a politician although he taught me to have the courage to say 'I don't know'; David Burns who went on to a chair in Newcastle; Herbert Paul, brilliantly versatile, who turned from an academic career to enjoy life, principally in a unique hospital venture, at Millport on the larger Cumbrae – an island in the Firth of Clyde; Noah Morris who succeeded Stockman in the chair of Materia Medica and who, at the time of his premature death, had made a name for himself as teacher, clinician and researcher; George Wishart who became Dean of the Faculty of Medicine. Through the wall, so to speak, was David Campbell who went on to Aberdeen and was, as Sir David, for many years President of the General Medical Council.

I know all this sounds like a roll-call of dear old pals on one or other side of the grave. That is not the idea. I am trying to demonstrate that in Medicine as in Art I kept good company. When I returned to Glasgow in a new profession all our paths crossed very frequently in the course of mutual interests.

Others, engaged solely on research work, found the department a congenial place to work in and the team spirit was strong. The basic remuneration for a university assistant in the early 1920s was £150 per annum. It could be, and generally was, augmented by research grants. Noah Morris and I were in a dilemma. Each of us wanted to get married and found a family. We decided, therefore, to have a spell in general practice, still keeping a foot in the academic field. In turn I served on the outdoor medical staff of the Royal Infirmary, taught Physiology at Anderson's College, succeeded Geoffrey Fleming (he became Professor of Child Health) as assistant to John Cowan at the same institution. Probably the most illustrious student was the celebrated missionary-explorer David Livingstone.

John Cowan was in many ways remarkable. Tall and slender, slightly bent at shoulder level as if to reach down to lesser people, he reminded one of a question mark. His quiet mode of speech seemed to be sprinkled with queries. He was the last of a long line of Glasgow doctors, a pioneer in modern methods in cardiology with a bias towards the scientific approach in clinical investigation. He took me into the cardiac clinic set up by the Ministry of Pensions after World War 1 and thus gave me the chance to profit from his great experience. I was actually being paid to learn. Some years later, on the first day of my new career as an art dealer John Cowan called at Reid's Gallery. We missed each other but he left an envelope containing a halfpenny to wish me luck, and three guineas for 'any old print' so that he would be on record as my first customer. He has left behind him a very enjoyable mixty-maxty kind of book *All our Yesterdays*.

Morris and I were leading rather a hectic life – sixteen hours a day sort of thing – but we both managed to steal the odd moments of respite. His consulting rooms in Whitehill Street, Dennistoun in Glasgow's East End, were almost opposite our door at No. 14. Regularly he would pop in for a talk, and not infrequently would try to pacify our first-born to let Cath and me finish our meal. Tim, the said first-born, notwithstanding his noisy beginnings grew up into physically robust manhood. When 'Uncle' Noah, in reminiscent mood, reminded him of the days when he was a babe in arms and had to be comforted, Tim grabbed the then eminent professor, carried him in triumph round our dining-room, observing 'Fair's fair! It is an honour now to do the same for you.' Morris got out of general practice before I did. He went back to where he belonged – the lecture room, the laboratory and the hospital ward. His successor, Professor Stanley Alstead, closed the most moving tribute to a colleague I have ever read with these words 'The unspeakable misfortune of Morris's premature death, in 1947, deprived him of the joy of seeing the full fruits of his labour.' He had been among the first to create and develop an interest in the aged sick – i.e. geriatric medicine.

The phrase 'He does good by stealth' applies more to Stanley Alstead than to any other man I know. He was President of the Royal Faculty of Physicians and Surgeons (now the Royal College) (1956–8), and in his quiet gentle way performed a great service in restoring the finances to a healthier condition.

The Royal Faculty paid me the great compliment of establishing a new post and elected me to fill it, 'Honorary Curator of the Art Collection'. They forgot to give me a collection. However, I took over the care of a number of portraits of Presidents, Fellows and Members, promoted a small picture fund and eventually helped to acquire some works by contemporary artists. The City Corporation was most helpful, and among other gestures of support agreed to the exchange of a large portrait of Sir William MacEwan, Glasgow's illustrious surgeon, for the smaller version, which was less than appropriate in the rearranged College hall.

The general amenities were greatly improved. In the Alexandra Room are two portraits of Honorary Fellows, HRH Princess Alexandra and Sir Hector Hetherington. Both are fine examples of the work of Stanley Cursiter, and make superb decorations in a restful room.

Geoffrey Fleming (President 1946–8) thought we must do something about a serious gap in our pictorial history. There was no portrait of King James the Sixth (First of Great Britain) from whom the College had received its Royal Charter in 1599. According to Horace Walpole the King was 'lavish with meanness'. Professor J. D. Mackie, H M Historiographer in Scotland, says of him:

'The Tragic Queen was followed by one whom history, not uninfluenced by the pen of Sir Walter Scott, has tended to regard as a King of comedy. Spindle-shanked, goggle-eyed, sloppy-mouthed James shuffles across the Scottish Stage, witty of speech, irresolute in action, influenced by personable young men, flinching at the sight of a drawn sword.'

However, I kept a look out for a portrait, and thanks to a London friend Francis Howard, who enjoyed haunting auction rooms, we picked up an excellent portrait by Van Somer (or Somern) at a bargain. It cost £20. Painted on panel, it arrived in three parts, but was excellently cradled and restored by Harry McLean at the Art Gallery. There are several portraits of 'Jamie the Sixth' by Van Somer. Five are in Holyrood Palace. None in my opinion are as bright or as interesting as the Royal College example.

I find it impossible to conclude this University Interlude without a reference to more recent events.

In 1953 I was elected Rector. I was supposed to be a working rector, which is another way of indicating a regular attendance at meetings of the Court and participation in its affairs.

My immediate successors were R. A. Butler and Quintin Hogg, indicating a return to the tradition of a remote political celebrity. Then, in 1962, the student body elected Chief Albert Luthuli, and the SRC (Students Representative Council) invited me to be his assessor on the Court. The invitation was confirmed by the Rector. We never met. The South African Government refused permission for him to come to Glasgow to deliver the customary Rectorial Address. For many reasons it became clear to most of us that Chief Luthuli was one of the greatest men of the century, far greater than most of those who dared to call themselves his masters.

More recent than that the conclusion of the W. A. Cargill lecture – already indicated as the occasion which sent me off on this adventure, was this:

'Let me finish with a piece of news. Less than three months ago it was announced that Mr. Paul Mellon had made a gift to Yale University of his collection of British paintings, drawings, prints and illustrated books. Valued at around thirty-five million dollars, the collection will be housed in a multi-purpose Art Centre for which twelve million dollars have also been donated. I need not give details, for Mr. Dennis Farr, the curator of the Mellon British Art Collection, has recently joined the staff of this department.'

(He is now the Director at Birmingham, where he has been joined at the Barber Institute by Hamish Miles, also ex-Glasgow.) What impressed me was the opening paragraph of the Press Release. Paul Mellon speaking:

'It was at Yale as an undergraduate that my personal interest in Art began in earnest, and I have always been deeply grateful to the University for this fact.'

This great gift must have been regarded by Andrew Ritchie, the Director of the Art Gallery at Yale University, as the finest thing to mark his retiral from a fascinating post. We first met Andrew and Jane Ritchie when he was at the Museum of Modern Art in New York. He is a Scot, originally from somewhere around Coatbridge; but the only things that pull him back to the land of his birth – and they do so with great regularity – are the trout in a highland stream.

In these days when the menace of state interference in the freedom of our Universities becomes a matter of anxiety, it might not be a bad idea to breed a race of grateful graduates.

In Glasgow University the General Council has over 40,000 on its register. Among its most important statutory duties is to elect the Chancellor and four assessors to the University Court. It once elected a woman, Dr Flora Tebb, late head of the Girls' High School. I proposed her. It seems odd to me, that she has never had a successor when women now form a very important proportion of the student body. A number of years ago a Graduates Association was formed, presumably to sustain post-graduate contacts. Notwithstanding an attractive and very valuable journal *The College Courant*, has it developed as its begetters hoped and expected? Concealed among these 40,000 there must be some Paul Mellons.

I first knew about Lord Boyd Orr, Glasgow's Chancellor, when he was in the Department of Physiology. I followed him there and I have been following him ever since (see illustration between pp. 40-41).

There may be other universities with Chancellors as distinguished in learning or politics, but none has collected to himself a more universal respect, admiration and affection. And that also goes for his family.

In any case, no Chancellor possesses eyebrows as remarkable in luxuriant grandeur as our John Boyd Orr. James Bridie was fond of 'recalling' an occasion when they sat together at one of Bridie's first nights in London. Before the curtain rose Boyd Orr turned to a lady in the seat behind him and said, 'Madam, are my eyebrows obstructing your view? I can raise them.'

6

After the Blitz

Every time I think of the wreckage which confronted us on the morning after the blitz (March 1941) I am reminded of what one comforter said. 'Well, you remember the Phoenix fable. It's up to you to determine what will rise from the ashes.' This was another way of planting the idea that we should do something more than think of restoring things as they were. On the night the Art Gallery got it, a land mine sailed down from the skies and exploded on the banks of the Kelvin. The blast was terrific. When daylight came we saw the place as a shambles, except for the corners most remote from the river side of the Gallery, where we had placed the Scott Collection of armour.

Apart from broken windows the structure of the University remained intact. Some of the Gallery towers had moved slightly, and with a few freak exceptions, windows, roof lights and display cases had the glass reduced to fragments. In fact, 50 tons of broken glass were subsequently removed from the building. We know this to be correct for we received 10 shillings a ton by way of salvage.

One blessing, I think, resulted. The Sculpture Hall, the central feature of the building was, to me, an eye-sore, with so many pieces of bad sculpture and plaster casts dotted around like men on a chess-board. When we had extracted the really good works they were totally insufficient to fill the large space. The re-thinking done then has remained as evidence of the value of using the central space for the multiple purposes of changing displays. We had quite a number of largish marble ladies who had originally come out of Italy – a survival of the days when Glasgow merchants did the Grand Tour and came back with Eves, Satyrs and Nymphs to decorate their grand glass conservatories. And they looked not too bad in these very necessary extensions to the large mansions in Kelvinside, Dowanhill and Maxwell Park. The setting at least, was appropriate enough.

The next generation had no use for them and they found a home in the Art Gallery. I thought I knew of a better home and, with the co-operation of the Director of Parks, we had them placed in the large glass house known as the Kibble Palace in the Botanic Gardens. Although generally approved, my friend Professor John Walton had other views. As Professor of Botany John Walton had a special interest and affection for the Botanic Gardens. We had spoiled the overall vegetation climate of his beloved Kibble Palace and turned it into a cheap imitation of Palm Court, Grand Hotel type of presentation. It led to the exchange of some unusual forms of greeting when we met, and, at a distance, the perpetration of defiant doggerel verses.

This recollection has, I imagine, arisen from the fact that our ship is on the point of entering the Panama Canal. Some years ago Dorothy and John Walton did the same voyage. While in one of the Canal locks he asked a fellow-passenger a leading question. Would she prefer to be embraced in a lock or locked in an embrace?

Now enjoying retirement in Dundee, Professor Walton is still Dean of Faculties at Glasgow University, where an excellent portrait by Albert Morocco can be seen in the College Club.

Another reason for including the Waltons in this narrative is that John is the son of E. A. Walton, one of the founders of the Glasgow School. The Waltons were for a time near neighbours to Whistler in Chelsea. When Whistler received intimation of the University's intention to confer the honorary degree of LL.D., he was highly delighted. He immediately got in touch with E.A., to find out all about the procedure, what he should wear at the graduation ceremony and how he should word his letter of acceptance. This and other pieces of fresh information I got from John Walton when I compiled the Whistler pamphlet in 1951.

With the memory of what I had seen in Science Museums, especially in America, I conferred with Dr R. G. Absalom, the curator in charge of our Natural History Department. He became Director of the Newport Art Gallery. Once we got over the usual stumbling block 'we'll never get the money for it', everyone concerned became keen on the project of building large habitat groups. We found we didn't need much money. Under war conditions no firm was able to accept a contract, and we had therefore to do everything with our own staff, working with whatever material could be scrounged. The Parks Department gave us all we required in the way of vegetation. Through some old theatrical supply friends from amateur drama days (I mean Bambers of Charing Cross) we got some discarded scene canvas. Joiners, painters, electricians, taxidermists, tackled this new job with enthusiasm and eventually the first group was completed.

With my publicity bias working hard, I thought this effort was worth a brochure. Another reason was that publications on very interesting museum exhibits were almost non-existent. I insisted on due acknowledgements being made of the tradesmen's part in the project, and their names were included. I also got the committee – all the members were delighted with the result – to sanction a small bonus to each of the tradesmen who had made the experiment possible. Then, for the first time I came up against Trade Union rules and regulations. A bonus is contrary to the basic idea of a wage structure. Evidently I could find no way to make a distinction, through occasional extras to first-class men with the ability to do something beyond the strict limits of their trade – and the time-servers. Every now and then I had to play a part in trade disputes, mostly minor issues, since our relatively small department was governed by a more central authority.

In all the meetings I had with Trade Union officials, the discussions were conducted in a most friendly and understanding atmosphere. This was due, in some measure, to the fact that the official was well aware of the fact that his most vocal and active members were also our most vocal but inactive members. I have never forgotten one occasion when, after a sound briefing, I had to explain to a very good and efficient tradesman, deputed to be spokesman for others, the special situation in Corporation employment. I pointed out that they had other benefits denied to their trade outside, such as the privileges of superannuation with a pension on retiral. He interrupted me very politely to say, 'Please don't make too much talk about pensions. So few of us live long enough to enjoy them. Then we only get our own contribution back and without interest.' He was right, for when I looked into the matter I found it was the exception rather than the rule for anyone in our department either to reach the pension age of sixty-five or to enjoy it for more than a brief space. I also found that, with some officials, the later years of service were clouded by a state of mind which I can only define as 'pensionitis'. Thrift, with an eye on security in old age, is an excellent virtue, but when it becomes an obsession it acts as a handicap to clear thinking and effective work.

The 'Habitat Group' idea continued to expand into one of the museum's most popular features. There was also restored to the architectural qualities of the building a sense of space and an attractive vista extending through the East and West Courts. Previously this had been blocked by huge cases containing elephants and giraffes. These huge animals looked far more comfortable in their new setting, and their old central site was put to much better use. One of these uses was to put on, every summer, a display of wild flowers with popular as well as botanical labels. I had seen something of the kind elsewhere – I think in Birmingham. In our case we had the good fortune to win the enthusiasm of a very well informed 'amateur', William Rennie by name. Stocky in build, his gait always reminded me of the line 'with measured beat and slow'. For several years he brought in most of the specimens. These were displayed openly on tables and I was warned that we were asking for trouble. It was said that the kids would pinch the vases as well as the flowers. Nothing of the kind ever happened. I used to wonder if we had taken the precautions recommended and erected some kind of barrier, whether we would have enjoyed the same result.

When we began to speculate on the right procedure for the rehabilitation of the Ethnography Room we came up against the snag of nobody in charge. This was very happily solved by the re-appearance of Dr Henry G. Farmer, who made himself available to do what he could on the lines of creating a new approach to the selection and display of the material which had survived the blitz, and anything else he could find in store.

Before I record what he did for Ethnography, I must go back to the first 'post-blitz' exhibition, opened by Lord Provost Dollan on 21st May 1941. This was 'Instruments of Music', the first complete thing of its kind to be held in Britain. Our debt to Dr Farmer was immeasurable as it was to various lenders. It was a very ambitious and somewhat risky venture. I learned a lot. Among other things, I was told to be careful not to describe it as a Musical Instrument Exhibition – there is no such thing as a Musical Instrument! Instruments of Music, yes!

We had over a dozen lecture-recitals on Tuesday afternoons throughout that summer and when it was all over, from the belated accounts in various journals we were made increasingly aware of the

fact that the gallery had contributed in more ways than we thought
to museum and music history. Whenever we remembered the
recurrent snags, the comic solutions and the compliments, we
always thought of it as Farmer's Show.

The Instruments of Music Catalogue has become a rarity. One
important sequel, and again through Dr Farmer's good offices, the
Museum was able to acquire the famous Glen Collection of
Instruments for little more than a nominal figure. The nature of the
collection and its significance for the music lover are explained in an
article contributed to the first number of the *Scottish Art Review* in
1946.

Another thing this exhibition did for me was to increase my
admiration for the remarkable man who made it. Out of our
association grew a friendship which developed with the years. I had
seen Henry Farmer, particularly the view of his back, on several
occasions. He was conductor of the orchestra at the Empire Theatre
in Glasgow from 1914 to 1947. (I think our first handshake was on
an introduction by my sea-faring brother Gilbert.) He spoke crisply,
as if to match his short dark moustache, and seemed anxious to hide
his scholarly pursuits. Subsequently, I became very interested in the
other side of the double life he was leading, especially when I heard
that when experts in British, Continental and American circles
foregather to discuss Arabic music, they frequently conclude by
saying 'We had better ask Farmer about that.'

I happened once to pick up in a London bookshop, a little book on
Modern Art. It had wandered from the USA to the Charing Cross
Road. The title *Zarathustra Speaks on Art* was its sole link with
Nietzsche. Opening the book casually, I came across this bit of
dialogue between the painter and the doctor.

'It is a historical calamity that the Arabs' presence has been so
ignored. Why, even the Crescent was cut from the Cross.'

'Oh! Tell us something about it, doctor?' I urged.

'What little I can,' he replied. 'You must read the works of
H. G. Farmer.' . . . and so on.

How did all this come about? What led a man whose main
occupation, apparently, was to maintain contact with the elite of the
music hall 'stars' – he knew them all – to become an Orientalist of
very high standing? He was also interested in Scottish Music, witness
his *History of Music in Scotland*, the first complete treatment of the
subject.

I gathered that under pressure from a London publisher, who had issued two Farmer books on military music, he did a translation from the French *La Musique Arabe*. This led to appeals for more information, to which he had to make reply 'Look up so-an-so'. It was when he found confusion among the so-called authorities that he decided to learn Arabic. This was the only way, he thought, to be able to form his own opinions on Arabic Music – by being able to read the old treatises in their original form. An MA in 1924, PhD in 1926, DLitt in 1941, all from Glasgow University, to be crowned by the Doctorate of Music (*Honoris Causa*) from Edinburgh. The late Dudley J. Medley, Professor of History, once greeted him with 'From Risibility to Research'. My curiosity on his Jekyll and Hyde way of living brought the explanation, 'Save for a couple of hours at a Monday morning rehearsal, my livelihood is made from 6 pm to 11 pm, which means that the morning and afternoon can be devoted to my avocations.' The summary in scholarly achievements is in *Who's Who*. I hope the full, fascinating story of an extraordinary life will one day be told.

To bring Dr Farmer back to Kelvingrove and Ethnology, I have to begin by saying that he devoted himself to this very painstaking job for over two years. He was in the gallery at the back of eight every morning – before any of the rest of us had made an appearance. We had often to drag him away to have some lunch, and he disappeared only when it was time to go to spend the rest of the day at the Empire Theatre.

The cost to the Corporation was negligible. We had to reglaze the smashed show-cases and adapt their shapes. At the same time we got rid of the funereal black paint which in every case had hidden some beautiful light mahogany. Getting down to the natural wood helped the final overall colour scheme. The interiors or cores of the cases were made up from the wood of packing cases covered with hessian or the remnants of the torn window blinds. Even if we had wanted new material we couldn't have got it. But in adapting what was there and in adding a colour scheme which, while being easy on the eye, also served a descriptive purpose, Dr Farmer transformed the place. As an aid to easy reference he designed a large wall-map with a colour key indicating the distribution of races in the different areas of primitive and civilised peoples. By glancing at the colours on the map and picking up the same colour in the case interiors, the visitor could at a glance quickly relate the exhibits to the country. This map almost led to a serious international situation.

The ambassador of one of the South American republics, following a visit to the gallery and without demonstrating anything more than extreme pleasure, afterwards sent a strongly-worded complaint to the Foreign Office. Evidently, misreading Farmer's wonderful map, he deplored that his mother country had been marked as the home of an uncivilised race. Due explanations were forthcoming and all was well.

Farmer had been given *carte blanche* to dig into the accumulation of acquisitions in the stores. He unearthed quite an amount of valuable material which had never seen the light of day since the building was opened in 1901. One box of Persian tile fragments, showing a beautiful sense of design, appeared to have been received in the eighties of last century. I was excited myself to find some unique examples of Primitive African Sculpture which was probably brought home by Scottish missionaries. No one appeared to have noted their significance as works of art, and I was only able to spot them because of my association with the first important exhibition of the kind we had put on at the Lefevre Gallery in May 1933. It was then I met Louis Carré for the first time. The show was under his direction. The prices of most of the exhibits struck me as fantastically high, but Carré's invariable explanation was '*très rare*'. It became a form of greeting between us and has lasted down the years. Anyone interested in contemporary French Art must eventually find his way to Carré's gallery in Paris.

The reconstruction of the Ethnographical section was done voluntarily, as a labour of love. However, I had to regain some peace of mind and suggested to my committee that the least the Corporation could do was to pay Dr Farmer some kind of honorarium. Following a good deal of discussion, and another fall-out with Tom Kerr, the handsome sum of £200 was voted for two years' work! Some time later we worked it out and with perfect good humour Farmer confirmed that the rate of pay was very much less than that of the boy who helped him, namely 2d an hour. All his life this charming scholarly man has never valued his work in terms of money. For some years before his death, and following active efforts by a number of friends, he was persuaded to accept a Civil List Pension.

Before leaving Ethnography it should be added that the finishing touches to the new room were some special relevant murals by a number of young Glasgow artists. This was my idea and I thought they were novel enough to give an added interest, but they failed to meet with general approval and have disappeared. As a sentimental touch we placed, prominently, Bourdelle's portrait bust of James Frazer as a salute to the author of *The Golden Bough* – a native of the city.

The final 'splash' was the catalogue or descriptive booklet. This was designed by T. Johnston Walker, head of the Stow School of Printing. He produced one of the most striking covers ever to be seen on a museum publication. He did the same for the Instruments of Music Exhibition. His knowledge of typography and layout was like a breeze of fresh air. One of my enduring regrets is that we were unable to come to some arrangement whereby he could continue to advise and help us. It was a case of 'Barkis is willing' but the demands of his important and growing post were too great.

Every now and then I would hear criticism of the Ethnography Department. There were several errors. Some of the items were in the wrong cases; others were wrongly described. So! Dr Farmer never imagined that such a large and exacting operation would be completely free from imperfections or errors. The best answer to the critics would appear to be 'Do you remember what this section once looked like? And how much money was then available?'

Our blitz and post-blitz experiences were varied, multiple and memorable. We made a host of new friends. Dining out was ruled out through rationing and a new social formula. We met in each other's houses for snacks, coffee and conversation. I recollect especially many happy evenings in the Robieson home. Sir William, as he became before the war ended, was Editor of the *Glasgow Herald*. His finger, so to speak, was right on up-to-date news. His visitors made up a formidable range of celebrated and interesting people and we were always sure of a rewarding spell when we crossed their threshold.

It was there Cath first met the Waltons. Mabel Robieson had whispered an introduction to John Walton and Cath fancied she had heard the phrase 'Professor of Pottery'. In a one-sided conversation she spread herself on what we had both acquired from Staite Murray, a leading figure in the revival of the Art. The response was polite but negligible and, taking Mabel aside, Cath asked 'What did you say he was Professor of?' 'Botany,' replied our sweet hostess. 'Goodness me! I thought you said Pottery. That explains it!'

7

Some Exhibitions and a Prize

I had my share of chips on the shoulder. But they were never fixtures and I always had plenty of friends ready to brush them off when they became too big. I recollected a few when browsing through the gallery news-cuttings book. How insignificant they are now in re-living the delightful experiences which were part and parcel of a more or less continuous flow of special exhibitions. It is easy to get cluttered up with irrelevancies, not to mention embarrassments, in reading over-generous notices. To get a semblance of order I have fallen back on the Caesarian device (nothing obstetric) of dividing the fifteen years at the Art Gallery into three parts. If the great Julius Caesar, who made life miserable at school, can push Gaul around in this way, nothing may be lost and something may be gained if I follow suit.

The first five years were not the worst. The war was a challenge, which the Art Galleries and Museums all over the country accepted. In the face of many handicaps they made a great contribution and they found a public response which was most encouraging. It has been defined as a 'spiritual hunger' arising out of indefinable needs which followed from the strain and anxieties of war. In a sense I had two models – Sir Kenneth Clark of the National Gallery in London, and Stanley Cursiter at the National Gallery of Scotland in Edinburgh. Deprived, as with us, of their greatest treasures they succeeded in various ways in focusing public attention on escape routes from war efforts. Perhaps there was more to it than escape, as a considerable number of people were to discover.

Ours was a municipal gallery and probably because of that we could go further in forgetting what was supposed to be traditional or seemly. Encouraged in every way by Convener and Committee we were able to put on a number of exhibitions not ordinarily identified with an Art Gallery.

From the outbreak of war in 1939 until well after the end of fighting, special exhibitions, that is to say those organised and circulated round the country by outside bodies in addition to those thought up from our own possessions, reached a total of fifty. The majority of them had special opening ceremonies with the Convener of the Committee in the chair and some prominent public personage to declare the exhibition open. This ensured a fine blast of preliminary publicity. I often thought it would have been a louder blast if the distinguished visitors had refused to open the exhibition. In some cases they would have been amply justified. The opening gambit in our defence was to assert that one of the first things a public gallery should aim at was to get the people inside. When they are attracted or tempted to come in to see a particular thing they are likely to wander around and become curious about other things.

I have glanced down the list. The titles of some indicate cooperation with government Information Services – e.g. 'British War Artists'; 'RAF in Action'; 'BBC at War'; 'Battle for Freedom'; 'Vegetables for Victory'; 'The Stalingrad Sword'; 'Princess Elizabeth's Wedding Dress'. Most of them depended on photography to communicate information and to lend support for propaganda. But painting and sculpture were not neglected, nor were the efforts of our allies. Noting the exact dates when the Air Raid compelled us to close the doors – 13th March to 21st May 1941 – and following the 'Instruments of Music' (already referred to), I find the first Art Exhibition was 'Art of our Allies'. This was followed at intervals by others. 'Czechoslovak Art'; 'Poland'; 'Spirit of France' (a fine show greatly helped by generous private lenders who faced the risks involved with commendable courage in the circumstances); 'Belgium'; 'Greek Art'; 'Chinese Art'; 'Norway'; 'Jugoslavia'; 'American Art'.

None of these exhibitions was without incident of one kind or another. Just to see the names again revives memories of a host of fine people. Invariably some member of the armed forces of the various countries, with a special and often professional knowledge, would be seconded for this special duty. It was a pleasure and a rewarding experience to meet them. The British Council and the Arts Council (CEMA – Council for Encouragement of Music and the Arts – in the early days) were often the responsible organising bodies. The contacts made – and, I like to think, the friendships formed – were among the highlights of an exciting and very active period. Resisting the flow of recollections which have in their train an abundance of anecdotes I must permit a few to pass.

The exhibition of Greek Art was the work of Professor Charles T. Seltman, assisted by Mrs J. Chittenden, under the auspices of the Royal Hellenic Embassy and the British Council. I, of course, discovered he was one of the leading authorities on the subject, and we looked forward to getting his views on the small Greek section in the Museum, and if he thought there were any items worth including in his show, so much the better. There was one outstanding exhibit, which he immediately recognised. This was a vase, well documented and well known to Greek art scholars. In our ignorance we had left it in a show-case throughout the blitz. No one on the staff knew much, if anything, about Greek Pottery. The collection – rather mixed – had come through gifts and perhaps as a reward for donations to earlier exploration funds. In a survey of the museum's unique exhibits, when we had to consider safety measures, I had been told this particular vase was 'too good to be true'. It was a 'fake'. So we left it. Thanks be to heaven it survived the 'blitz' and if Professor Seltman entertained a low opinion of Glasgow's Art Curators, he very kindly kept it to himself.

The Chinese Art Exhibition in the summer of 1944 (organised by the Chinese Embassy and the British Council) brought us the bright Dr Yeh. Small, vivacious, with the Oriental capacity to employ the entire face in raising a smile, he was then second in command at the Chinese Embassy in London. This was the Chiang Kai-shek period. The last time I saw Dr Yeh's name mentioned he was the Foreign Secretary in the exiled Formosan Government. He, too, was anxious to augment this exhibition with any items in Scottish Collections. My friend, Herbert Paul, had some years before introduced me to John Houston, who was living in retirement in Millport. Houston had been over forty years in China and had brought back what looked to me and a lot of other people as an extraordinary range of fine Chinese Art, Pottery and Paintings in particular. Down we went to Millport – Dr Yeh and myself – and there, interrupted by the hospitality of Dr and Mrs Paul, inspected the Houston Collection. I gathered that several pieces were outstanding, much more important than the owner understood or appreciated. On the way back to Glasgow Dr Yeh was very entertaining. From what he had seen he could trace friend Houston's travels in China and the places where he was stationed. I never forgot his summing up: 'Of course Mr Houston has acquired one or two very fine pieces; he told me these were gifts. But oh! the remainder! If he had only known or been guided he could so easily have made a wonderful collection.' In fairness to John Houston it must be said that he never once pretended or professed any expert knowledge. He had bought what he liked. None of it was negligible from a decorative point of view, but he had missed the masterpieces. And in this respect he was not unique.

Probably the 'Spirit of France' Exhibition was my own favourite: perhaps because the picture part of it was 'all my own work'. I mean the organisation, collecting, cataloguing and hanging. Apart from aesthetic and historical considerations the sideshows, so to speak, emphasised the spirit of 'The Auld Alliance'. There had been built up in Glasgow a very active Friends of France organisation. The late Lord Inverclyde made it one of his chief interests. But we all knew that the driving force, aided by his wife, was Etienne Vacher. As Manager of the Central Hotel – where so many of the VIPs were entertained as they halted either going to or returning from the USA – Monsieur Vacher was well situated to keep in touch with every movement. Above ground or underground it was all the same to him, as long as he could advance the cause and welfare of his native country and its citizens. General de Gaulle paid several visits to Scotland and on those to Glasgow we were privileged to meet him – mostly a short gracious greeting from him. His aloofness not to say arrogant attitude in small company was a first impression which never became erased. Recently, when the General was speaking on television, my wife remarked to a group of grand-children, 'I have met that famous man. He once kissed my hand.' A small voice piped up, 'What was the matter with your face?' The links with France and the people of France were not merely a war-time sentiment. Practical efforts were constantly being devised to strengthen them. On instructions, particularly through Lord Provost Sir Hector McNeill, the Art Gallery and Museum con-tributed a number of objects from our store of treasures to help to restart the Brest Museum, which, like the city itself, was a major war casualty. Franco-Scottish House continued in Glasgow for a number of post-war years as a memento, in some cases a memorial, to mark a great amount of self-sacrifice on the part of a number of noble people.

The 'Spirit of France' Exhibition made the month of June 1943 exciting and busy. The evidence is in the programme of events. Lectures and Recitals of Music twice weekly, to large audiences, seemed to indicate a service which was appreciated by the public. It still looks well on paper. 'Cézanne' by Sir Kenneth Clark, 'Impressionism' by Stanley Cursiter, 'French Painting – its background of ideas' by James Laver, 'Painting since Cézanne' and 'French Paintings in Scotland' by T.J.H. In Music, 'Quartets by Ravel and Debussy' – Scottish Chamber Music Players led by Mouland Begbie, 'Piano and Violin Music' by Couperin, 'Cesar Franck and Debussy' by Wight Henderson and Bessie Spence, 'Concert of French Music' by the BBC Scottish Orchestra conducted by Ian Whyte. In many ways they were memorable events.

Activities were not limited to what was happening inside the building. As part of the role of showman – one of my important functions – I was ready to accept invitations which would give me a chance to show off elsewhere. Some of my worthy masters again thought I was directing too much of the limelight on myself and not enough on the job. A member of the Committee defended by saying something like 'Honeyman has made the Art Gallery and Museum,' to be met with the retort 'Don't you think the Art Gallery and Museum has made Honeyman?' To which someone added 'Well, they don't seem to have made anybody else.'

There were, of course, a number of well-intentioned and interested citizens who did not like many of the things we were allowed to do and, I admit, we sometimes risked getting permission after the event. If one is entitled to judge from the press, national and local, weekly and daily, and from public response, we were having a successful time. And I mean *we*. For again it is obvious, more than one man is involved in running an Art Gallery. Around me was growing up a warmth of loyal support which made it possible to forget the fading number of disgruntled 'passengers'. I was reminded the other day of a favourite remark with which John Fleming used to enlighten the proceedings. The expression was enhanced by a mixture of his slight stutter and the freezing conditions due to inadequate heating in his office, 'We're all jjjust one bbbig happy fffamily!'

When the innovations I thought desirable were accepted as being worth a trial, smoothness crept into the machinery. I had been trained on the platitude 'The secret of organisation is delegation'. The first step towards this end related to correspondence and led to

an early difference of opinion with the Town Clerk's Department.
I was advised, in a friendly way, to follow the Corporation rule as
printed on the letter-heading of their department, 'All letters must
be addressed to the Town Clerk'. I tried to point out the differences
existing in our relations with the public. I had to be more personal.
The proof was forthcoming some years later. My friend Victor
Cumming decided to present his collection of silver to the City. His
eminence as a collector and expert on the subject is reflected in the
catalogues of the Empire Exhibition in 1938, and of the Scottish Art
Show in London in 1939. It was a great and generous gift – featured
in one of our special exhibitions in 1945. All he received by way of
acknowledgement was a brief formal letter from the Town Clerk.
It was so brief and so formal that Victor Cumming carried it in his
pocket for a long time, as a No. 1 exhibit of Glasgow's 'appreciation'
of his kindness. Gradually, and quite amicably, I was able to take
over what I considered a very important duty, requiring some kind
of expansion into the realm of courtesy and warmth of appreciation
and understanding.

It struck me as elementary to recognise in a gift which the donor
has treasured for years and which represents a high market value, a
public spirited gesture meriting something more than:

'Dear Sir,

———————— an extract from a minute ————————

Yours faithfully,'

In all probability I may sometimes have spread myself overmuch in
sending letters of thanks. Nevertheless I must have thought it
important for I seem to have suffered from an urge to give guidance
to the staff. One of them, when he moved to another and more
important job was good enough, in a farewell letter, to thank me for
stressing the importance of how to say thanks to other folks.

The second award of the St Mungo Prize came my way. This
prize, awarded every three years to the citizen who has done most
in the preceding three years to promote the amenities, welfare and
prosperity of Glasgow, was created by Alex Somerville. A quiet,
reserved, soft-speaking little man, with painting in water colours as
a relief from manufacturing shoes, he was a member of the Art Club.
No one bothered to take much notice of him. At first he tried to
preserve anonymity; but it soon became an open secret. In addition
to a gold medal the winner is given a cheque for £1,000. Lord
Provost James Welsh who was, ex officio, chairman of the selectors

later informed me, in the course of a bit of chaffing, 'It wasn't your work at the Gallery won you this prize. You are paid for that. It was your interest and work in other social and cultural enterprises which impressed us.'

All the same, it was my colleagues at the Art Gallery, not to mention my tolerant family, who had lent me their aid. Consequently I divided the cash among them. The medal and the honour remain with me as does the sweetest compliment raised by the occasion. One of our handymen who did odd jobs of cleaning and watchman duty was Jimmy Motherwell. At one time a well-known professional footballer, he had failed to make the grade in any big sense. Given to silence, he was asked what he thought of the distribution of a week's wages all round, to mark the chief's winning the St Mungo Prize. Jimmy replied, 'It's all right! It suits me. But he didna' need tae dae it.' Among the flood of congratulations, I received three letters from Corporation departments and four from City Councillors. One of my colleagues comforted me with, 'Don't let this worry you. It's like the Highlands. They don't take to you unless you've lived with them for a very long time. You're too fresh. And you can take that just as it appeals to you!'

Sir Patrick Dollan, as he became, was the first winner of the St Mungo Prize. He was, in my view, the most successful Lord Provost in living memory (a close runner-up was our first Lady Provost, Dame Jean Roberts). During the difficult early war years Pat (as we who were accepted as his friends could address him) won for himself the added title 'The King of Poland'. This reflected his energetic efforts to do everything in his power to welcome and sustain the Polish officers and men who arrived in large numbers in the West of Scotland. Among other things he helped them to organise the celebrated Male Voice Choir, saw to it that they were taught the classic songs of Scotland and arranged concerts, large and small, for the delight of innumerable audiences.

I have already mentioned the opening of our first post-blitz exhibition by Sir Patrick on 21st May 1941. There is a small menu card in front of me dated exactly a year before, Central Hotel 21–5–40. It is signed P. J. and Agnes Dollan, W. J. Jordan, High Commissioner for New Zealand, and his wife Winifred Jordan. My wife and I completed this small dinner party. It was two days before the serious war situation in France was made public. We were pledged to secrecy and told of the government plans for the immediate future – in consultation with the Commonwealth countries. The prospects of a German invasion were discussed seriously and the possible sequelae appreciated. Pat knew he was on their list – a marked man. But he was optimistic or resigned in the face of the gloomy tidings Mr Jordan kept bringing to us from the frequent phone calls to London.

Pat whispered to me, 'I have a box at the Empire, offered to me to entertain our distinguished visitors. You take the ladies there. We will join you later, but if we don't show up take them to your home and wait.' The Empire was packed. The chief performer, I remember, was George Formby, Junior, singing some of his father's songs. The audience roared and laughed with delight, while three very depressed ladies and their equally depressed escort shrank back into the shadows of the Stage Box. Nothing was capable of persuading us that all was well with the world. P.J. and W.J. joined us in the small hours, determined to put on a brave show in the face of impending catastrophe.

This war-time incident has been recalled by a passage in Leonard Woolf's final volume of autobiography *The Journey not the Arrival Matters*. It is part of the bundle of 'arrears' in reading I have brought aboard. Woolf recalls a meeting with his wife, Virginia, Rose Macaulay and Kingsley Martin talking till 2.30 in the morning:

'Kingsley, diffusing his soft charcoal gloom prophesied the defeat of the French, the Invasion of Britain, within five weeks. A Fifth column would get to work; the Government would move off to Canada leaving us to a German pro-consul, a concentration camp or suicide. We discussed suicide while the electric light gradually faded and finally left us sitting in complete darkness.'

In her diary, a month before she committed suicide, a tragic event in every sense, Virginia Woolf wrote 'This is my conclusion. "We pay the penalty for our rung in Society by infernal boredom".' It throws me back to the thirties when I met from time to time, as on the fringe of their affairs, Vanessa Bell (sister of Virginia), Duncan Grant, Maynard Keynes, Roger Fry, Clive Bell and some others who made up the Bloomsbury Group. I was afraid of Virginia Woolf, not of any of the others, but her sad conclusion seems to me an appropriate epitaph for art history makers in my young days.

Pat Dollan was never harassed by boredom. He was too much an extrovert; too full of ideas which could be expressed in practical applications. Constantly, throughout his term of office he filled in

the time of VIPs waiting for planes to carry them across the Atlantic
or for the late night train for London. Sometimes there would be a
little private dinner party and I would be summoned, on short
notice, to represent the civic cultural enterprises. At one of these
I met Jan Masaryk, a fortnight before his mysterious and tragic
death in Prague.

Probably the most significant occasion in Glasgow's history as
host to eminent war-time visitors was when Prime Minister Winston
Churchill brought Mr Harry Hopkins (President Roosevelt's personal agent) to the city. The PM had been touring Scotland with the
frail, delicate-looking representative from the USA without getting
from him the slightest inkling of America's intention of becoming an
active participant in the war. Glasgow's reception was tumultuous
and impressive. City Councillors, officials and eminent citizens had
been invited to the Municipal buildings to hear an address from
Churchill. His summary of the war situation, at home and overseas,
was masterly; but to most of us who had to stand throughout the
proceedings it became a trifle irksome. Harry Hopkins, in a non-
committal acknowledgement of his welcome, boasted of his Scots
ancestry.

There are three accounts of what happened at the dinner party in
the evening – John Winant, American Ambassador, in his autobiographical *A Letter from Grosvenor Square*, Harry Hopkins in his
White House Papers and Tom Johnston's *Memories*. In my view the last
of the three is the most accurate. Tom Johnston presided. Under
pressure from Winston Churchill he succeeded in getting Harry
Hopkins to say something, bringing in a reference to the grandmother from Auchterarder.

In the course of his short speech Harry Hopkins, looking straight
at the Prime Minister, quoted from the Bible the celebrated passage
from the Book of Ruth which begins 'Whither thou goest I will
go . . .'.

Tom Johnston concludes 'That was all. He sat down in dead
silence. Churchill's eyes welled up with tears. Here was the first
news that the United States was throwing its weight on the Allied
side.' The secret was well kept and the delay led to a variety of
versions of an outstanding historical incident.

It was brought back to my mind when I lectured on Art Appreciation at Kirkintilloch, Tom Johnston's home town. It was my custom
then to quote this beautiful prose passage from Ruth as an example

of the idea of communication, in an Art Form, of the profound notion 'I love you and always shall'. T.J. did the honours of the evening and whispered to me afterwards 'Do you remember the time when Harry Hopkins used that quotation from Ruth with a different application and significance?'

The Lord Provost made a point of building an image of Glasgow which was new to most of his visitors. Partly to augment this he persuaded me, and the publishers Faber & Faber (without much difficulty), to present to him the second edition of *Introducing Leslie Hunter*. This I had written in 1937 with fair results, which scarcely justified an orthodox second edition. With a specially designed cover and a foreword by Pat it was very well sold on behalf of the Central War Relief Fund. Some were presented to distinguished visitors interested in the Arts. Apart from augmenting the fund, the chief aim was to boost Scottish Art in general and Glasgow artists in particular.

A week before I left home on this trip, on St Andrew's Day the present Lord Provost, Donald Liddle, declared open at the Westminster Theatre in London the Dollan Memorial Library – a tribute to Agnes and Pat Dollan who in their life-time had devoted so much time, energy and affection to great causes. Lady Dollan had found in the Moral Rearmament Movement comfort and opportunity she had failed to find elsewhere. Pat encouraged her efforts in every possible way.

In recalling the Bloomsbury Group – a few pages ago – I must add a postscript. In the early thirties it had become, for a spell, less important. New groups with the odd isolated individual began to appear. I had heard and read of the Vorticists, but I did not meet those who were regarded as the leaders until later in the thirties.

Wyndham Lewis was a strange genius. He scared a number of people. He didn't scare us. He puzzled us. So keen not to be observed or overheard, he favoured a style of dress – particularly in hats – which made him conspicuous in any company. Constantly in need of funds at a time when paintings were hard to sell, I extended my patronage to a commission to do a portrait of my wife. We were both near broke. I had returned from a visit to the USA and may have had in mind an advertisement I had seen outside a restaurant 'Come in and eat before we both starve'. I do not like to remind myself of how little I paid for this family heirloom. Later, I was able to make amends in a number of ways, notably in persuading the

Durban Art Gallery in South Africa to acquire the celebrated portrait of T. S. Eliot – the rejection of which by the Royal Academy led to the resignation of Augustus John. The lead in Durban was taken by a fellow medical student, Walter May, who returned to his native South Africa and became a leading cardiologist in Durban. We had, together, our beginnings in appreciation of art in the Art Gallery at Kelvingrove. When Walter became chairman of the Durban Art Gallery we renewed contacts on his visits to London, when he always looked in to see me in King Street. I introduced him to Wyndham Lewis and when the chance of the Eliot portrait came along he seized it for Durban. The Tate Gallery ought to have jumped at this opportunity.

8

Innovations

On very many occasions, as part of the 'Chairman's Remarks' I have been introduced as the man who brought the famous painting by Salvador Dali to Glasgow. While there is no need to apologise for the part I played in this piece of civic art history, I would like to be remembered for other things accomplished in my fifteen years.

I do not boast 'I did this or that'. I was part of an organisation – the chief part maybe – but nothing could have been done without the willing collaboration of those working with me.

How few of us have the ability to listen to others, undisturbed by our prejudices. We can never gain complete freedom from pre-occupation with our own ideas, affairs and concerns, and cannot therefore achieve a true objectivity and a sound discernment on every occasion. Words, I discovered, are not the most effective means of communication. A look, a touch or a shout may be eloquent of emotions too deep or strong for the limitations of language. Repressed resentment tends to disappear when it is seen that the idea is feasible and can be made to work. Rumblings of 'stubborn devil' sometimes did swell up into opposition.

Here is a list of the activities which were started in my time. With a smaller staff we reconstructed the whole administration especially with regard to storage and records. We established (1) Schools Museum Service; (2) Conservation Department; (3) Art Galleries & Museums Association, with its journal *The Scottish Art Review*; (4) New methods of presentation (advances continue in this); (5) Public contacts through lectures, group visits in evenings, etc.; (6) Creating habitat groups in Natural History; (7) Exhibitions – some broke all attendance records; (8) Advised several important acquisitions; (9) Influenced gifts from generous donors.

I know that this must read like the appendix to a Blue Book. It is intended to function as an aid to memory. We must expand on some of these if for no other reason than to give credit where and when it is due.

Schools Museum Service

One of the first books dealing with museums to reach my notice came out of Boston (USA). Published in 1923 by their Museum of Fine Arts and written by Benjamin Ives Gilman, with the title *Museum Ideals of Purpose and Method*, it contains a reference to the main hall of Kelvingrove. He quotes Sir W. Armstrong, who describes the ground floor plan as 'more successful than anything else of the same kind in Europe'. That warmed me to friend Gilman as did some of his views on publicity. The ground floor plan is excellent; but the upper floor, the Art Gallery part of the structure, is as old-fashioned as the total architectural quality of the building. And I thought a long time over this: 'A Museum should announce its opportunities but not force them on the public notice.' Later I was to hear Charles Carter, recently retired from many years as Director of the Aberdeen Art Gallery, say at a Scottish Museum Federation Meeting, 'We have ourselves known of museums and art galleries whose officials seemed almost to regard the collections as their own property to be maintained principally for themselves and a few specialists.' I would like to think he was reporting a departing phase, but I am not so sure.

During the war and for some time afterwards when in London, Birmingham, Manchester, Glasgow and perhaps some other places, the special exhibitions with crowds of people were described as 'stunts'. Some people deplored the large number of visitors – forming queues on occasions – who ordinarily have no use for Art Galleries. Quality of visitor not quantity, it was said, should be the aim of a well-run gallery. However, I became rather intrigued with the notion that sometimes quality may be concealed in the quantity. When I had some years of experience to back me up I presented some conclusions on the matter to a Museums Association Conference and later, somewhat expanded, they appeared in *Museum* (the international publication produced by UNESCO).

To the question 'What kind of public do we want?' was added the further question, 'Do we take what we get?' or 'Do we try to make some of our visitors into what we think we want?' In discussions, which often took the wrong turning, I have been known to say that

I envied my colleague, the City Librarian. At least his customers had learned to read. Ours arrived with an intelligent interest but with more or less abysmal ignorance. There must be some place for educational methods at school level to become an integral part of a museum function, without in any way conflicting with the prime function. Having seen, especially in the USA and Canada (notably in Toledo, Ohio) visits from school children in classes featured as an important activity, I kept wondering how we could go about organising something of the kind in Glasgow. I wanted something better than some of the docents – the name given to the ladies who were in charge. Most of them were untrained and seemed to me as if they were merely enjoying a pleasant little interlude. We must have, I thought, trained teachers and a solid piece of organisation. And that meant a direct approach to the Department of Education.

Dr R. M. Allardyce, who was then Director of Education, listened to my proposals with great sympathy and courtesy and then said 'Nothing doing! The school curriculum is already crowded and we have no provision for paying transport costs to and from the gallery.' I had to take 'no' for an answer, but the following year, by government decree, school holidays were cancelled. The authorities were glad to find some extraordinary ways to keep their dear little charges occupied. So back I went to Dr Allardyce. He smiled and this time said, 'I've got a Headmasters' Conference on. Come and join it and tell them what's on your mind.' I was brief. 'Here we have a building full of interesting material, with untapped possibilities. Telephone us and we will arrange mutually convenient times for class visits. They can be taken round either by their own teachers or by members of our staff, who are prepared to volunteer. If the response is good we may have to plan accordingly and offer you specific hours to suit everybody.'

The response was slow at first, and then we became almost overwhelmed. The teachers were a bit doubtful of the capacity of the members of our staff; but very quickly they acquired the habit of handing the children over while they enjoyed some relaxation in the tea-room. As I had landed the staff with this extra I felt I had to do my share. I soon discovered that it was no easy job to keep youngsters interested. Indeed, with anybody below fifteen I was rather pathetic. John Dunlop Anderson, then Depute Director of Education, I had known for years. He was keen to see how this holiday enterprise was working and, after following me and my group around he summed

up my efforts as a teacher in a word – 'Rotten!' He had taken notes
and produced some of the words I had used in explaining the things
I was showing. 'It took *me* all my time to know what you were
driving at. How do you expect these kids to understand?'

I took myself in hand, and selected some of the outstanding
exhibits from each department and made a simple and informative
talk round each of them. For example, I made the mongoose my
star turn in the Natural History section with memories of India and
Rudyard Kipling. Stroking the stuffed animal until I nearly rubbed
the fur off its back, I think I brought it back to a new kind of life.
It was all very exciting. The reports which I knew would drift back
to Bath Street – the Educational Offices – must have been satisfactory.
Conferences followed and with the whole-hearted support of both
committees we were allowed to proceed with the experiment of
having a Schools Museum Service started at the Art Gallery. There
was much less palaver about it than I had expected. None of the
usual 'remit to a sub-committee for examination and report';
'Instruction to Town Clerk to find out what they do in Birmingham
and Manchester' (never Edinburgh).

The business was immediately delegated to Dr Allardyce and
myself. More than that, we were allowed to cut through the usual
committee procedure and, in joint consultation, select the man who
was to be officer in charge. We interviewed quite a large number of
candidates and made a very fortunate choice – a middle-sized, cheery,
round-faced, confident sort of chiel named Sam Thompson. He was
seconded from the staff of Bellahouston Academy in June 1941 and
by the middle of October in that year the Schools Museum Service
was in business. It could not have continued in business and have
developed as it did without the continued support and encouragement
of Dr Allardyce's successor, my good friend Dr Stuart Mackintosh.
A sandy-haired Scot going grey, with a face that looked as if it had
been knocked around a bit – he was a Rugby International in his
youth – his smile, when he was on your side, was magnetic. He used
his eyes a lot, and I liked the music of his laugh. Although no longer
colleagues, but fellow honorary doctors of Law of Glasgow, we have
continued to be associated in more than one adventure, ranging from
doubtful haunts in Hamburg to TV 'rackets'!!

One must not forget that in all this, we had the blessing of the
Scottish Education Department. HM Inspectors gave us every
encouragement, particularly through the late J. D. Macgregor. As a

tribute to all he did to help us, there is now a prize bearing his name in the annual art competition, held in the Art Gallery.

The trouble was to find a place to accommodate the active and energetic enthusiast who had joined us. We were still probing and searching for space for our own administrative staff. Literally, Sam Thompson started to build up what became a very important part of museum life in the basement. We cleared out dumps, masquerading as stores, and made for him an office and a small class-room. We turned one of our handymen, Harry Willies by name, into a general factotum, lantern operator, specimen collector and distributor, and performer of all the odd jobs. Harry Willies educated himself and eventually became the Curator of the Kirkcaldy Art Gallery.

In course of time Sam Thompson acquired a number of assistants, all of whom shared his ambition to make their department outstanding. I was to discover that there was nothing quite comparable anywhere else in the country. And very soon we began to have visitors eager to inspect what was being done. The difference, basically, when comparisons were attempted was that in Glasgow the Schools Museum Service was staffed by trained teachers, paid by the Education Department. In addition, those responsible did not limit themselves to rigid rules of educational methods. They tried things out; they expanded the interest to cover anything which even hinted at an educational aspect. Sometimes this catholic interpretation led to arguments, not all conducted with the decorum one expects in cultural institutions. When was education not education? What gallery or museum activity was there which fell out of the realm of education? For a time I was almost scared that Sam Thompson would approach the Corporation with a take-over bid for the entire outfit. However, we managed to retain our balance, if not our sense of proportion. Gradually, and in the face of exasperating delays, we won more space and made it easier for this fine piece of work to grow and prosper. The story of the first ten years is on record in *Educational Experiment* (published by the department in 1951).

I like to recall some of the names and some of the spectacular achievements of those who were in at the beginning and continued until I left. I remember especially Miss Jean Irwin, elegantly tall, attractive and distinguished looking, with the ability to convert a frown into an enchanting smile. She was and still is a brilliant judge of quality in children's painting. Under her guidance Saturday

morning Art Classes for the young folks started. With ages ranging
from four to sixteen it was a delight to see them at work and at the
end of the session a pleasure to see the results. Very soon there was a
formidable waiting list. Often I was pestered by parents asking me
to use my influence to get their child, or a friend's child, into Miss
Irwin's class. This I seldom dared to do because I had to store what
influence I had in order to bring it forth at the right time on behalf
of my own grandchildren.

There was Tom Lindsay, who made a speciality of creating models
of the American Indian Tribes, with replicas of tribal dress. The
bony structure of his fresh-complexioned face made me think of
Indians to the extent of wanting to greet him with outstretched
palm and 'HOW'. (Surprisingly enough, queries regarding authenticity of the various habitat details reached Glasgow from individuals
and museums in America.) W. G. Beaton, whose chief subject was
Civics, and whose interests now are in Television as a feature in
education; Miss Louise Annand (affectionately known to us all as
Dick), accepted in Scotland as an artist of distinction in her own
right, and now, following Sam Thompson's retiral, in charge of the
department.

After the three years' trial period, the 'seconding' procedure
faded out and the new Glasgow post of Museum Education Officer
was created. At the same time the evidence of interest in our
experiment became emphatic, leading up to an invitation to the
Education Officer to the first UNESCO seminar in New York.
Moreover this new department inherited a 57-year-old annual
Schools Drawing Competition, which was on the point of petering
out. It has been raised in numbers of participants from a few hundred
into an average of 5,000.

To Sam Thompson and all his team I shall remain grateful for the
excellent work which allowed me to bask in a reflected glory. Sam
is an FEIS (Fellow of the Educational Institute of Scotland). So am I!
The honour I am sure came to me in great measure because of the
educational aspect of the gallery work. Some things I was able to do
in other places may have contributed. It is likely too that many new
departures and developments have taken place, and I have failed to
mention others worthy of notice. I still cling to the memory of a
very successful experiment started in my time.

Cleaning and Restoration

The Clydeside had a remarkable freedom from air-raids while other parts of the country were getting a pasting. Then in those concentrated few nights, in March 1941, Clydebank in particular and some areas in the centre of Glasgow suffered devastating damage and a great number of casualties.

Some thought we would, at the Art Gallery, be out of business for at least a year. They were wrong. With remarkable energy and, let it be said, cheerfulness, the staff got to work and we were able to open again to the public within a month. This was made possible by very great and imaginative assistance from the City Engineer. Very quickly he made us wind and water tight and gradually, by giving us more and more light in the roof of the picture galleries we were able to continue with exhibitions which seemed to draw more and more of the public.

We learned several lessons from this situation. One is recalled because some earlier fears had proved to be groundless. Under ordinary circumstances the best way to inspect a painting is to look at it without the barrier of a sheet of glass. Sometimes the glass acts only as a mild interference, but, especially in the case of the Dutch and Flemish masters, the reflections are often so disturbing as to compel one to engage in a series of contortions. Unfortunately in public collections glazing is a necessity. If the pictures were unglazed the irresponsible visitor would finger or even scribble on the paint surface. The proof of this was generally forthcoming on Monday mornings when, following the crowded galleries on a Sunday, the cleaners would have a much more onerous task in removing the finger marks on the glass. Moreover the inevitable dirt would collect, and to have this cleaned off a paint or varnish surface by inexperienced people with cotton dusters seems to me to be the acme of bad conservation. We were able to demonstrate the dirt menace when we had the Van Gogh Exhibition in Glasgow. At any rate we proved it to our satisfaction and probably to others, since the results of our investigation were accepted for publication by the Editor of the Museums Journal.

With air-raids in mind, we debated for a long time on the wisdom or otherwise of removing the glass as a safety measure. I am referring of course, not to the top level irreplacable pictures which had been removed to various places outside the city, but to the 'reserves'. In the blitz, the roof glass – two layers of it – was smashed. Many of the flying splinters also smashed the glass on the paintings, but with three exceptions the paintings themselves were unscathed. It seems reasonable to conclude that if we had taken the glass out the splinters would have penetrated the canvases.

The greatest damage was done to a very large painting which, possibly because of its size, had been left on the stairway wall. This was Sir John Lavery's historical document of the opening of the 1888 Exhibition by Queen Victoria. It was left in shreds, apparently beyond repair. However, in the belief that nothing should be regarded as hopeless the tattered canvas was rolled up to await the day when someone qualified in pictorial plastic surgery would attempt the impossible.

Shortly after these events I was talking to Sir Kenneth Clark, then Director of the National Gallery. As always, when I unburdened myself he was most helpful. The particular point on this occasion arose from a growing conviction that now was the time, when our notable pictures had to be taken from public view, to have them where necessary cleaned and restored. It was on his recommendation, having persuaded my Committee on the soundness of the project, that Mr Helmut Ruhemann came to Glasgow for a period of two years. I had already met him in London and knew he was a man of wide and long experience, fully informed on the history and practice of 'scientific methods'. He was chief picture-restorer at the Kaiser-Frederich Museum in Berlin in 1929. Arriving in England in 1933, he became associated with the Courtauld Institute. Trained as an artist, he was aware of all the current trends as well as being expert in the technical methods of the Old Masters. Recognising that the cleaning of pictures is still regarded – in a decreasing measure maybe – as a controversial subject, to establish a department seems to me to mark an important chapter in the Art Gallery's history.

We started, very tentatively, in a makeshift studio on a section of the balcony which, as part of the reconstruction, we had adapted for administrative offices. In acquiring Helmut Ruhemann's services, on a part-time basis, we also acquired a considerable number of critics. They, artists and laymen, did not 'believe' in cleaning. One of them addressed me in the gallery when I was making some re-arrangement. In rather scathing terms he condemned us for having 'spoiled' one of his 'favourites'. He talked airily about 'glazes' and 'the pass' – i.e. the gentle rhythm of one tone leading into another. I doubt very much if he will ever be convinced of the truth. He was sure I was kidding him when I told him that nothing whatsoever had been done to the painting. We had simply removed the glass, cleaned the picture side of it – there was a forty-year-old film of dirt on it – and replaced it. On another occasion, when we were bold enough to give, at the Glasgow Art Club, a demonstration of the processes involved in cleaning, two members deplored the cleaning of a painting by Paul Bril. They insisted it had not been improved and that they preferred it in its 'original' state. Somewhat nettled, I challenged them to go further than a mere statement of opinion. Then it came to light that neither of them could remember when they had last seen it.

Probably one ought to approach polemical occasions with due regard to the place and circumstance. Yet, when one is thrown back on the defensive it is necessary to try to give as good as one gets. Besides, I was beginning to grow restless under the nonsense being spoken and written on the subject. Here is what Arthur Laes of the Brussels Museum of Fine Arts said about it. (We had him in Glasgow throughout most of the war. Indeed, he arrived in the country in evening dress, having just managed to escape from Holland before the Germans poured in. He had been attending a party to mark the opening of an Exhibition.)

It was with his emphatic support the Bril was cleaned and some years before his death, after he had gone back to Belgium, he favoured us with an article containing this passage:

'The most outstanding success achieved at Glasgow was the "resurrection" of a work dated 1602 by the Flemish landscape painter Paul Bril, which had formerly been hidden under a coat of brown varnish and which can now be seen in all its pristine freshness; this picture which is more than three centuries old, is in a perfect state of preservation.'

I must take you back to the dawn of my interest in cleaning and restoring works of art. In my student days we had already started the craze for reducing everything possible to initials. O. H. Mavor was always O.H., and in some circles, then and now, I am described as T.J. Then, as mnemonics, initials had their uses. 'The Florentines for Form' became FFF and 'the Venetians for Colour' became VFC. It was when we began to measure this up in galleries, at home and abroad, we had to take the form for granted because we didn't quite know what it meant. What seemed absolutely clear was the dirt and brown varnish between us and the form and colour which go together to make great paintings. Then, when I listened to artists, scholars, historians and the queer section of humanity known as 'art experts' I began to wonder if the accumulation of surface grime and the discoloured varnish was the whole story. Glazes began to mean something almost sacrosanct, until someone pointed out that they were often added to cover deficiencies.

A lot of things required looking into and when I began to be more concerned with the care of valuable paintings, I looked into them. Nothing like being financially involved to make one very interested. Thus I eventually found the surest guides among those who had taken the trouble to study the science of picture cleaning and restoration. They were among dealers, collectors, curators and especially among the active practitioner whose job it was to apply, in action, the facts, testimony and experience which are combined in the science and art of picture restoration. Just like medicine and surgery with a sick picture as the patient. Artists who, because they are artists, presume to know all there is to be known about the conditions of painting, had not been in the past very reliable witnesses. It is exceptional to find a mother more competent than a physician in the treatment of a sick child – her own or another's. This bogey of the removal of glazes drove me to look up the diaries and records of the period when the European Old Masters began to arrive in this country. A reference to Whitley's 'Artists and their Friends in England from 1700 to 1799' will reveal that Sir Joshua Reynolds was entrusted with the supervision of the cleaning and relining of the Duke of Rutland's recently imported Poussins. He, in turn, entrusted them to a Neapolitan who had 'an extraordinary secret for cleaning pictures' and eventually reported the pictures as 'now just as they came from the easel'. Other references in biographies and histories show that many distinguished artists deplored in vigorous language the destruction of masterpieces by irresponsible cleaners. There have also been as many who have showered their blessings on fashionable charlatans. One result is that today the custodians of many famous paintings have, in addition to preserving works entrusted to them, to arrange for the restoration of those which have been damaged by bungling amateurs or inefficient professionals.

In Reynolds's time much too great a reliance was placed on empirical methods, and cleaning was something in the nature of a mysterious process. Glasgow's 'Man in Armour' by Rembrandt was at one time in Reynolds's possession. He thought it was 'too dark'. I think he was right, but I wonder if, when the picture was restored in Holland in 1930, some of the problems, very competently solved, were not created by Sir Joshua's faith in secret processes.

I got to know something of the work of the late Dr A. P. Lawrie, Professor of Chemistry to the Royal Academy of Arts. It was he who fitted up the first laboratory of its kind in this country for the scientific examination of pictures. The equipment included the necessary microscopes, cameras, ultra-violet light and X-rays. He was more concerned at the time with the detection of fakes and forgeries. G. L. Stout in the USA was another pioneer. Stanley Cursiter re-kindled my interest with his well-known account of the cleaning of the Franz Hals in the National Gallery of Scotland. It was through him also that I became aware of the wax-resin method in re-lining, i.e. reinforcing with a new canvas.

In the ordinary run of picture cleaning, elaborate scrutiny and investigation, with physical, chemical and historical aids are not always necessary; in the case of accepted masterpieces and treasures the utmost care is essential. Nevertheless, we cannot ignore the fact that, from time to time, some people become seriously disturbed. They are not all nitwits and busybodies.

With this thought in mind I once barged into a correspondence in *The Times* when the National Gallery was under fire from the 'anti-cleaners'. I was ticked off very severely by Lord Crawford, the Chairman of the Trustees. I had, mildly I thought, criticised the authorities for ignoring the sincerely held views of the opposition. Evidently the charge of 'cynical aloofness' got under somebody's skin. The chief reason for being completely unrepentant was and is that the policy of cleaning pictures in public collections has been open to attack ever since there have been public collections, and as the policy was not peculiar to the National Gallery, the interest was universal rather than metropolitan.

Part of our job as curators is to keep on reassuring the uninformed so that when they become informed criticism will disappear. I was later restored to favour in high places when I made it clear in an article in *The Studio* that I was convinced our National treasures were in the keeping of qualified responsible people. In the course of my advocacy I poured ridicule on those with preferences for particular varnish solvents. It is not the solvent, but the man with the swabs or pledgets of cotton-wool in his hand who is the crux of the matter. Those who are wise after the event have only a remote idea of what has been done unless they have been there when it was done. It is like surgery again. One hasn't the foggiest idea what a surgeon is doing when he is rummaging around inside an abdomen. This analogy led me into fantastic bursts of rhetoric for I concluded my 'come-back' with something like this: After all, our civilisation, wobbly as it is, rests on Trust. When we lose that we shall indeed have returned to barbarism. Inasmuch as I am prepared to entrust my child's body to the surgeon, his mind to the teacher, and his soul to the preacher, so will I entrust my share in the nation's treasures to the Trustees of the National Gallery. They are aware of the risk and I am all for encouraging them to take these risks because of the evidence that the consequences more closely approximate the work as the artist finished it. In any event, sweet are the results of bitter controversy when more people are made aware of the significance of masterpieces in Art.

This is a long way from Helmut Ruhemann and the start of our Department in Glasgow, but I had to insert these leaves from memory in order to make it clear we had become part of a movement. We were satisfied, too, that we were going the right way about it. To see Ruhemann at work was both a pleasure and a reassurance. The deliberate and careful examination as a routine preliminary led to a course of action where restraint was looked upon as of the highest importance. Retouching was always reduced to a necessary minimum. Records were kept and published in the Annual Reports. (Incidentally Annual Reports of the Department which I regarded as fulfilling the joint purposes of publicity and reference had ceased to be published. In fact none had appeared for 26 years. They were resumed in 1943.)

Ruhemann divided his time between the Art Gallery and private work. He cleaned some of the University pictures, notably their famous Chardins. I had reason to remember their inclusion in the Paris Exhibition of 1937. As a Glasgow man I was teased by the French authorities for the deplorably dirty condition of the paintings. Of course I passed the blame to the University, but they got their own back. Ruhemann, in the cleaning process, revealed a date on one of the Chardins which put the French experts twenty years out in their catalogue entries arranged in chronological order.

He also did a great service in giving lecture demonstrations at the School of Art and elsewhere. 'The Artist at Work' Exhibition

inaugurated at the Art Gallery under the auspices of CEMA which toured the country was in the greatest measure Helmut Ruhemann's idea. He did most of the preparation of a Penguin volume, in collaboration with the late Mrs Ellen Kemp. It is a permanent witness to a first-rate performance.

It was impossible for us to hold Mr Ruhemann in Scotland, but before he returned south he had started to train a young man, William Hood. He, too, in turn went south and after a spell with a firm of restorers received an appointment at the Bowes Museum at Barnard Castle. We lost a few of our young and up-coming members of the staff when the war finished. Better pay and prospects exercised a natural pull. We got a little comfort in the reports that their Glasgow association was regarded as a recommendation.

Having started on this particular enterprise we had no intention of abandoning it. There was plenty to do, and a vast amount of arrears to be overtaken.

In museum work of this kind – it applies also in some degree to technicians – you have to train your own men. One day I got a phone call from an old friend and neighbour from my medical practice days. He wanted to tell me about a patient of his, who might be useful to us. The patient, a graduate of the Glasgow School of Art, temporarily under the weather and not quite certain what kind of career he should aim at, carried an unqualified assurance in the matter of reliability. I said, 'send him along and if he is still in need of a doctor you have lost a patient'. That was how we met Mr Henry McLean who, from the ground floor so to speak, began to build for himself a reputation which is becoming increasingly well known within and beyond art gallery circles. Of course Harry – as he very soon became known to us – had an excellent background of training. Very few in his newly found profession start off with a Diploma in Art. He got a little guidance from me in the role of enthusiast rather than executant on the lines of directing him where to look for information. Naturally, and this was always made clear to the Committee and the public – not one of the city's masterpieces would be subjected to any treatment prior to consultation and investigation.

Now, with a funded experience and a fully developed talent, Harry has become the first person to be consulted. Two outstanding cases stand to his credit, but as they occurred after I left they are not in detail part of this story. Before he had reached the level of full mastership in his craft we had arrived at the momentous decision to clean the greatest painting in the collection, viz. 'The Woman taken in Adultery' by Giorgione.

I think it would be fair to say that my hopes that this very important operation would be completed in my time, were first raised by Philip Hendy. When we were rivals for the job I succeeded in getting, he said, in course of a friendly letter '. . . Glasgow is a great opportunity. Merely to get that Giorgione cleaned would be a great work.' I must have kept this in mind, but as it turned out it was pure coincidence, or maybe the inevitable march of events, which led to Hendy – now Sir Philip – having a share in the successful conclusion of a very excellent piece of work.

Before reaching the preliminary stage of recommending my Committee to give the necessary authority to proceed, I consulted a number of leading art authorities. I put two questions to them, (a) should we clean the Giorgione? and (b) who should do it? To the first question the answer was an unanimous and unqualified 'yes' – nothing half-hearted. Make a thorough and complete job of it. The unanimity disappeared in reply to the second question. Three or four names were suggested, all of them men with high qualifications. Before reaching a decision I recommended a complete investigation of the present condition of the work and then determine the correct procedure. In other words, let's have an overhaul, arrive at a diagnosis, and then decide the treatment.

There was only one place in Britain with the necessary full equipment – the National Gallery in London. The full report with X-ray photographs, micro-chemical analysis and all the rest of it are now in four portfolios in the Gallery archives. In charge of the investigation was Mr Ruhemann and when the final decision was made to proceed with a thorough cleaning and restoration, it was obvious that he was the man for the job. His previous experience with other paintings by Giorgione, his association with the National Gallery, the trustees of which allowed the work to be done there, and personal knowledge of his integrity and competence made the choice irresistible.

A full account of what was found and what was done is described in an article, 'The Story of its Restoration' in the *Scottish Art Review* (1954) and I need not paraphrase it here. It is repeated in Ruhemann's authoritative work *The Cleaning of Paintings* (1968). There are, however, some side issues worth mentioning for several reasons.

In the first place, when the painting came back to us – it was away for over a year – I was delighted with the result. We had, of course, visits from those who 'seriously questioned' or 'deeply regretted' what we had done. I made available to them the reports, the arguments for and against cleaning which had been put before the Committee. I showed them photographs in colour before and after treatment. I pointed out passages which for years were green and which now, with the old brown varnish removed, were blue. I asked them if they accepted the finding which emphasised that the picture was not in a good state of preservation, that many bits of paint were becoming detached from the canvas, and that if something were not done, the conditions would continue to deteriorate.

Some of the critics were men of standing and we had to pay attention to their views. Nevertheless I can think of no occasion when I was confronted with a greater demonstration of unreasonable and irrational opinions. We were enveloped in prejudice.

Mr Michael Ayrton has made two critical assaults, on the BBC, in 1962 and 1966, without reply. (On art affairs the BBC suffers from quite a number of prejudices.) By way of example, Mr Ayrton has twice said, 'Cleaning has caused the blue robe of the central figure to advance from its proper tonal place so that it seems nearer to the eye than the shadowed arm and knee of the armoured man in front of it.' Now, at a distance of three to four feet from the picture this is quite correct. But at the proper viewing distance for a picture of this size it is not so. When the dirty brown varnish was removed from this painting not only were the colours restored, the space relationship of different passages appeared to regain the original values which had been lost. Test this for yourself in front of the painting. (Indeed the argument may be sustained by comparing the 'before' and 'after' reproductions.)

One unfortunate result of the controversy in some respects was a loss of confidence in connoisseurs and scholars. This led me to play a game with some who favoured me with a visit. But first of all I ought to report one aspect of importance. Ruhemann told me of visits paid to him when he was engaged on the work. Several eminent authorities, British and foreign, were unanimous and emphatic in their opinion that the painting was entirely by Giorgione's own hand, although two of them had expressed serious doubts before they saw the cleaned picture. Following on this we got a letter from Dr Louisa Vertova, assistant to the great B.B.

(Bernard Berenson), one of the foremost authorities on Italian Painting. He had always resisted the Giorgione attribution. I think it was B.B. who first drew attention to the missing portion – a head in the Sach's collection. This is what Dr Vertova said:

'The impact of the picture was such – in spite of the missing bits revealed by cleaning – that I too feel utterly convinced it was by Giorgione and couldn't be by anyone else . . . all the X-rays were sent to us. The result is that in the new edition of the Berenson Lists (on which we are working) the Glasgow "Christ and Adulteress" will be listed as Giorgione.'

And B.B. never saw the cleaned picture. This, and other experiences, made it easy for me subsequently to agree with Malraux when he stated, 'The history of art is the history of that which can be photographed.' This was confirmed on a number of occasions and from correspondence. Apparently it is not at all necessary to inspect the actual works before spreading oneself on an analysis of treatment and style.

Sometimes we got a little impatient with the 'high-hat' technique extended by some of the young and not so young visitors from the south, especially when we sensed that their prejudices were inclined to rest on personal animosities. I remember one such visitor (name withheld because I have no desire to hurt anyone). As we walked round the gallery he said, 'Ah! I see you have been cleaning some of your paintings. Who for example cleaned that one?' – pointing to a Dutch landscape. Deliberately making a mis-statement I said, 'Ruhemann.' 'I knew it. He has ruined it.' Then I corrected myself. 'Oh! I'm wrong. It wasn't Ruhemann. It was . . .' mentioning the name of a restorer I knew he held in very high regard. In a grim silence we continued the tour.

One of the first things Helmut Ruhemann tackled when he was with us in Glasgow was the huge altar piece 'Virgin and Child Enthroned'. It came with the McLellan collection and has been discussed extensively in standard works with various attributions. We label it 'School of Bellini'. I remembered it from my student days and wondered what had happened to it. Eventually I found it covered up in the basement and was told that because of the extensive blistering and generally poor condition it had been removed for treatment. Apparently it had been forgotten. Over the next two years Ruhemann endeavoured to salvage the wreck. The painting is divided into two large panels. He was only able to complete, more or less, one section, and nothing was done to the other for a long time.

When Harry McLean had, so to speak, served his apprenticeship, I said to him one day, 'What about finishing this semi-wreck? We must exhibit it again and at least we can arrest further disintegration.' I suppose at the back of my mind, a sentimental liking for the huge painting kept bubbling up. In any case Harry did a heroic rescue and the result has, for many years, been on view above the left stairway. A slight manipulation of light, or shifting the angle of inspection, makes it easy to identify the scars resulting from extensive repairs on the badly blistered surface. Retouching is just as extensive. Regarded as a period piece it is, in my opinion, worthy to be exhibited. Anyhow, it created a great deal of interest. One of our young 'scholars' from the south was especially attracted by it. Evidently he knew a good deal about it or had read it up shortly before. Among his qualifications appeared the fact that he once had tea in Florence at I Tatti, Settignano, the home of B.B. He struck a very professional attitude, and said, 'I am positive it is the work of Bellini himself. Look at the shepherd's head for example. Only Bellini could have painted that.' As a matter of fact the head in question had been so mutilated by blistering that most of it had to be repainted – and very well repainted it was – by Harry McLean. For a long time afterwards Harry had to suffer a daily greeting, 'Good morning, McLean-Bellini!'

At no time had I any difficulty in obtaining a favourable response to requests for equipment for the Conservation Department. We did not need much, nor was there any sense in Glasgow creating an elaborate laboratory when the occasions for using it were not, at this time, likely to be frequent. I had some idea that, one day, we might grow into a centre, offering service to the West of Scotland – Edinburgh looking after the East – and maybe we could undertake to train the rising generation. Our first need, however, was adequate studio accommodation, and this would have to take its priority chance against some very formidable claims. As in many other cases we did the best we could with what we had but the essentials were always forthcoming. One of these led to another appointment, a staff photographer. We got Rupert Roddam who came from the laboratory of a steel works where his speciality had been to X-ray welding jobs. Very quickly he adapted himself to our particular work, which stretched from publicity on special occasions including snapping at celebrities, to infra-red photography of paintings and to demands from every department on the museum side. He too, in the matter of accommodation, dark room, etc. had to be pushed around from pillar to post.

Although it was not primarily part of our business to be concerned with the detection of fakes and forgeries, as a matter of interest we could not resist testing our suspicions when these were aroused. In any case, for the first time we could supplement simple visual examination or put a hunch to the test. When the sensational Hans Van Meegeren forgeries became public news they were, for a long time, the subject of discussion in and out of gallery circles. As always happens, the experts who had been taken in were subjected to a great deal of ridicule. It was a fantastic story. Van Meegeren confessed to having painted nine canvases which were sold under the name of Vermeer or de Hooch. The first one, 'Christ at Emmaus' was sold to the Boymans Museum in Rotterdam. It was acclaimed enthusiastically in an article in the Burlington Magazine in 1937. The author was Abraham Bredius, an outstanding authority, who among other things dated it about the same time as the Edinburgh Vermeer 'Christ in the House of Martha and Mary'. (This was once in the Coats Collection.) That led some of the 'experts' to cast doubts on the painting in Edinburgh, and to ask me what I thought. They could, as we say, have saved their breath for, apart from knowing practically nothing about Vermeer's work I had already learned the lesson to keep out of print in controversial issues not primarily my concern.

Alas! My friend Thomas Bodkin had taken the side of Bredius (note, by the way, that not all the experts had been taken in away back in 1937) and in a popular art book he had praised the wonderful find. We agreed later that experts must be allowed a few mistakes in their lifetime. Besides, one must not interfere with the pleasure of the laity when the expert goes wrong.

Meegeren is said to have sold pictures forged by himself to Goering for no less than eight million florins. It was this 'collaboration with the enemy' which brought the whole amazing story to light.

The main reason for recalling this, at this point, is to stress the fact that we were in the process of developing a new and necessary branch of Art Gallery work, when the public were being compelled by the press to be curious about what went on behind the scenes.

For a long time, after an address or lecture, when questions were invited the first question was generally directed at some aspect of the Meegeren case – especially the financial aspect. How did the speaker – me – explain this or that? On one occasion the mover of the vote of thanks let himself go. He congratulated the Gallery on its cleaning and restoration activities and proffered the view that not even a fake Vermeer would be allowed to pass through our portals. I ought to be ashamed to confess that I lapped it all up with a benevolent grin. In the cause of publicity I suffered it all very gladly!

From outside sources and reports from a number of people I know that Harry McLean's work is highly appreciated. It is difficult therefore to understand why the Museum authorities appear to 'pipe down' on the Department of Conservation. On two counts at least it is worth sustained publicity – (a) the restoration of the slashed Dali painting –the records of the whole process are fully informative, and (b) the transfer of a painting from one canvas to another. The account of this was filmed, step by step, by Mr Charles Palmar, Curator of Natural History. These are things I would have wanted to tell the whole world about.

There is something else I must tell some of the world about. At a meeting of UNESCO in Paris some years ago I heard the delegate from the Lebanon tease the man from Poland, who was being somewhat obtuse, not to say obstructive, by telling him of an old Proverb which was 'You cannot stop the birds from flying over your head; but you can prevent them nesting in your hair.' Ever since Professor McLaren Young brought to my notice a neglected Scot named William Buchanan, I cannot get the fellow out of my system. I find him mentioned in all the diaries and records around the beginning of last century. A graduate of our own University, he became a lawyer in Edinburgh and then, as an Art Dealer in London, was responsible for the importation of some great masterpieces of Art. In 1824 he published a two-volume account of his adventures in Art. He inscribed it to the *Amateurs of the Fine Arts.*

'At a period when a taste for the Fine Arts is rapidly spreading through every part of the British Dominions; when the Sovereign himself, a Prince of refined taste and extensive attainments, takes a lead in the establishment of Institutions calculated to diffuse a general knowledge thereof and to promote their culture; when the Galleries of a public nature are forming in several of the principal cities of the empire, and a desire to cultivate these Arts increases with the growing prosperity of the country; some details concerning these works which are now objects of general regard may not be unacceptable to the Amateurs of painting.'

Buchanan says, in justifying his memoirs and speaking of paintings:

'To fix their history, to ascertain their origin is to enhance and to ensure their value.'

He quotes the Duke of Orleans (Brother of Louis XIV):

'No man could perpetuate his name so effectually with posterity as by a just and liberal patronage of the Fine Arts.'

Therefore, if you seek immortality you know one way to achieve it.

When I began to wonder why the Art historians had overlooked Buchanan for so long, his name kept cropping up in references, articles and most recently in 'Christie's Bi-Centenary Review of the Year'. There was reproduced the Van Dyck painting of Charles I. The 'three in one' idea was in order that it be sent to Italy for Bernini to execute a bust. (Is execute the wrong word in this case?) It was brought back to England by Irvine – acting as agent for Buchanan, who put it up for sale in May 1804. It fetched 490 guineas. Eventually it was acquired by George IV in 1822. He paid 1,000 guineas. (Kenneth Clark talked about it on television some time ago, when taking us round the Royal Palaces.)

The other day, when refreshing my memory in the sensational case of Van Meegeren, I came across Buchanan's name again. The first outstanding case of Art forgery to come to my notice was the celebrated bust of 'Flora' – supposedly a genuine Leonardo da Vinci. It was acquired in 1909 by Wilhelm Bode for the Kaiser-Frederich Museum in Berlin. In 1909 I was more interested in a Dr Walford Bodie, the music hall medical magician who had fallen foul of the Glasgow undergraduate body, the affair terminating in the famous Bodie Riot. The similarity of the names perhaps made me especially eager to investigate the story of the fake 'Flora'. It was proved to the satisfaction of the vast majority of informed art experts that Bode of Berlin had made an error. The Leonardo Bust was made in 1846 by Richard Lucas to the special order of *Mr William Buchanan*, who supplied the sculptor with a painting 'in the style of Leonardo' to serve as a model. Neither Lucas nor Buchanan can be described as forgers. The work was never offered for sale by them as a genuine work. It was made in 1846 and it was not until the experts proclaimed it as by Leonardo that it became a forgery.

Buchanan was among those who campaigned for the National

Gallery. His memoirs appeared in the same year as the opening (1824). It has been stated that some of the finest paintings in the National Gallery passed through Buchanan's hands. You should know more about him. You might care to start at his tombstone and work backwards. He is buried in the Glasgow Necropolis – the date is marked as 1864 and his age eighty-seven. Very soon you are likely to know more about him; a book by Mr Colin Clark is in the offing. An advance note on his researches has appeared in the *Scottish Art Review*.

Glasgow Art Gallery & Museums Association

In March 1942 the Committee and then the Corporation gave its approval to the formation of an Association which might play an active part in the cultural life of the City. That was the beginning, but it was September 1944 before we got down to the end of the beginning – or in other words, before the Association became an accomplished fact.

We had got into the habit of dating every fresh effort as after 'the Blitz'. It also functioned as an excuse for postponements. There were other excuses for delay. I was subjected to a number of cross-examinations on the need and purpose of such an Association and the nature of its constitution. It was pointed out, more than once, that it was the Corporation's job to run the Art Gallery, and no outside body was going to take over. I was rather amazed at the amount of suspicion and misunderstanding. This did not arise in the Committee. It came as a result of *official* warnings that nothing would be approved which might undermine the authority and responsibility of the Corporation. Glasgow had got along quite well in the past without this kind of thing, so why bother? To the new Convener I put the 'ulterior motives' in something like this:

(a) a new form of publicity;

(b) the creation of a mailing list to ensure good audiences for exhibition openings, lectures and the like;

(c) probably the creation of a fund to allow us to produce up-to-date literature and new catalogues;

(d) form some kind of link between existing societies, clubs and associations and persuade them to make greater use of the civic collections;

(e) cultivate private collectors with the obvious end in view, and anything else that might emerge as we went along. I added that the Corporation was giving nothing away. The council of the Association could be so formed as to make the majority of its members town councillors – the City Chamberlain can be the Treasurer, in control of the finances, and in the event of winding up all funds would pass to the Corporation. Moreover, the whole enterprise would add nothing to the running costs of the department. To Convener Burnett I raised this question, 'Why all this suspicion and obstruction about something you and I and a great number of people think is an excellent idea?' He gave me a grin and said, 'By this time you ought to know the Corporation and how it works. In any case it's going on.'

It went on. Two people, Isabel Mackintosh and myself, were chiefly – almost exclusively – responsible for getting it going. When names and descriptions were all being reduced to initials we were a bit apprehensive about the title we should give the Association. There was only one possible and we just had to face the risk of 'Gagma'. It has, fortunately, never been twisted either in conversation or reporting.

The minimum annual subscription of 1/– was criticised; but I was acting on a psychological hunch partly to demonstrate our anxiety to attract the young through a nominal subscription, and partly to assess the amount of support likely to be reflected in donations and subscriptions in excess of the minimum. It worked out in that way. The average subscription was around 5 shillings and in a short time – without any other form of appeal – we had over £2,000 in the kitty. The financial nucleus had been created by fees received by myself for newspaper articles and outside lectures.

When, in subsequent application forms we added 'A single payment of at least £5.5.0 qualifies for Life Membership', I was chaffed for daring to ask for 'a hundred times the annual subscription'. Nevertheless this hint on how to make a gesture was taken with very satisfactory results. At no time were we anxious on the score of finance. The Hon Treasurer, generally through a member of his staff, was there to keep a kindly eye on us. Sometimes our eyes didn't look at things the same way. I wanted to spend the money. It had been given for that purpose. But, 'Take things easy'; 'Be cautious'; 'You never know' were the phrase formulae which kept us in check. The Treasurer wanted money to be idle. I wanted it to work. At an Annual General Meeting the Treasurer once reported 'You lost money on the Calendar of Events'. I nearly became speechless. 'Lost money, my foot! This is an outlay for which we raise the money.'

I think I must suffer from a complex on 'money in reserve' – I am a Scot and I believe in thrift. It is a good policy to pursue, whatever we are, and wherever we may be. But far too often money is stored by charitable associations and the like when it was intended to be spent in the lifetime of the donor. Churches and comparable institutions with reserves of funds far in excess of their ordinary requirements, means some work is left undone. For example, if an individual church doesn't know how to spend it, the Church as a whole has need of it. Besides, 'Oh ye of little faith' still strikes me as a good text.

The Association, from its inception – and I am delighted it is still going strong – has never received any grant or donation from the City. The Calendar of Events has continued to be issued regularly since 1944. Its format, still unchanged, was 'borrowed' from one issued by my friend the late Martin Baldwin, for many years director of the Toronto Art Gallery. It took a little longer to get the illustrated magazine – an important item on our list of promises. The first number appeared in 1946, and was called 'The Glasgow Art Review'. Although we rather fancied the cover design which allowed the reader to understand he was looking at the official journal of the Glasgow Art Gallery and Museums Association, we recognised that it was only a beginning. But it was very well received. The Press gave the effort a warm welcome – every member of the Association got a copy free of charge (they still do), the general public paid half-a-crown for their copies, and we made a profit. This of course was made possible by the support of advertisers with a charitable rather than a commercial outlook. One thing I was immensely pleased about – the decision to reproduce on the frontis-piece of No. 1 the portrait of Fra H. Newbery, famous director of the Glasgow School of Art by Maurice Greiffenhagen, RA, who exercised a great influence on the artists of my generation. The name Fra, like the tight frock coat and the Whistlerian straight-brimmed top hat, might have been a mild affectation. His energy, his devotion to the School and his enthusiasm were persistent and fruitful. These might never have been the monument of Modern Architecture but for Fra Newbery. The background of the portrait is a silhouette of the School designed by Charles Rennie Mackintosh. Old Man Newbery, in rather feeble health, was living in retirement in the south of England. From him and others we heard that he derived a great amount of pleasure in having been thus remembered.

A considerable amount of thought and midnight oil went into the perfection of my first Art Review editorial. The closing paragraph was this:

> 'Therefore, because we do not feel disposed to treat the bulk of our visitors with indifference, the emphasis of this review will be practical rather than theoretical. In effect we shall say to the scholar, whether he be archaeologist, geologist, ornithologist, historian or aesthetician, "The road up to you is a bit steep. Come down and meet us sometimes!" '

This may seem a long harangue about a very simple affair, but I have to emphasise the fact that the production of this new art magazine and its successors was the work of two amateurs, Isabel Mackintosh and myself, and one professional, John M. Jack of MacLehose & Co, our printers. I had known John M. Jack for a long time and we had many mutual interests. His firm, official printers to the University, were said to be 'very good but not cheap'. This 'saying' gave us plenty to argue about, but I am sure we would often have been sunk if it had not been for John Jack's valiant rescues, not to mention his wise direction on practical affairs. His son, Ian, following a distinguished Army Career was looking for a civilian job with, of course, prospects. I got Etienne Vacher to take him on at the Central Hotel. He started in the kitchen, survived a period of aching feet and other numerous trials and tribulations. Now, he is the head of British Railways Hotel Service.

At first it looked as if the Association might founder on the question 'Who was to do our printing?' The Corporation had its own printing department, and every now and then party politics took a hand. One side was opposed to this apparent interference with private trading, the other upheld the economical advantage in having their own show. All printing therefore had to go through the official channels. The check on this was simple. If a department presented for payment a printing account from an outside firm it was asked 'why?' and a dim view was taken, whatever the excuse. The Corporation Printing Department was very busy. There was nobody on their staff who could guide us on the kind of layout and typography we wanted to have. Nothing would have pleased me more than to be able to boast that everything in the way of publications issued from the Art Gallery was produced by a

Corporation Department. But the kind of production we were aiming at was much too special a job, and I think they were quite relieved when we went elsewhere. This was, in another sense, easy, for the Corporation was not called upon to pay the account. The Association paid its own way on matters of this kind.

Quite clearly we were acting under the impression that we were doing something original and terribly important. There were a few who thought it would quickly fade away and that I would get tired of it. How wrong they have been and how I rejoice in the fact that fifteen years after I handed it over quite a number of our bright young critics and historians are delighted to appear in its pages.

When I look up the list of contributors to the Art Review I experience a glow of pride in recalling how many distinguished men and women thought it worth their while to prepare articles for a nominal fee or no fee at all. Our own staff and those on other Scottish Galleries and Museums were encouraged to say what they liked on their special subject. Some welcomed the opportunity. Others held back. As there was nothing comparable to the magazine being produced in Scotland, and as it was clear we could not limit ourselves to Glasgow and the West of Scotland, I put a proposal before the Scottish Museums Federation. Why not make this new journal common to us all? Each of us could create his own local association, and in some way we could take turn about with a quarterly featuring different collections or areas. We could change the name to 'The Scottish Art Review' and find a way to ensure that editorial supervision would not centre in one man or in one place. It came to nothing. Perhaps it was premature, or I was too much of a new boy. However the proposal did not beget any hostility and my colleagues in other cities made the very friendly gesture of putting each number on sale in their respective galleries. We did, nevertheless, change the name to *The Scottish Art Review*. There was nothing defiant in this decision. We had discovered that the Glasgow School of Painters – the group which flourished in the eighties and nineties of last century – had issued a journal under this title. And we were convinced that even with a Glasgow bias it was possible for us to be of service to the whole of Scotland.

One other important result followed in the course of time. This was the increase in the number of museum publications which were received from museums and galleries all over the world. Nothing can equal the importance of knowing how other people think and act. Inasmuch as we had now something to send out the list of exchanges grew in volume. There were critics, of course; some expected a more scholarly production. These had missed the point and purpose of what we were trying to do. On balance, however, we had every reason to be pleased with the nature and source of the congratulations received from many correspondents – especially those from overseas.

I see that I said farewell in the issue marked as Vol. V No. 1 1954. In the concluding paragraph of my last editorial I wrote this:

'Reviews in art and literature appear to come and go with lamentable frequency. This is the 17th issue of our particular contribution to art conversation in Scotland. The present editor is about to take his leave but he feels confident that the journal will continue to serve the interests of the Association, and of a very much wider public.'

It is a special pleasure to report that the confidence was more than justified. Although nowhere indicated, it is an open secret that Isabel Mackintosh does both the editing and the collection of advertisements. She has not lost her enthusiasm for the Association and has added to its range of operations. For example, she has for a number of years conducted tours abroad, giving opportunities for members to visit art centres in different European countries. I have seen this at first hand. Some years ago the party was in Denmark. Among them was my wife and her friend Jean Singleton – wife of George Singleton, founder of the Cosmo Cinema. On my way back from Sweden I halted for twenty-four hours in Copenhagen. It seemed to me that some of the party looked as if a concentrated week on art treasures had been too much for them. At least, that is my story and excuse for taking some of them to a 'flea circus'. It took a little time to get back again to 'the cultural level' where I thought my reputation ought to rest!

I had a special interest in the issue of the *Scottish Art Review* which had to be my farewell performance. The contents show that we celebrated in print the centenary of Archibald McLellan, the real founder of the civic art collection. This was done in a well-illustrated, delightful historical essay by Elspeth Gallie, curator in charge of the Old Glasgow Museum. She is now Mrs William Buchanan, wife of the Deputy Director of the Scottish Arts Council.

The front cover – designed by W. J. Macaulay, then Curator of Art, was most successful in recapturing the spirit and character of the Glasgow of a century ago. Without showing them, for the drawing is that of composite west-end terraces, he makes one think immediately of antimacassars and aspidistras (the biggest in the world of course). I sometimes wonder if Bill Macaulay designed this cover with his tongue in his cheek. On the left is a male figure, doffing his hat, and to the right is a cab, waiting for someone to depart. This 'Hail and farewell' gag could have applied to either of us. He got out three months before I did. He joined our staff as Curator of Art in succession to Andrew Hannah who had become the first keeper of the Burrell Collection. A graduate from the Edinburgh School of Art with some experience in archaeological expeditions in the Middle East and a spell with the Council of Industrial Design, he was just the kind of man we needed. He brought with him a special quality of personal taste, which was demonstrated in the framing of paintings, in the hanging of exhibitions, and in the arranging and planning of objets d'art. Moreover he was an entertaining and loyal colleague. He had an incisive wit. Sometimes those at the receiving end of it imagined they felt a barb when there was none. I thought he was happy with us. I had ideas that Glasgow would do well to promote him to greater responsibility. When he announced, some time after it was known that I was resigning, that he was leaving, I expressed some surprise. His comment, 'I saw what was happening to you and I lost my desire to continue in the Corporation's service.' When we compare notes or exchange gossip on people and affairs incidental to our Art Gallery adventure he can always put me in my place. He has a letter from the City of Glasgow thanking him for his excellent work during his six years of service. Alas! I, with my fifteen years, have no such document. Bill Macaulay went back to his native Edinburgh, oddly enough, to become an art dealer. He is now the sole partner in what is probably the most prominent art dealing firm in Scotland. I left business for local government service. He reversed the process and, as far as I know, has no regrets.

9

A Note on Collections and Collectors

In the first number of the Art Review, with great pride and satisfaction, we had stretched beyond the bounds of caution to produce a colour supplement. I see that I had grabbed the first page of this to reproduce the diagram which was the background of all my efforts in talks and lectures to spread the gospel of Art Appreciation. The centre piece – and in largest lettering is – WORK OF ART: on one side is SPECTATOR and on the other ARTIST. From the beginning I made it clear that my business was with the SPECTATOR.

Art, we have been told, is communication. It follows therefore that a work of art does not come to life until and unless it is seen or heard. I do not think enough attention is ever paid to the receiving end. We too often disregard the audience. I have said something like this already and I expect to return to the bee in my bonnet. Meanwhile, I am always interested in the views of our succeeding race. I have noted two observations by Professor Quentin Bell of the University of Sussex. A son of my friend Clive Bell, I last met him, when he was a schoolboy, in Duncan Grant's studio. He wrote an article in *The Listener* following a visit to the Glasgow Civic & University collections. His conclusion was this: 'Glasgow certainly has the pictures; all that it lacks is the galleries.'

More recently, in the *British Journal of Aesthetics* in discussing the aesthetic diversity of the nineteenth century, he has this to say:

'The patron was, in the Middle Ages, an institution; by the nineteenth century he had become a market, a market composed of innumerable individuals most of them united by a prevailing taste in art, but with many varieties of individual feeling.'

Still thinking of patronage and taste, I recall hearing some years ago the late Mr Hugh Gaitskell say at a Royal Scottish Academy Banquet, 'The age of the Private Patron is dead. The future life of the artist lies in the patronage of the State and of the Municipality.' I was sitting among some active Scots artists, one of whom remarked, 'That is a gloomy outlook for us.'

In the House of Commons before she departed therefrom, Miss Jennie Lee said, 'In a mixed economy the arts ought to be financed from the Central Government, from local government and from *private* patrons.' She might have added Industry. I think I know the bias of her successor, Lord Eccles. His father was a famous surgeon and he married the daughter of a famous physician – all of which information has nothing to do with the case, or has it? He is well known to me as a collector, and I particularly remember his early adventures in art.

I do not know what attempts were made a hundred years ago to answer the question 'Is there a standard of Taste in the Fine Arts?' The question continues to be asked. For my purpose, when talking of patronage I rely on this working definition: 'Taste is the result of intuition working in and out of partnership with experience.'

The great collectors of Art, when they die, win for themselves obituary notices in which, generally, they are acclaimed as 'men of discerning taste'. Very few of them had any taste. Knowledge? Yes! The sporting instinct? Yes, and often very well developed. Ability or good luck in selecting advisers? Most important. Surplus money? Essential. Critical bias – the great Berenson had it – is frequently another name for prejudice. It is all part of the make up of the successful collector.

There may be hidden motives resting on some confused ideas on immortality. It is a fact of Art History that the Collection lives longer than the Collector. If it bears his name it becomes a monument to a public-spirited citizen, whether he thought of it in that way or not. In the long run we, the art historians, educators, students, enthusiasts or casual spectators, inherit the treasures.

On many occasions, before and since, I have also been asked 'Why do people buy pictures?' Starting from the well-worn platitude that collecting anything is man's response to one of his deepest urges, there opens up a great variety of explanations and defences. Before leading the answer in the direction of public collections in general, and the Glasgow collection in particular, I could start at No. 3 Kensington Gate, then the official residence of the Director. The contents of course were ours. One evening I was asked by a visitor, an unashamed philistine, 'Did you actually buy that?' – pointing to a painting by Jean Lurçat. It was painted in 1929 and we got it in Paris on our first joint visit without either liking or understanding it. I had been told that Lurçat, Dufy, Marcoussis and some others to whom I had been introduced were 'up and coming' men. This particular picture, 'La Charette', was inexpensive (less than £20). I thought I would make it function as a text-book, arguing to myself, 'One buys a book on the recommendation of a friend. It is an act of faith. Why not the same with a picture?'

When I said this or something like it, our visitor looked as if he wanted to say 'All baloney'. However, he was very polite and turned to look at our Lurçat tapestry. This is a three panel screen, probably the only one in Scotland, and interesting as reflecting the revival of the art in France and Scotland. He liked it immediately, and never thought to ask 'What is it meant to be?' Most of our visitors react in the same way. The screen is admired at a first glance, but they take much longer with the painting. What happens is this! First visit – 'Goodness, what's that?' Subsequent visits – 'That picture intrigues me', or 'I'm beginning to see something in it', or 'D'ye know, I think I like it'.

As a small and hesitant collector, but grateful for so many chances to see the world through an artist's vision I have missed opportunities galore. I am not thinking solely of increased values; but who isn't pleased when he has acquired something within his financial capacity to find later it has become worth much more?

On this very point I have to break away again to reveal our sad experience with squandered treasure; partly provoked into doing this because of an article 'The Passionate Quest of an Art Dealer' (in the November 1969 issue) of *The Reader's Digest* – a copy of which is floating around this ship. There is an illustration, in colour, of 'The Pool of London' with this caption:

> 'Vollard commissioned Derain's "Pool of London" in 1906. He later sold it for £100; bought for the nation by the Chantrey Trustees for £1,500. It is now worth over £60,000.'

The only correction I have to make is to substitute £45 for the £100. That is what I paid for it, and it belonged to us for twelve years. Because of the 'tight squeeze' in trying to live as the Corporation and our humble tastes required us to live – plus the pressure of Family Insurance Premiums, some things had to go. The Tate got our Derain, because it was the Tate. Another of our treasures also came through Vollard. It is the large Pissarro 'The Marne at Chennevieres' now in the Scottish National Gallery in Edinburgh. We used to call it 'Our Country Cottage', for we had hoped one day it would help us to buy a small place in the country. We have neither picture nor cottage but we are glad we eventually said 'Yes' to Stanley Cursiter who had long wanted it for Edinburgh. Near the point of his retiral he tried us again and, without any resistance from his Trustees, who were given the full story of how it came to be our property, this fine picture remains in Scotland. It cost us £542.17.1. What the National Gallery paid is their secret. We made what looked like a handsome profit. Today, it is worth more than ten times what it cost the National Gallery. We have no regrets, for we think there is comfort of sorts in daydreams. Besides, we owe so much to artists, many of them no more, who have helped to keep our home fires burning.

During my 'apprenticeship' in Glasgow with Reid & Lefevre before going South I had to regard the question 'Why do people buy pictures?' as important. It was then my job to make people want to buy. I had to know something about their motivating impulses. I listed a few.

There is the casual, quite insensitive man, who buys pictures because it is the proper thing to have some in his house. When the walls are covered to his satisfaction he is finished.

There is the man whose glance has been caught and caught again by something which pleases him. He sees it in a window or in an exhibition to which he may have been unwillingly dragged. He can afford it, but he wonders if he is not a bit foolish in spending money on art. There comes to mind the comment made by the Duke of Wellington when he bought a painting for a thousand guineas from Sir David Wilkie. 'For Heaven's sake don't let my banker know.' Sometimes a 'foolish' purchase is the first step towards the creation of a genuine interest. Once bitten never shy again.

There is the well-to-do citizen who may be persuaded as a duty to society to support young artists of promise. Either discreetly or through an agent he becomes the owner of a number of works and then he doesn't know what to do with the 'damn' things'. I often used to wish his type was more numerous. It is also remarkable how the 'damn' things' in the long run find their rightful place.

There is the man who has heard that pictures can be good

investments if he is prepared to risk a bit of money. That is when art masquerades as currency. I remember when the Art Institute was having its first exhibition at Kelvingrove I was asked to advise a prospective 'investor' who thought he might spend some money on contemporary art. Always keen to encourage anyone who had a mind to buy the works of living artists, whatever the motive, I asked him what exactly was in his mind. 'Nothing in particular,' said he. He did not object to spending £1,000, but he wanted paintings by young artists, whose works would eventually go up in value. 'Who are they?' he asked. The only answer I could think of at the time was 'Do you think if I knew the answer to that I would waste my time and opportunities showing pictures? It would be enough to store them.' However, he took the plunge and some young painters had a better year.

The kind of collector who became important to me for several reasons was William McInnes. I got to know him around the time I had switched from medicine to art. I think he was one of the few who knew that I had become an Art Dealer to 'get a kick out of it'. Throughout a long and successful career in the shipping industry his leisure interests were centred on the appreciation of music and painting. Rather reticent on his ability as an executant in any of the arts (he had played the church organ in his younger days), slowly and deliberately he acquired a standard of taste which is reflected in his collection of paintings. Music competed with pictorial art for the leading place in his affections. If you want to know what he looked like there is a drawing of him seated at his piano in *Introducing Leslie Hunter*. Chiefly via gramophone records and a Pianola he became familiar with the classics and he seldom missed the Saturday evening concerts promoted by the Scottish National Orchestra. McInnes was a man without ostentation, modest in his bachelor way of living, fearless in criticism, but without bitterness, and anxious above all things to evade the limelight.

When he travelled, especially in France and Italy, he spent much of his time in galleries and treasured the catalogues. His art library was small but it was used. From the day he began to collect paintings he endeavoured to make himself an informed and discriminating buyer with confidence in his own judgment. Chiefly through and because of the Scots artist Leslie Hunter we became friends. For two years, off and on, before I went to London we met, apart from holidays, almost daily. It was customary for a group of us to meet

for morning coffee in the 'Bon Bon'. That was the comic name
for a very ordinary little café in the Central Station. It is now no
more and most of the company has gone. I think I am now the sole
survivor.

It has just occurred to me to note how many of Glasgow's art
collectors were connected in one way or another with shipping, as
builders or owners. The Scott Collection of Armour came from a
member of the famous Greenock Ship-building firm. The Burrell
Collection – of which more later – was the lifetime preoccupation
of a successful shipowner. The firm with which McInnes was
associated was known as Gow Harrison. The head of the firm,
Dr Leonard Gow (LL.D. *honoris causa* from Glasgow University) was
a very well known art collector with some great pictures – old
masters, nineteenth century French (Manet, Degas and Renoir). He
also collected Chinese Porcelain. Much of it was, for a period,
exhibited at Kelvingrove and is recorded in an elaborate, beautifully
illustrated catalogue. Dr Gow had stopped collecting when I first
met him. His treasures were dispersed (some are now in the Burrell
Collection).

It may well be that he first created the interest which grew into an
enthusiasm with William McInnes, and some others. Whenever I
looked in at the office in Gordon Street I seemed always to be
interrupting talks on Art, not on shipping. Ion Harrison, son of
Gow's first partner, also extended to me a warm friendship. A
strongly-built, fine, handsome man he had a largish nose which took
part in the smile which could, and generally did, illuminate an
expression which to some seemed severe, but which I always found
comforting. He was keen on the Boy Scout movement and looked
splendid in a kilt. Like his colleagues, Ion Harrison too was interested
in French painting, but with due deliberation he decided that the
masterpieces in this field were likely to go beyond his financial
resources. He confined his collecting adventures, almost exclusively,
to the works of Peploe, Hunter and Cadell. An account of his
experiences and friendship with these artists is given in *Three Scottish
Colourists*. The book stands to me as a constant reminder of many
very happy occasions when we enjoyed the pleasure always to be
found in a delightful home and in such grand company.

Talking of Three Scottish Colourists, meaning Peploe, Hunter and
Cadell, I have often been asked 'What about J. D. Fergusson?' Of
course he is a notable Scottish colourist: but when I first coined the

descriptive phrase, J.D., unlike the others, was living abroad. He came back to Scotland in 1939, and led me to believe that my appointment to the Art Gallery was partly responsible for his decision to try in Glasgow to win for the younger artists, with something new to say, the recognition and support which was their due.

Before I joined the Lefevre Gallery I was well acquainted with J.D.'s history and work: we had a number of mutual friends. And, of course, I was intrigued by the discovery that he had matriculated in the Faculty of Medicine at Edinburgh University. The practice of medicine was not, however, to be his role in life.

I have written and spoken a good deal about Fergusson's life and work in forewords to exhibition catalogues and in opening a number of 'one man shows'. In his own book *Modern Scottish Painting*, J.D. expresses the view that the Glasgow School's achievement was wonderful. It petered out because of the atmosphere in which it was impossible, or nearly impossible, to carry on. He argues that they should not have surrendered to the Academics. Neither Whistler nor Sickert gave in.

While he was in no sense a recluse, my mental pictures of him have been composed more in studios than at ceremonial parties. My first visit to a Fergusson studio was in Paris. It was the tidiest, cleanest studio I have ever visited. His painting is like his mind and surroundings – clean. It is free from the dust of irrelevancies. There is no cluttering up with odds and ends, which belong to something other than the art of painting. (In a different way from the Harrison home in Helensburgh – a visit to the McInnes flat in the Maxwell Park suburb was also a refreshing interlude.) The host would never indulge in superlative claims which are liable to lead to awkward silences. A proper pride in having got this or that painting was often balanced by an expression of regret over something which had been missed. One could discuss with the utmost freedom the lesser things which had won a place more on sentimental associations than on inherent worth.

One of the ties helping to bind our friendship was the sharing of an admiration and affection for Leslie Hunter. It was due to persistent pressure from McInnes that I wrote the monograph on Hunter in 1937. When I came back to Glasgow as Director of the Art Gallery he presented the Matisse 'Head of a Young Girl' to the City. McNeill Reid had picked it up in auction for £60. When McInnes heard of it he acquired it for Glasgow. In his letter to the Lord Provost he stated that he was doing so to mark his approval of my appointment. When he died in 1944 his entire collection became part of the civic collection and greatly enhanced the importance of the gallery devoted to French Art.

It would be a poor return for his generous benefaction to use this occasion to exaggerate or lose a sense of proportion when describing the McInnes Collection. Some things, however, have to be remembered. Although more than comfortably well off, McInnes was not what would be described as a wealthy man. When he bought a picture it was for something it meant to him, and that something was not primarily related to the price. His main object was to acquire works of art for the enjoyment of himself and his friends. The acclaimed masterpieces by artists whose works he was beginning to appreciate and to like were not specially coveted. They were either beyond his conception of what they were worth or outwith the range of funds reserved for picture buying. He was also convinced that often the less *important* productions of an artist were the finest and most original work. The special value of his bequest may be summarised thus: The names of the following artists appeared in the gallery catalogue for the first time: Bonnard, Braque, Cézanne, Van Gogh, Jongkind, Matisse, Picasso, Renoir and Seurat. The Braque and Matisse are outstanding, and the Cézanne landscape small but text-book in treatment.

As an introduction to a school of painting in and around which controversy continued for many years, the McInnes collection is invaluable. In it there are several small 'minor' works which are gems. The Van Gogh is of the Paris period and is perhaps historically rather than pictorially important. (Incidentally Van Gogh did six versions of the subject – Le Moulin de la Galette – two of which came to Scotland.) The Monet and Sisley landscapes contain the whole purpose and achievement of Impressionism. The three Renoirs – portrait, still-life and landscape – constitute an excellent guide to more famous paintings, and the 'blue period' Picasso (I saw a reproduction of it in Stockholm two years ago) gives, to the surprise of many when they note the name of the artist, unqualified delight. There then we have an exciting range of paintings, drawings and prints, a fine memorial to a lover of the arts and a public-spirited citizen.

In recent years a somewhat different if not altogether new kind of art collector has appeared. He is in the millionaire class. Some, buying through the auction rooms of the world become well known; others acquire their treasures quietly through agents or dealers. Sometimes years elapse before their possessions or the extent of them are made known to the public. I am glad to think that in the majority of cases the ultimate owners are the public.

Probably in the thrill of collecting lies the chief pleasure. The peculiar whims and fancies are absolutely a man's own affair. It is certainly a privilege, if not always a pleasure, to meet this kind of collector. To be shown their treasures, and to hear accounts of how, when, where and why they were acquired is a very important part of one's education. That being said, it is necessary to go on to say that not a few of the great private and public collections of art in this and other countries might be properly described as accumulations. Very few collectors have succeeded in keeping out the odd 'curio' and most of them abhor the idea of admitting they may have been taken in. The situation is by no means peculiar to Art.

It was not generally known or understood how the great industrialists in the West of Scotland filled their houses with nineteenth century French and Dutch paintings in advance of British appraisal. I knew a little about some of the collections, Coats, Brechin and Burrell, but only got to know about the David Cargill Collection when I joined Reid & Lefevre. When I made my first visit to the Cargill home, near Lanark, I was amazed at the quality and importance of what I saw. I had heard that he had Cézanne, Renoir, Van Gogh, Seurat, Courbet, Toulouse-Lautrec, Gauguin and others. Some were familiar through reproductions in the catalogues which I had to swot up as part of my training, but I did not know they were in Scotland. David Cargill was a kindly man. He was burly in build, baldish, with a fringe of dark hair and a short trimmed moustache. His voice was gentle, and he never indulged in lengthy sentences. His questions, answers and comments were short and to the point. His family was associated with the founding of the great Burmah Oil Company. He had other business interests in the Far East, where he spent some time in his younger days. David Cargill's usual response to the enthusiasm of visitors, informed or otherwise, was a gentle smile and a sentence, 'It would appear that I have been well advised.' If one as much as hinted to him that an expected visitor to town was a picture lover, he would say, 'Bring him – or her – or them – out for lunch on Saturday or Sunday.'

One Sunday the party included C. B. Cochran (to become Sir Charles). He was highly impressed by more than the paintings. The unaffected simplicity of the household arrangements; the two elderly serving maids who reminded him of Rembrandt or Hals – Mrs Cargill's enthusiasm for the theatre, and a host of other incidents supplied him with ample material for the account C.B. gave of the day's outing at a small party on our return to Glasgow. I thought then what a pity C. B. Cochran did not write plays as well as present them. He was a very acute observer and, in his quiet way, communicated the essence of a reminiscence with lucidity and sparkle. C.B. was, of course, a showman. Maybe, when I thought I had to try to be a showman, 'Cocky' was the model I selected. Certainly I turned more towards him than to the great Lord Duveen, the persuasive dealer in magic.

There are three pictures from the Cargill Collection in the French section of the Art Gallery – the Cargill Trustees allowed me to choose them: an important Corot portrait, 'Mademoiselle de Foudras'; a large Courbet 'Flowers in a Basket' and a well known Seurat 'Boy Sitting on the Grass' (a study for the large painting 'Sunday at the Grande Jatte' in the Art Institute of Chicago). The others were disposed of mostly in America, and the proceeds used to augment the Cargill Fund. This is a Trust which continues to come to the assistance of a number of Scottish charitable institutions and stimulates various interests concerned with the Arts.

One cannot leave the name Cargill without mentioning a half-brother of David, who lived at Bridge of Weir. He was William Alexander Cargill, generally known as W.A. When his collection of paintings was sold in London, following his death in November 1962, it was by way of being the Art Event of the year. A total of £1,043,590 was reached (£105,000 for a Degas), far in excess of what had been paid for the forty odd works. William was smaller in height than David, reserved to the point of shyness, physically active – tennis and golf were his chief recreational interests when young and gardening throughout his life. Completely disinterested in dress – nothing pleased or suited him more than a well-worn jacket and flannel slacks – he remained a bachelor and was devoted to his mother. When she died he withdrew more and more into a spartan mode of living which bordered on the eccentric. He resisted seeking medical advice when 'below the weather'. He neglected himself, but responded in many quiet ways to the needs of others. His last words, said at the close of the fatal illness, without venom but with rather a sad smile of resignation, 'I could murder that night nurse!'

When I came back to Glasgow the outbreak of the War created an unsettled state of affairs in the world of Art. Very soon we got busy with organising exhibitions. This included borrowing from private collections. The first step was to find out where the collections were. Of course, I knew about the magnificent French Paintings at Bridge of Weir. A difference of opinion with old Alexander Reid had led William Cargill away from the Reid & Lefevre Gallery. Among his most notable acquisitions were those he had bought from Etienne Bignou.

In response to a tentative enquiry I was invited to Carruth. Most of the paintings acquired in the thirties were still in the packing cases, concealed in wardrobes or under the beds in various out-of-use bedrooms. I was allowed to sort out the collection, tidy things up generally and hang the paintings in some kind of order. He was grateful for the use of the gallery resources in cleaning, recording, photographing and other services. For all of us on the art side at Kelvingrove it was an unusual and exciting experience.

From then on William Cargill relied on our help and guidance on minor and major issues concerned with his collection. Certainly I was hoping that, eventually, he would emulate my friend McInnes and bequeath the pictures, or some of them, to the City. Two things killed that hope. The first was the Corporation's decision to elevate the Museum side at the expense of the Art side following my retirement. His comment 'They don't seem to think much of their Art collection' perhaps reflected the opinion of a number of people. The second factor referred to the Burrell Collection. 'Look at what they have done – or not done – with Burrell's magnificent gift!'

One other illustration from the 'modest collector' group: A few years ago there was much excitement in London art circles over the purchase for the Tate Gallery of a small portrait of André Derain by Matisse. It cost £8,500, and came from the collection of William Jeffreys, who bought it for £280 in 1939. Between 1924 and 1939 Mr Jeffreys assembled a group of paintings – Picasso, Lautrec, Bonnard, Dufy, etc. His total outlay was £3,300; when realised the total was £44,320. This kind of thing reminds one again of Oscar Wilde's epigram in reply to the question 'What is a cynic?' 'A man who knows the price of everything and the value of nothing.'

I had developed a strong sense of national and civic pride over our Art Collections and Collectors, but I was frequently being provoked by the disdain which greeted my boasting. I expected to be encouraged to expand, but some of our English visitors – I mean the professionals – critics, scholars and officials – struck the 'high-hat' attitude and played us all down. This still continues. When we indulge in the laudable effort of telling our friends at 'headquarters', i.e. London, about Art in Scotland, we are listened to with a sweet courtesy which fails to conceal an inability to accept our claims. When they come to Scotland their surprise is mixed with incredulity. Among the young and upcoming historians, studying the 'old masters' the assumption is that since they are in the 'provinces' they are probably spurious. Here is an example of what I am trying to convey.

In one of Sir Osbert Sitwell's enchanting autobiographical volumes *Noble Essences* he tells the story of a Glasgow millionaire who was visited by Sickert. Professor John Wheatley, who is given as the authority for the story, was with him. They saw a portrait by Renoir, and to their amazement recognised the subject – a well-known London model. The picture therefore was a fake. Following a further inspection of the contents of the house, Sickert is alleged to have remarked to the host 'I really don't mind you hanging one of my paintings in your bathroom, but you might ensure that it is genuine.'

It is an amusing anecdote. It began to go the rounds, appearing in a magazine and some newspapers, never omitting that it was a Glasgow millionaire. I was often being asked 'Would it be Burrell or Gow or Cargill?' It was only then it dawned on me that some people were beginning to put two and two together, and also beginning to wonder if the Renoir 'dud' had passed through old Reid's hands. I thought I knew every Renoir and Sickert in Scottish collections, and my curiosity had become irresistible. I took the matter up with John Wheatley. In due course, after a couple of efforts, he replied saying that the story was perfectly true, but it did not happen in or near Glasgow. As a matter of fact he had never had the pleasure of a visit to Scotland. I turned, therefore, to Sir Osbert Sitwell. His reply, very gracious and courteous, was to the effect that I was over-stressing the amount of interest in the Sickert story. All collectors everywhere are making mistakes, together with the rest of humanity; in future editions of his book he would make it

'Glasgow or Birmingham or Sheffield', and in any event he was sure 'Glasgow can take it'. The last bit was particularly entertaining, for I had discovered that in the realm of public controversy the last people who 'can take it' were the Sitwells. Moreover, when I moved from private to a public appointment in the world of art, I found that 'Glasgow can take it' is expected to operate as a one-way traffic.

While Glasgow has benefited greatly from the big collectors it would be a serious omission if I failed to acknowledge how much the City owes to those who, as evidence of goodwill, have given or bequeathed one or two works. Often these have filled gaps, which for financial or other reasons might have continued to be passed over.

On the matter of acquisitions my interests were directed towards building up a strong representation of nineteenth and twentieth century French painting. This was the period I knew most about and none would deny that in the last hundred years the dominant school has been French. Although we might receive the news with what we imagined was a nonchalant air, we enjoyed the thrill of hearing our visitors from France say, 'No student of French Art can afford to miss seeing what is in the Glasgow Art Gallery'.

The occasional gift or purchase plays an important part in building up a comprehensive collection just as the elimination of errors strengthens and enhances the total effect. For example, among a number of excellent pictures given to the gallery by Sir John Richmond is a first-rate Vuillard – I always think the test of this kind of reporting is to measure it against what we might hear in other places. For instance, if a group of people anywhere happen to be discussing the work of any great artist and someone is moved to say 'Ah! Have you seen the one in Glasgow?' The Vuillard is that kind of picture.

Through the operation of the Hamilton Trust some notable additions have been made in recent years. But what chances the Trustees have missed! This Trust is entirely a law unto itself. The total amount of the original gift was considerable, and it had to be spent in buying oil paintings for the City's art collection. The Art Gallery Committee has the right to refuse or accept what is offered. I think I may hazard the claim that the Hamilton Trustees with whom I was always on the best of terms have no reason to regret any of the acquisitions which came through my recommendation. Some would,

I believe, be prepared to admit regret for not having taken my advice more often. That leads me to my own regrets.

On going round the gallery a few weeks ago and recalling with pleasure a number of works bought for a few hundred pounds and now valued at several thousands, I began to make a note of the missed opportunities. True, we had very little money. The annual grant for purchases when I arrived was a few hundred pounds per annum (that is what I was told but I found later (see page 208) that I had been misinformed). It was raised to £2,000 before I left. With the Hamilton Trust and other funds available Glasgow is not too badly off. In my view the city should keep out of the 'fantastic' art market. Filling gaps at high prices is an expensive way to make good the sins of omission perpetuated by those who had authority and power and did not use them. It is also good to remember that the sources of private benefaction have not dried up altogether.

If I had been more persistent, more courageous, more persuasive, Glasgow would have had many more fine paintings at the reasonable prices of the immediate post-war period. There is some consolation in the thought that every gallery in the country is in like situation. All of us 'missed the boat' with Picasso, Braque and many other great figures who have changed so profoundly the nature, purpose and conditions of pictorial art. In spite of that, and thanks in many instances to my friends, I am glad when anyone admires and praises the French section at Kelvingrove, to be able to reflect that something happened in my time.

This morning in Cristobal, the Caribbean side of the Panama Canal, I received the news of the death of George Primrose, chairman of the Hamilton Trust. In the course of a sympathetic and kindly obituary in the *Glasgow Herald*, of which he was Commercial Editor for twenty years, is the following:

'He had a family interest in the Hamilton Bequest, the accumulated funds of which are used to purchase works of art for Glasgow's art gallery. The trust was founded in 1927 with £60,000 contributed by his uncle and two aunts. As a trustee and chairman he was one of the discerning art lovers whose purchases, including many French Impressionists, are valued at more than £500,000. One Picasso Mr. Primrose insisted should be bought for £2,000 was rejected by the other trustees. It was recently valued at £60,000.'

I wonder where they got the £500,000 figure from. It would be very, very interesting to have this in some detail. How well do I remember George Primrose's valiant fight for the Picasso. Not one of his fellow trustees would listen to their chairman or to me.

It was in 1944 that Sir William and Lady Burrell intimated the gift of their entire Collection to the City of Glasgow. Not so long ago a leading article in a prominent Scottish newspaper was devoted to the Burrell Collection. It was headed 'Glasgow's Disgrace'.

10

The Burrell Collection

When Sir William Burrell decided to give Glasgow his great collection in the name of Lady Burrell and himself he sent for me. One December evening in 1943 he got me on the telephone. On his instructions I travelled, in great secrecy, to Hutton Castle at Chirnside, near Berwick-on-Tweed, without the foggiest idea of what it was all about. When he told me that Lady Burrell and he had finally determined to present the entire collection to the City of Glasgow plus the sum of £450,000 to provide a gallery for its display, I must have said something. Whatever it was is of no importance, for the one certain thing about the occasion is that I was too excited to be coherent.

On getting back to Glasgow I immediately made contact with Bailie Burnett, the Convener of the Art Gallery Committee, and, together, we passed on the information to Lord Provost James Welsh. Small wonder I still feel a thrill whenever at any time, anywhere in the world, I hear the Burrell Collection mentioned. I like to remember that this wonderful gift should have come in my time as Director. For, whatever you may have heard to the contrary, that is how the good news was brought from the Borders.

The subsequent history of discussions regarding conditions and the selection of a permanent site will come later. Meanwhile, and principally because it has never been done, I want to go a little further back in my recollections of the man behind one of the most remarkable collections of art to be found in this country. It is also well to remember that it was assembled by one man in the course of a long, busy and interesting life. To remind us of the range, here is a summary of the categories. The numbers in brackets represent the total in each category.

ANCIENT AND ORIENTAL ART

1. Ancient Civilisations:
   Mesopotamian   (80)
   Egyptian   (293)
   Graeco-Etruscan   (197)
   Roman   (82)

2. Far East:
   Chinese Pottery & Porcelain   (1397)
   Chinese Bronzes   (172)
   Chinese Jades   (139)
   Japanese Woodcuts   (30)

3. Near East:
   Persian Pottery & Metalwork   (232)
   Carpets & Rugs   (122)
   Coptic Textiles   (18)
   Ismik Pottery   (39)

EUROPEAN ART

1. Textiles:
   Continental Tapestries   (176)
   English Tapestries   (21)
   Continental Needlework   (30)
   English Needlework   (220)
   Samplers   (25)
   Lace   (120)
   Curtains   (51)

2. Metalwork:
   Bronze & brass wares   (217)
   Bronze statuary   (20)
   Candelabra   (8)
   Arms & armour   (130)
   Limoges enamels & copper-gilt   (37)
   Silver   (292)
   Gold   (15)
   Knives & forks   (265)
   Iron & steel   (61)
   Pewter   (43)

3. Glass:
    Stained glass   (585)
    European table glass   (74)
    English table glass   (426)

4. Woodwork:
    Wood carvings   (240)
    Furniture   (510)
    Panelling, Screens, Ceiling, etc.   (11)
    Doors   (41)
    Clocks   (7)
    Treen   (14)

5. Stone & Ivory:
    Stone Sculpture   (79)
    Alabasters   (47)
    Ivory & bone carvings   (29)
    Lintels/fireplaces   (17)
    Architectural   (22)

6. Pottery:
    Continental   (51)
    English & porcelain   (452)

7. Pictures:
    Oils, watercolours, pastels etc.   (659)
    Etchings/engravings   (37)

8. Other Art Objects: (97)

Grand Total: 7,930 items.

By the time I had my first meeting with Sir William, in 1929, he had already become a legend among collectors of works of art. His home was no longer in Glasgow, but he still had a house in Great Western Terrace (a 'Greek' Thomson structure) in which the panelled hall and staircase were designed by Sir Robert Lorimer. For a long time it functioned more as a store for furniture and became rather derelict. The Corporation bought it as a temporary measure to relieve storage problems which have now been solved in other directions.

If business did not detain him overnight in the city, Sir William generally caught the four o'clock train for Berwick-on-Tweed. A further nine miles took him to his home in Hutton Castle, beautifully situated near the River Tweed.

Sometimes between lunch and train time, he would call in at Reid's Gallery in West George Street. As the firm was then in the process of centralising its activities in London, there was seldom anything important enough to capture his interest. But he would always look at anything by Joseph Crawhall, one of the members of The Glasgow School. (There are no less than 132 Crawhalls in the Burrell Collection.)

On a visit to Reid's, a month after I had joined the firm, Sir William put me through my paces in what must have been the forerunner of BBC quiz programmes. He also gave me some illuminating views on art and art dealing and, finally, after some bargaining, bought a Crawhall drawing. Throughout the afternoon I glowed with satisfaction – my first contact with the Burrell Collection. Two hours later I got a telegram from Edinburgh cancelling the purchase of the Crawhall – he had plenty of them – and ending with 'good wishes'.

Every time he came into the Gallery I tried to hold him for as long as possible in the hope that some thing or some observation would give rise to a reminiscent mood. It is well known that he was among the first to appreciate nineteenth century French art, but he always gave credit to Alexander Reid for introducing him to the finest examples.

It could hardly be expected that two strong characters like Reid and Burrell were always in agreement with each other. On certain members of the Glasgow School and the French Impressionists they would share enthusiasm, but I feel certain that with the nineteenth century Dutch also favoured by Sir William, the arguments would be fierce and recurrent.

In recalling these early days, Sir William never forgot the great supper-party given by Reid when he moved to new premises in St Vincent Street. All the leading members of the Glasgow School were there – Guthrie, Lavery, Hornel, Walton, Henry, Stevenson, Kennedy, etc. 'I was the only non-artist invited. It was a very, very merry evening.'

When I appeared on the scene Sir William had become less interested in painting and, although he made some important additions later, I think he regarded the picture side of his collection as more or less complete – his one and only Cézanne was one of the few exceptions. This painting, 'View of Medan' or 'House of Zola', is mentioned in Gauguin's journal in an amusing anecdote, repeated by John Rewald in his biography of Cézanne. The painting had once belonged to Gauguin, and much later was acquired in New York by myself on behalf of Reid & Lefevre in exchange for a painting by Toulouse-Lautrec 'L'Accroche-cœur'. I hoped it would find a home in the National Gallery, but they were not then interested enough. Burrell got it for £3,800.

Everybody knows that there is a public interest in money values: what did it cost? how much is it worth today? This kind of enquiry is not necessarily a wicked approach to Art appreciation. The most recent example is the discovery, last year, that the Raphael portrait of Pope Julius XVIII is the original and might *now* be worth millions ('£5 million would not be regarded as an impossible price').

While on the subject of the Burrell Collection and prices, there is an urge to intrude a general comment. We know that an aesthetic doctrine can be a good servant but a bad master. We also know that private and public patrons may not always buy a thing of beauty if they are more concerned with historical documents. We can never be wholly objective or impartial. Such an approach is the peculiar privilege of the auctioneer who has become increasingly important. His records are sometimes the most reliable when one is assembling a long pedigree.

If Sir William Burrell had been less of a hunter after bargains, had been more aware of what was happening to art and artists, had been occasionally more courageous, or less prejudiced, the painting section of his fabulous collection would have been even more notable than it is in French painting – think of the times he was living in. I have to tell you what he paid for them to stress the point. For instance, 'The Empress Eugénie on the beach, Trouville' by Boudin, bought in 1923 for £250; Portrait of Duranty by Degas, also bought in 1923 for £1,900; 'The Rehearsal' by Degas (this was ac-quired in competition with Felton Bequest of Melbourne, Australia) bought in 1926 for £6,500; 'Jockeys in the Rain' by Degas, bought in 1937 for £3,885. (This came from the Gow Collection.) I think Sir William Burrell had missed getting it earlier. He once said to me 'It's no use being an "also ran" in the Art Race. You have to be first.'; 'Self Portrait' by Rembrandt, bought in 1948 for £12,500; and Portrait by Franz Hals bought in 1946 for £14,500. The Rembrandt and the Hals were late purchases. £14,500 seems to have been the highest price he paid for any item.

There was nothing casual or haphazard in Sir William's collecting. It is certain that he had a policy in building and expanding – here and there filling some obvious gaps in sections that he thought were weak, but always appearing to be pleased if his attention was drawn to some item which might be an appropriate acquisition.

Until advancing years made it impossible for him to visit Paris and London, Sir William was a regular visitor to important exhibitions organised by the leading art dealers and to the pre-views of auction sales. Catalogues were scrutinised with care, and his amazing memory made it easy for him to identify works which might have eluded him on an earlier occasion. I do not recall a single case where his name is associated with a startling purchase at an extravagant price, but I remember several instances where his wide and exact knowledge led to the purchase of an important item at a bargain price. There is an example of this. Some years ago there was acquired from the Randolph Hearst collection a restored Romanesque (XII century) portal $15\frac{1}{2}$ feet in height. It cost Hearst about £5,000 and was sent to America. It re-crossed the Atlantic to St Donat's Castle in Wales and, when the Hearst Collection was dispersed, Sir William got it for £550.

This policy of 'building a collection' is of special significance at the present time when, with the advent of new collectors with, apparently, inexhaustible resources, fantastic and unrealistic prices are being paid for names rather than for masterpieces. As a well-known Paris auctioneer recently indicated, the time will come soon when it will be wise to get out of the 'blue chips'.

Before Sir William and Lady Burrell made their munificent gift to Glasgow, many of the treasures of the collection were on loan to various cities throughout the country; some of the tapestries were shown in a number of cathedrals. For reasons of safety and preservation, limitations had to be put on the innumerable requests for special exhibitions, but there never was any doubt that the owners derived much pleasure in the enjoyment others experienced, even for a short time.

To hear Sir William's account of the history of a particular picture, tapestry, sculpture or art object was an education. But alas! not nearly enough is, as yet, on record. And it is a matter of regret that he resisted all suggestions to have prepared a factual record of his unequalled experiences as a connoisseur. Moreover, every attempt to get him to sit for a portrait by painter or sculptor met with an emphatic refusal. I had in mind a fitting place in the gallery which, one day, would be built, but the idea was repugnant to him. 'The collection,' he would say, 'not the collector, is the important thing.' The only photograph – apart from very early studio portraits – is that taken with Lady Burrell when Sir William received the Freedom of the City. He was tall, slender in build, distinguished looking, with a long narrow face, white hair and short moustache. He spoke with a pronounced burr and a nasal twang.

Many business associates have told me that in his active life in Glasgow shipping circles Sir William's foresight and enterprise belong to the realm of romance. Remember, too, that he was for seven years a City Councillor, Consul for Austria and Hungary before World War I, a Trustee of the Tate Gallery in London and of the National Galleries of Scotland. Provand's Lordship, the period museum in Glasgow's oldest house, opposite the cathedral, is also greatly indebted for timely assistance at a critical point in its history. It so happens that I am the Honorary President of the Provand's Lordship Society. Professor J. D. Mackie, Historiographer Royal, is the President. It is not run by the City but by a society of private individuals who saved it from demolition at the beginning of the century. The bulk of its interesting period furniture contents has been acquired through a 'Burrell Fund'.

I doubt if anyone outside his home and family ever influenced Sir William Burrell. From time to time and in special circumstances he would seek advice, but confirmation rather than opposition to his own views was the operating factor. More than once I fell from favour and found it difficult, not to say impossible, to convince him that as a servant of the Corporation there were occasions when I was bound to defend a course of action contrary to his instructions. Sometimes one opened a letter with an anxious 'What now?' to find that differences had been forgotten and we were launched on a new adventure. Often have I wished that more frequent meetings rather than correspondence had been our method of communication. One learned so much from him.

He resisted all approaches by the press to get a 'story' on his experiences as a collector; but the occasional reminiscence with which he illuminated conversation was often delightfully amusing and always historically important. I know too, that Sir William could turn the story against himself. One day when we were walking round the gallery at Kelvingrove he recalled his earlier gift of pictures (in 1923). He had stipulated that they were all to be hung together and, as can be seen from the 1935 catalogue, the then 'Burrell Collection' (an interesting but not very important group of French paintings) was housed in Gallery IV. He told me that some time previously he had been in the building. No one had recognised him, and in the Burrell room he asked a uniformed attendant to tell him about the collection. In the course of his observations the man is reported to have said, 'Ach! I don't know much about them. We've got to keep them together, that's the condition: but we'll likely scatter them when the old buffer dies.'

It was this gallery I had decided must be reserved for 'The Glasgow School'. Surely, I thought, it had to be one of our duties to create a 'library' of works by this School of Painters so closely associated in name and residence with the City. Owing to the perpetual problem of space the proposition has not been sustained in recent years.

Among my happiest memories of Sir William are those related to his visits to the Lefevre Gallery in London. For some years Lady Burrell and he enjoyed cruising in the West Indies, and on the way out or back spent a few days in town. We were just along the street from Christie's, and I was frequently taken there, and to Sotheby's, to inspect and discuss some of the lots coming up for sale. There were other things to attend to, and it was his custom to list them on odd sheets of paper. One day he asked me to decipher a line of writing which had defeated him. It was in the middle of important memoranda which looked to me like stock market prices. All I could make out was 'Get your hair cut'. He confirmed this with a chuckle and advised me never to let domestic instructions get tied up with affairs of business.

On the way home one summer he came in to tell me that a friend of mine had been on the same ship. 'He must be very well off,' said Sir William. 'He had a suite de-luxe – I can't afford that, but I have always got to have a separate cabin on a ship or a room in a hotel because, you see, I snore! Wherever I go I have to face up to the extra expense of a room to myself. Let me tell you, Honeyman, that snore has cost me thousands of pounds.' I discovered later that the friend was W. G. Riddell (see page 67), by no means as well off as Sir William. W.G. had no great regard for his fellow-passenger (business-wise) but he knew a lot about the art collection and wondered what would happen to it.

One fine day, when the complete Burrell Collection, in its permanent home, will be on view, all that has been said and written about the munificence of this great gift to Glasgow will be regarded as under-statements. Of that I am sure. And bear in mind the good fortune that has come my way in having seen many famous collections. I find it easy to confirm what the late Lewis Clapperton – a Glasgow business man who collected pewter, and who had known Sir William Burrell over a great stretch of years – wrote me on 25th January 1944: 'This will put Glasgow on a level with any non-capital city in the world, except perhaps New York.'

The more I think of it the more amazing becomes the fact that so many works of art have been studied, appreciated and acquired by one man – and that at the end of it all he does not squander his accumulated treasures. In partnership with Lady Burrell, he gave it away. It now belongs to Glasgow.

We know that the Corporation has been very severely criticised – and most of the criticism is ill-informed – for mishandling the business of the Burrell Collection.

'It is really a scandal that so long after the original bequest Glasgow should not have made a home for the Burrell Collection according to the wishes of the donors.'

Thus the opening sentence of the indictment in the article already mentioned. It went on:

'Is a collection worth £10 or £12 million not worth the extra million for a gallery? Would any city outside the benighted philistine British Isles allow such a treasure to be buried, because the local council feared the ratepayers might not think their money well spent on a gallery beyond the city limits?'

Better to get the facts right. On two counts this article in a prominent newspaper is misleading.

In a letter dated 20th January 1944, when very necessary discussions regarding some of the conditions were taking place, Sir William wrote:

'I find I omitted to mention to you that a collection worth today £1,000,000 (and mine is worth considerably more) will at a rate of an average of $2\frac{1}{2}\%$ per annum, be worth 2 millions in 40 years – 3 millions in 80 years.'

Even Sir William was well out. In the world of Art there is

nothing certain in the ups and downs of market assessments. How conservative he was in the face of so much nonsense when we keep on confusing values with prices. It is often forgotten that in addition to the collection the donors gave a sum of £450,000 which, plus accumulated interest, was to be used for building the new gallery. The Corporation was to acquire the site and that site had to be in the Killearn area not less than sixteen miles from the Glasgow Royal Exchange. All the subsequent difficulties, differences of opinion, and delays stem from Sir William's emphatic condition: maybe not all.

Throughout January 1944 there were many exchanges of letters and telephone calls. Sir William had put me under obligation to see to it that there should be no fuss or publicity. I had to point out that the Corporation must follow certain procedures which he, as a past town councillor, would appreciate. For example, the Town Clerk had made it clear that the terms of the gift place the City under certain commitments, and these must be approved and minuted. A telegram asked me to arrange a meeting between his solicitor, Mr Logan, and the Town Clerk, Mr Kerr, without delay so that the matter should be 'off or on' with Glasgow before the end of the month.

I was present at the meeting and was very pleased to hear Mr Logan say that Sir William's decision to give the collection to Glasgow had in part been reached because of the successful work I had been doing at the Art Gallery. From time to time I was to hear a number of claims on the subject of who or what influenced Sir William to choose Glasgow.

On the way to Mr Logan's office the Town Clerk asked me 'Why did Sir William send for you?' The obvious retort was, 'Why ask me?' but it seemed more polite to say I had known him for several years, and well enough to ask him to allow me to use his name as a reference when I had applied for my present post as Director. Further explanations were not sought at the time, but two years later Mr Logan's observation was confirmed in a letter Sir William wrote (May 12th 1944) to my Convener (on the occasion of my resignation for reasons not germane to the present issue):

'I read with the greatest regret that Dr Honeyman may cease to be Director of the Glasgow Art Galleries.

I have known him for many years and his great knowledge of art was one of the principal factors which decided my wife and myself to offer our collection to Glasgow. I have always looked forward to his putting the collection in order. He has already done so to a considerable extent, but a great deal has still to be done and I feel that if he leaves the service of the Corporation it will be nothing short of a misfortune. I sincerely hope that any difficulties will be overcome and that we shall have the benefit of his knowledge and advice for years to come. –

Yours etc. William Burrell'

This is the kind of thing which should be left to someone other than myself to make public. But no one has, nor will – and it is part of my story.

After Convener Alex Burnett and myself had our interview with the Lord Provost and the Town Clerk, we were both made aware of a 'high up' decision on the Town Clerk's advice, that the Art Galleries Committee could not handle such an outstanding gift. It was being made to the City and, with the addition of the important money aspect, it became essentially the concern of the Finance Committee. At the time I did not care very much how the Corporation dealt with the matter. As a piece of hindsight I now think a very serious mistake in procedure was made. Is it not now obvious that the officials responsible for advising the city to complete the terms of the gift are the Town Clerk and City Chamberlain? It may not be their function to determine policies but it is their duty – not that of the Museum Committee, as now named – to point out to someone, 'There is still some unfinished business on the agenda.'

There were then a number of legal points to be considered. The Town Clerk, very properly, had to advise caution on the site condition. For example it might not be possible to provide a site within the narrow limits of the specified area, especially in view of the uncertainties of post-war planning and regional development. It could however be agreed that the Corporation would undertake to acquire a site in such a position to ensure amenities and atmospheric conditions to the complete satisfaction of the Trustees appointed by Sir William. Discussions went on for some time with Sir William alternating between annoyance and exasperation.

In answer to direct questioning from my convener and later the Lord Provost I expressed several doubts about the conditions, but I recommended very firmly the acceptance of the gift on the terms indicated, for two reasons:

    (a) The importance of the Collection, and

(b) The conditions reference site might turn out to be, taking a long view, a very wise precaution.

It all depended on the extent the Corporation would be prepared to go in developing an estate in the country with the Collection as the chief, but not necessarily the only feature. Nevertheless, in the light of my own experience (at home and abroad) I thought it might be worth while to put before Sir William some considered views on the subject, not so much with the intention of asking him to change the conditions, but rather with the idea of persuading him to leave more power to his trustees to alter or modify them as might be seemly and sound in the face of unforeseen circumstances. I was instructed to prepare a memorandum, the terms of which were approved by the Town Clerk and Mr Logan. The latter, however, made it clear that in his view Sir William, having given all aspects long and serious consideration, was unlikely to make any changes. How right he was. It was a lovely memorandum, but when it reached Hutton Castle it almost set the place on fire. The telephone buzzed for days.

At this time I did not know of earlier proposals which Sir William had discussed with government representatives on what was to happen to the Collection. During the thirties, when I lived in London, I had heard various speculations and forecasts; but it was not until 1946, when he came to Glasgow to visit the Burrell Collection Exhibition arranged in the McLellan Galleries, that Sir Eric Maclagan (Victoria & Albert Museum) passed on some interesting information. Sir Kenneth Clark also took part in conferences but it was not possible to reach a satisfactory agreement. Sir William often consulted Sir Kenneth Clark, who more than once suggested that his native city might be the appropriate place. The London County Council also made proposals, including a site on the South Bank of the Thames near Waterloo Bridge. None of the suggestions appealed to Sir William and Glasgow became the fortunate recipient, plus the large sum of money. There is no doubt that uppermost in Sir William's mind were the tapestries and the menace of fog and perhaps other atmospheric impurities.

I had spread myself on 'air conditioning' and modern museum methods. The late Sir James French of the well-known Glasgow firm, Barr & Stroud, prepared an elaborate scheme covering every contingency for a safe gallery in the City, and Sir William wouldn't even glance at it. So, when one reads that, in 1960 -- sixteen years having passed – the Corporation decided to ask the Ministry of Works for a report on air conditioning in public buildings in order to enlighten the Burrell Trustees, it was difficult to suppress a growing alarm over the increasing evidence of civic ineptitude.

All these things had been considered. All of them were worth examining. It was Sir William's conclusions which, in my opinion and that of many others, were completely unrelated to evidence or to museum experience. Not only that, both before and after the offer to Glasgow, Sir William and the Trustees have departed from the rigid conditions which were laid down and accepted. Looking back now on the exchange of letters ('voluminous correspondence' would be an inadequate description) and the telephone calls early and late, I wonder what all the fuss was about. My position could be summed up in this passage of a letter to Hutton Castle:

'25th January 1944. (I should have been quoting Burns)

I would be failing in my duty if I did not express the opinion, based on a considerable experience, that conditions which are as the laws of the Medes and Persians should not ignore the fact that unforeseen circumstances are liable in the end to make things go contrary to the original wishes of those interested.'

Sir William naturally had the last word.

'I have today (4th February) received a letter from the Town Clerk informing me that the Corporation have accepted the collection on the conditions stipulated by me.

I am sorry you should think I was a little unfair to you. Nothing was further from my intentions, my only desire being to state the position clearly so that there should be no misunderstanding later on.'

(The last paragraph is a reply to a 'dressing down' which I could not take 'lying down').

When everything was happily concluded the Corporation delegated the affairs of the Burrell Collection to a special committee. The Art Gallery and Museums Committee would handle the gathering in of the various items, scattered among different galleries, museums and cathedrals. The administration of funds and decisions thereanent were Finance Committee business with the City Treasurer in command. It seemed all right at first but it did not work well. It added to the difficulties in reaching amicable decisions on a number of matters regarding new purchases (all made exclusively by Sir William) and plans for conveying, storing and insuring the collection. Even more significant was the factor which eventually led to the severe criticism of the Corporation over the delay in implementing its side of the bargain. The City Treasurer, who holds office for a three year term, is responsible for taking the necessary action. He is probably the busiest man in the whole structure of civic administration. Art and the Burrell Collection have to be regarded as minor matters. Indeed some time ago I was amazed to hear a past holder of the office, when subjected to queries like, 'When is the Corporation going to get a move on?', say 'Damn the Burrell Collection! I wish we had never seen it.'

With the passage of time, the work of registering, photographing, cataloguing, collecting, exhibiting and storing became far too heavy and exacting to continue under the immediate control of the Director. Sir William's interest never slackened. This is reflected in the correspondence and instructions on a great number of minor and major matters. Eventually the Corporation agreed to the creation of a new post – Keeper of the Burrell Collection. Mr Andrew Hannah was appointed, with Sir William's emphatic approval, and was eminently successful in winning and retaining his complete confidence. Mr Hannah did a fine job of work especially in organising the first large scale exhibition of the collection which was held in the McLellan Galleries in the summer of 1949. As well as supervising the great amount of checking, listing and other innumerable details the Keeper acted as a very valuable liaison officer when the Director (myself) had to take a stand as a Corporation official.

When the exhibition was first suggested – and the main purpose was to give the citizens of Glasgow the chance to see a part of the art treasures which were now their property – Sir William was doubtful. The Tapestries! I suggested leaving them out. But no! They are the chief attraction. He was willing to have an exhibition at the Fair holidays – for ten days. Then, because industry was at a standstill, Glasgow would be free of smoke. I had to explain the great amount of work entailed in planning, publishing and generally organising the large exhibition we had in mind. The expense involved could only be justified by a summer show of three months and that I could not seek the Committee's approval for less. He consented to a month. I tried the suggestion of limiting the show of tapestries to a month and replacing those on view with a fresh series. Sir William was not impressed. He saw, rightly, the dilemma in cataloguing and the disappointment likely to any specialists who might visit the exhibition in the later stages. Andrew Hannah and I both wanted to have this exhibition, and we were certain Sir William was just as keen on it. We stuck to the three months and, in the course of a very pleasant and amiable after-dinner chat, he agreed.

The exhibition was anything but a simple affair. By far the heaviest burden fell on the Keeper of the Burrell Collection but Sir William was most helpful in selecting and arranging, and even from the remoteness of Hutton Castle maintained close contact throughout the weeks of preparation. But note! *At one time he had insisted that at no time were the tapestries to be shown in Glasgow.*

The McLellan Gallery exhibition created a widespread interest more particularly, let it be said, among visitors to the city. Philip James, then head of the Art Department of the Arts Council, wanted to know if it was possible to have an even greater selection in London at Burlington House. The series of exhibitions held there were international events. With an eye, I suppose, on the publicity value, and with the chance of having the views of scholars and experts I approached Sir William. At first he seemed favourable. Then he made so many impossible conditions, e.g. the Royal Academy should abandon or postpone its Annual Summer Exhibition (the tapestries could only be exhibited in the summer. The risk of fog in the winter was too great, etc.). It was off.

In 1950 when I was in London to see the French Landscape Exhibition, Philip James raised the matter afresh; and without much hope I undertook to try again. In a longish, persuasive (as I thought) letter, I wrote this:

'. . . I had another look at Burlington House and it has made me more than ever keen for a great feature show of the Burrell Collection. In the French exhibition there are fourteen tapestries which are very well hung. I was in Birmingham, too, and saw some tapestries on the wall of the Gallery in the city centre. It is true that the climatic conditions this year have been exceptionally fine, but in this country we cannot be certain of anything. I am assured that the risk of atmospheric damage to the fine Burrell Tapestries is so negligible that no Continental or British Curator would have any worries on that score. The only qualification I heard referred to the question of fragility. In other words, the handling gave more concern than the exhibition.'

(Philip James gave every assurance even to the length of arranging
to put the Tapestries behind glass in hermetically sealed cases – or
have a show without them.) I concluded,

> 'Having kept my promise to approach you I await your views.
> Mine, for what they may be worth, are that the benefit would
> greatly outweigh the risks.'

In the course of his reply (dated 19th January 1950) Sir William
said,

> 'As you very rightly point out the climatic conditions have been
> exceptionally fine. In a normal year the damage would be
> incalculable. . . . People who talk glibly about the risk being
> negligible have no experience of Gothic Tapestries, and no idea
> of what permanent injury even two or three days fog can do.'

No further action could be taken. The refusal, I was subsequently
led to believe, was partly due to an anti-London attitude. Comparable to an anti-Edinburgh attitude, which persisted throughout my
term of office. Under no circumstances were we to lend any item
from the Burrell Collection to be shown in Edinburgh. (The reason
for this had something to do with the treatment Sir William received
from Government Authorities, with headquarters in Edinburgh, in
connection with the confiscation of the beautiful iron railings round
Hutton Castle.)

I know I lay myself open to the charge of daring to presume that
in the rigid conditions imposed – exclusively because of the
importance of the tapestries – Sir William had made himself captive
to an obsession. Such was and still is my considered opinion. But
obsessions never remain static, they can grow or diminish. They can
be affected by circumstance. Very rarely they can be explained away
without, however, any guarantee against their return. So much
depends on who does the explaining away.

In the early spring of 1950 I was in the USA and Canada. Over a
period of two months I visited a great number of Art Galleries and
Museums – a most valuable experience. With the future of the
Burrell Collection often in mind I collected what I thought might be
useful comparable information. Shortly after my return the Burrell–
Honeyman correspondence was resumed.

I do not propose to reproduce it. Much of it was concerned with
Sir William's reconsideration of the site conditions. He looked at
Mugdock Castle, in Milngavie. He turned it down and kept referring
back to the original agreement 'which must be rigidly adhered to'.

The full history will be in the Corporation archives. The Archivist, Mr Richard Dell, is a most helpful and well qualified official as is Mr William Wells, the present Keeper of the Burrell Collection. Between them they can supply the official memoranda and correspondence. I have kept some notes relating to telephone talks, usually conducted at a very early morning hour, and some private letters at a time when the 'official mind' had proved too much for me. Here are two extracts, in order to demonstrate that in spite of many differences I held the confidence of Sir William throughout the discussions.

'24th April 1946.

I am exceedingly sorry you are leaving the Gallery. You have put life into it and enthused the public as never before. I have had a severe blow.'

'26th April 1946.

I had looked forward to you settling on the style of building. . . . I know that your guiding hand will be badly missed and I shall not be here to help. It is a thousand pities.'

Something began to happen in another direction. Eventually it ended up in what appeared to be an eminently satisfactory conclusion. It can be summarised through an extract from the Press release which I was authorised to send out.

GIFT OF DOUGALSTON ESTATE TO THE CORPORATION OF GLASGOW

At a meeting of the Special Committee on the Burrell Collection, it was intimated that Mrs Therese Connell was prepared to offer the Estate of Dougalston, Milngavie, as a gift to the City of Glasgow, subject to her retaining a liferent interest in it. The offer follows on conversations between Sir William Burrell and Mrs Connell, and it is a condition of the gift that a site on the Estate will be used for the gallery to accommodate the Burrell Collection. *Sir William had expressed his delight at the gift and his complete agreement to the use of the Estate for the purposes of the Burrell Collection. The Agreement between Sir William and the Corporation will be modified accordingly.*

(The italics are mine, as is also the reminder that Dougalston is even nearer to Glasgow than Mugdock Castle.)

When we had first asked Sir William to inspect Dougalston, which everybody thought might be an admirable conclusion (my own reservations were related to the hope that the Corporation would develop the 360 acres into a larger scheme of a 'cultural centre' linked to Further Education with the Burrell Collection as the main feature), we expected a refusal. The Art Galleries Committee and Sir William met at Dougalston, inspected the estate and went on to the City Chambers to discuss the matter and await Sir William's decision. Jack Kelly, who was Art Gallery Convener as well as City Treasurer had prepared a persuasive and convincing speech in order to overcome the resistance. To his surprise and delight the speech was unnecessary and remained undelivered. Sir William concluded the proceedings almost before they had started by saying, 'All right! I approve. And I'm very hungry. When do we have lunch?' This entertaining anti-climax puzzled many members of the Committee who did not know that their distinguished guest and public bene-factor was a master in quick change-over from irresistible obstruction to benevolent co-operation.

Everything in the garden was lovely. The Parks Department took in hand to begin, then and there, to supervise the care and maintenance of the grounds. The Keeper of the Burrell Collection prospected the garage premises for temporary storage. On several visits the amateurs and professionals among us thought we knew the best situation for the gallery and the best uses for the mansion house and policies. Then the blow fell.

It was announced that the government had plans to establish a new coal mine in or near the Dougalston Estate. This was too much for Sir William. The whole project was abandoned and Mrs Connell's gift to the City was returned. By this time I was a back number, so it is without inside knowledge I express the view and ask the question 'Why all the rush?' The Corporation had spent £36,000 on the Estate. Mrs Connell's trustees might have been willing to allow the City to retain Dougalston – great are the needs of large cities to have places for recreation and relaxation. If this could not be considered, why the secrecy? The coal mine plan is still in suspension and may never materialise.

In earlier exchanges with Sir William, when I tried, without success, to persuade him to leave greater freedom of action to his Trustees, he appeared to find it difficult to understand what I meant by 'unforeseen circumstances'. The Dougalston Estate episode was a striking example. Sir William and Lady Burrell have gone and the City was back to where it was, still under certain specific obligations.

VE Day Celebrations by L. S. Lowry
Oil on canvas 31″× 40″
Purchased in 1946 for £136. Another Lowry *River Scene* was acquired for the collection for
the sum of £42 in 1943. A. J. McNeill Reid was the first to apprehend the genius of Lowry,
leading up to the first one man show at the Lefevre Gallery in 1939

Authors in Session by Stanley Cursiter, CBE, RSA, LLD
Oil on Canvas 38″ × 47½″
In this 'Conversation Piece' there are four distinguished Scots writers, from left to right
Edwin Muir, James Bridie, Neil Gunn and Eric Linklater. The artist, now retired to his
native Orkney, is H. M. Painter and Limner for Scotland and was formerly Director of the
National Gallery in Edinburgh

TOP LEFT. A. J. McNeill Reid and the author at an auction sale of paintings in Glasgow

OPPOSITE. Invitation to an Exhibition (1936) by Dali
A pictorial suggestion that the mind is a compartment of the brain. Therefore, keep an open mind in viewing the exhibition

ABOVE. *James VI* (of Scotland – 'Jamie the Sixth') – James I of Great Britain by Van Somern 45″× 34″
The Monarch who gave the Royal Charter to the Glasgow Faculty of Physicians and Surgeons in 1599

The Pool of London by Andre Derain
Oil on canvas 26″ × 40″ The Tate Gallery, London
This is one of a series of London scenes commissioned by Vollard in 1906. Most of the
Art Galleries in Britain missed the chance to acquire one of them. Leeds and Glasgow were
two exceptions – at £150. This one was for a time in the author's collection. In October
1970 one was sold in a London auction for £80,000

The Marne at Chennevieres by Camille Pissarro
Oil on canvas 37½″ × 56¾″ The National Gallery of Scotland
Acquired from Vollard and exhibited in several exhibitions in Britain and America.
For several years in the author's collection

It was also, more or less, constantly under fire for not facing up to them.

It is not true to say that the Corporation has done nothing. Let's summarise: (a) The gift was made in 1943; (b) For many years nothing could be done. Post-war reconstruction priorities found art galleries well down the list; (c) Items from the Collection have constantly been on view throughout the years; (d) Sir William in his lifetime agreed to depart from his original condition, thus justifying the Corporation's hopes that these might still be subject to amendments; (e) The Trustees have already agreed on two occasions to a departure from Sir William's instructions – Edinburgh Exhibition and Tapestries shown in London in winter months, not to mention the great display (1969) in Glasgow.

The Trustees are bound to hold the Corporation to the terms of the Agreement. In the light of Sir William's own adjustments on the original conditions I hope by the time this appears in print something positive will have emerged.

Some time ago I was challenged by a City Councillor to give an opinion on the line the Corporation should follow. I replied to the effect, 'This is no longer any affair of mine', to be told I was cowardly, irresponsible and not sufficiently concerned with civic welfare and reputation. I could not let it pass even though it was said with a friendly grin. And it is one reason for inflicting this account of one of the highlights of my fifteen years at Kelvingrove. This was my reply. It can have no bearing on what will be done, but perhaps some of it may assume the nature of a prophecy made before fresh events supplied the necessary amendments.

If Glasgow takes the view that its obligation is two-fold – one to the donors and one to the citizens – they could prove that Sir William's conditions were sound, wise and farsighted. He could have been right, even if he was right for the wrong reasons. The Corporation must begin to think big about the Arts generally. For example what provisions does it propose to make in re-planning the city for all the Fine Arts, Painting, Sculpture, Music and Drama? The Burrell Collection is only a part – a great part – of our inheritance from public-spirited citizens and from the foresight of some of our forebears. If, for instance, the city could show, on paper if you like, a scheme to include a new art gallery (already decided in principle around 1935), a shipbuilding and engineering museum (see chapter 'Memoranda Galore'), a new concert hall or opera house, a civic theatre and all the rest of fringe activities, all this would supply a convincing illustration of how to combine art and industry without compromise. Then we could say 'We need the Burrell Collection as part of it.' Future planning of large cities is an immediate and an acute problem. It has given rise to a fashionable and ill-sounding word 'overspill'. University expansion is part of the problem.

If the city – thinking small – acquired a site which will accommodate only the Burrell Collection and nothing else it may make a very serious mistake. Practical considerations suggest that it would only function in the summer months. But as part of a centre of a large educational and recreational scheme in the country – it could become the jewel in a crown of a unique cultural enterprise. What a wonderful thing it would be for Glasgow, to become distinguished in combining the aesthetic with the practical. As a business asset, what an advertisement! Instead of enquiring about what other cities do, for a change we might show them what they could do.

Glasgow could and should start now. It has government authority and rating power. Under expert guidance – and we certainly need it – it is conceivable that a joint step might be to erect the first of a series of 'pavilions' for the tapestries, and then gradually add other pavilions which finally would take on the character of a complete unity. It may not be a very bright suggestion, nor very original, although conforming to a contemporary tendency. The finest buildings in the world are not large. What then is the present situation? Following the great generosity of Mrs Maxwell Macdonald and family the site of the Burrell Collection has been finally settled. It will be in Pollok Park. I remember several visits there when Sir John Stirling Maxwell was alive. I think it probable that the last photograph of Sir John, before the infirmity of partial paralysis confined him to a wheel chair, was taken by myself. My wife and I were visiting to see the marvellous display of azaleas and rhododendrons.

In addition to the grounds Glasgow has acquired Pollok House with the contents. (I think especially of the El Greco and the Blake drawings.) With an eager and capable Director of Parks to develop the amenities of the estate and the chance of making Pollok House (an Adam building) a show-piece, this wonderful gift will make Glasgow more than ever notable for its public parks and Art possessions. Did you know we are the best equipped city in the Commonwealth in the matter of public parks and open spaces? I know, nobody told you!

The Corporation have decided to hold an Architectural competition for the Burrell Gallery. It is being sponsored by the RIBA. In addition to the Architect Assessors there are the Earl of Crawford and Sir Charles Wilson, Principal of Glasgow University. There have been a number of secret palavers to settle the extent of the necessary wall space and the overall area and to prepare a brief for the competitors.

When we are told (by the Town Clerk – as quoted in *The Times*) that Sir William wished the Gallery to look like a house rather than a Museum, and when Lord Muirshiel, one of the Burrell Trustees, said 'there was a clear intent in the deed of gift about the character of the Gallery and Sir William's wishes must be respected up to the hilt', the poor competitors are going to feel somewhat circumscribed. And all this is calculated to lead to a £4,000,000 Art Gallery.

In my view the Corporation have made a mess of the whole business. They have turned a generous gift into a burden and they are just floundering along. How I wish some city councillor, of any party, would have the courage to stand up in the council and ask 'What is this city spending on "expert" advice which it does not in the long run accept, on fees and expenses of specialists and how does it arrive at £4,000,000 for a Gallery which could be built for less than half that sum?' or something to that effect.

What would I do? I would cut my losses. Call the competition off and instruct one of our own Glasgow architects, acceptable to the Trustees and informed advisers, to design the Burrell Gallery. We are in danger of featuring the building and not the Collection, all contrary to Sir William's wishes and a commonsense procedure.

We are proceeding to make civic history repeat itself. A hundred years ago a bunch of amateurs selected a bogus Gothic project for their new University on Gilmorehill and all the time they had a brilliant architect, 'Greek' Thomson, on their doorstep.

Sir William and Lady Burrell's gift was not only to this generation, but this generation is responsible for the decisions. Let's hope our successors will speak kindly of the decision makers. If they were less concerned with secrecy they might produce some concrete evidence which would lead us to applaud performances rather than have to be brushed off with promises.

II

Spare Time

A Scottish Tourist Industry
One evening, in July 1944, as I was on the point of leaving for home, Sir Steven Bilsland (later Lord Bilsland) came on the telephone. He asked me if I could come to his office, right away if possible, to meet the Secretary of State for Scotland, Mr Tom Johnston. Both of them wanted to discuss with me a very important matter.

Following a short preamble I was invited to be Chairman of a Committee to investigate the post-war prospects for a Tourist Industry for Scotland. Tom Johnston is generally acclaimed as one of the greatest Secretaries of State Scotland has ever had. His chief concern at this time was to make the country economically independent. At one time an ardent supporter of Home Rule for Scotland, he had now reached the conclusion that a necessary first step towards achieving this – and I gathered he was still all for it – was a stable economy. He had set up The Scottish Council (for Development and Industry) and this under Sir Steven Bilsland's leadership was conducting, through different committees, a series of investigations on ways and means.

Tom Johnston indicated that he looked upon Tourism as a matter of considerable importance and was sure the government would not resist any practical proposals which the committee might include in its report.

My first reaction was in the form of the appropriate phrase indicating I felt honoured in having been selected: and I meant it. I was eager, then and there, to accept, at the same time wondering if it was wise to encroach still further on what was already little more than a figure of speech – my leisure time. (On the subject of Leisure, I had about this time accepted an invitation to address the Glasgow Rotary Club on this theme. A member of my family sent a telegram to the President, who read it in the course of his generous introduction: 'Your speaker today knows nothing about his subject. He doesn't believe in it!') However, a decision had to rest on something more than physical fitness and eagerness. I remembered I was a local government official and would have to seek the necessary authority. Tom Johnston, with a smile, said he did not think there would be much difficulty in getting it.

The next day I saw Convener Bailie Burnett, who immediately, and with some emotion, congratulated me. I may have neglected to explain the title Bailie. It is the Scottish equivalent of alderman or magistrate. Although the term of office is restricted to a few years, we have a saying 'once a Bailie aye a Bailie'. On some very rare occasions the holder of the honour behaves as if it should be spelt 'Bully'. Bailie Burnett also thought the invitation was an honour and would be an admirable complement to the work being done at Kelvingrove. There would be no difficulty in getting official permission. But there was. When the matter was raised at the Art Galleries Committee meeting, opposition was evident. A move was made to remit to a sub-committee, notwithstanding my request for an immediate decision and ample assurances that if I found this voluntary service interfered with official duties I would withdraw from it. The Minute of the meeting begins thus:

'The Director reported that he had been invited by the Scottish Council on Industry to act as Chairman of the Tourist Committee appointed by the Council.'

The minute puts on record that by the casting vote of the Chairman, the Director was authorised to accept.

It looked as if I were in the way of becoming a specialist in collecting casting votes. An explanation was forthcoming later. It would appear that Bailie Burnett was absent. In consequence the Chairman was Mrs Helen Gault, sub-Convener. Subsequently she became Convener and backed all our schemes with enthusiasm. Indeed she went the length of adopting an attitude of defiance against her own party's instructions and had the party whip withdrawn for several months. The opposition on the present issue very kindly told me nothing personal was involved. It was a matter of principle – I have been unable to discover what the principle was.

Without delay, but a little depressed, I saw Sir David Milne, then head of the Home Department at the Scottish Office. He briefed me thoroughly and along with Sir Horace Hamilton, top civil servant at St Andrew's House, cleared any doubts as to the importance of the remit. They had been trying to get this enquiry under way for a long time. And they hoped we would report as quickly as possible.

We got on with it. For two years Tourism was a big part of my homework. The steady accumulation of literature and memoranda led to formidable heaps on side-tables at home and in the office, but over the period it was a very happy and a very valuable experience. Blessed with a brilliantly efficient secretary in W. V. Stevens of the Edinburgh Chamber of Commerce, we thus maintained the inter-city balance of power. In his younger days he had played football for Queen's Park – leading me to chaff him by saying I remembered him as a 'dirty player'! Bill Stevens was a neat tidy man with a narrow face and dark hair beginning to go grey. With eyes looking straight at you and with a smile always ready to be switched on, he was a patient listener. We meet very occasionally now; but I recollect him attending the McEwan Hall in Edinburgh when I lectured on 'The Universities and the Arts' in the presence of the Heads of Universities visiting the Edinburgh Festival in 1955. When recalling the affair, at a later date, all Bill Stevens could remember of my 'memorable' oration was an anecdote to prove the present day brightness of student wit. I do not know where I collected it. Here it is: There was an International Conference of Obstetricians and Gynaecologists at Glasgow University. In the quadrangles were notices intimating the theme of the Congress – 'The Unexpected in Obstetrics'. Some student had scribbled at the foot of the poster 'Mary had a little lamb'.

For a period on the Tourist Board we went more academic than this. The Chairman Tom Johnston was Chancellor of Aberdeen University, Sir Malcolm Knox (most lucid and fluent in giving an opinion) was Principal of St Andrews University, I was Rector of Glasgow University, and Bill Stevens was on the Court of Edinburgh University. A unique situation, but what we really needed was money.

The Committee moved smoothly in collecting evidence. Regular meetings were held, alternately in Edinburgh and Glasgow. The Deputy Chairman, J. B. Crawford, Treasurer of the Bank of Scotland, arranged meetings and lunch in the Bank's palatial head office. The Glasgow meetings and lunch were held in the Art Gallery. I do not know whether the excellent Edinburgh lunches were on the bank or on J.B. The make-shift Glasgow snacks (imported for the occasion) were not on the Corporation.

Present at our meetings as an assessor, there would be a member of the Civil Service staff at the Scottish office. Always most helpful, some of them must have been entertained by my amateur efforts as Chairman of a semi-government Commission. Never, not by the slightest elevation of an eyebrow, did they show it. With the passing of the years it becomes difficult to recall the names which go with remembered faces. It is easy, however, in the case of R. E. C. Johnson (now head of the Home & Health Department, with a knighthood). Another bicycle devotee, always sounding as fit as he looked, his beaming bearded countenance was as reassuring and as comforting as a benediction.

Working under a sense of urgency we produced an interim report, and in a second interim report took the unusual course of saying, in effect, 'Don't wait for a final report. Get a move on now and set up a Scottish Tourist Board.' This was done, with Tom Johnston as Chairman. Nothing could have been better, nor have indicated more clearly the importance he attached to this new Scottish enterprise.

Tom Johnston published his memoirs in 1952. It is a fascinating record of a great career. It left most of us with the conviction that he had still more to tell us. (I gave a hint of this in a piece about him and some of his achievements in the *Scottish Field*.) Lots of people wondered why, when even greater political preferment seemed likely, he retired from Parliament. I repeat a diagnosis I proffered at the time and no one, including the 'patient', appeared to doubt it. T.J. had three special interests – all concerned with Scotland's welfare and development: (a) Hydro-electricity; (b) Re-afforestation, and (c) Tourism. He was also emphatic in holding to the idea of independent action. 'Let's do it ourselves, free from any risk of Government interference.' As a member of the Cabinet he was one of a team and would have to conform to government policy. As Chairman of these three post-war undertakings, and free from parliamentary responsibilities, he could practise what I have defined as the 'Daft Jock Technique'. In other words if he thought a specific course of action was sound and effective he would give orders accordingly. If, in the course of time it might be pointed out that subject to this or that statute, he could not do this or that, he would put on an expression appropriate to the occasion and say, 'That's too bad! But you see it has been done.' He came out of Parliament to regain freedom of action.

Among the founder members of the Scottish Tourist Board were

Sir Alex B. King, William Ferris, J. Ure Primrose, Lord Provost of Perth, W. V. Stevens and myself – taken over as it were from the Tourist Committee. We were joined by some fine people, among whom I remember Sandy Trotter, Editor of the *Scottish Daily Express* and clearly our leading expert on publicity. And there was Robert Wotherspoon, twice Provost of Inverness. From experiences ranging from the Channel Islands to the Holy Land we were to find in Bob and Poppy Wotherspoon the perfect holiday companions.

Starting from zero the Board had the good fortune to find the right man as its chief executive. William Nicholson took on a very difficult proposition. In addition to bringing to it the results of training in journalism he knew how to handle people – normal and abnormal. He must often have been tempted to call it a day, but throughout the years his loyalty, industry and imagination have been among the Board's biggest assets. I am sure he will remember the early days of tentative efforts – the struggle to find a descriptive title for the first regular publication. *Take Note* the 'it will do in the meantime' title established itself. The badge which was a feature of the letter heading took shape from an American cigar band. We were certainly thinking internationally. And the scrounging for money, with the Treasurer Sir A.B. giving personal loans to keep things going.

The Tourist Committee had produced a final Report which was published. The authors of it thought it was quite a useful production. It was soon forgotten, but for a long time thereafter when someone at a Tourist Board meeting would make what he thought was a bright suggestion – Ferris, Stevens and myself would exchange glances and smiles. We were silently indicating that it was all in our marvellous report.

For many years Bill Ferris and I represented Scotland on the British Travel & Holidays Association. We can go back to the days when Lord Hacking was Chairman – and a very fine Chairman. He was courteous, tolerant, practical and well informed. I succeeded in getting on the wrong side of a later chairman and some of the senior executives. I probably overdid the 'What about Scotland?' act or became too exasperated over the constant 'brush off' when quoting errors of fact reference Scotland in publications for overseas consumption. Bill Ferris, who died in 1963, never received anything like adequate appreciation for his persistence, and for his long and faithful service in the interests of the Scottish Tourist Industry. A great and fearless man to have on any committee. His accurate memory was often a menace to unprepared advocates.

Some day the story of the Scottish Tourist Board will be written. Whoever does it will find it impossible to dodge the use of a phrase which I have come to loathe, viz. 'a shoe-string budget'.

Tom Johnston's one mistake was his insistence on financial independence. He did not like our Committee's calculation with £100,000 as a starting figure. He could raise all that was necessary by standing at the top of the Waverley Steps in Princes Street, Edinburgh. Actually, the 'Waverley Steps Technique' as I came to define it was applied principally by Sir Alex King. He produced glossy publicity magazines with persuasive appeals for large-scale and expensive advertisements. Cinema premières, football matches and the like were held on behalf of Tourism. What a way to finance an Industry!

Of course it is only now that the British Government is beginning to recognise – well behind other countries – that Tourism is an important industry, highly competitive and economically beneficial. Money is now available and the important thing ahead is to see it is not squandered. For years Britain has been wasting money in futile efforts in a number of overseas 'campaigns' of the 'Come to Britain' class. Take New York alone: the number of agencies occupying expensive premises all concentrating on the one idea of selling Britain – British Information Service, British Travel Association, Thomas Cook, British Railways (same outfit), BOAC, Cunard, and other shipping lines.

Years ago when I first started fairly regular visits to the USA and Canada I investigated, for my own enlightenment, our different activities. I brought back two reports which did not lead to any action. Anyhow they cost nothing, but one did confirm that if you want to sell anything you have to send people to do the talking. Posters and publicity material – very costly – are heading for dim shelves 'below the counter' unless someone is around. I know this to be true. I have seen more effective results through the English Speaking Union and similar voluntary associations than the high powered expertise of 'specialists'. Indeed I know of a strip of a girl with a pronounced Glasgow accent, on an American Field Service Scholarship in the State of Washington, on the Pacific. She showed a bunch of transparencies on the beauties of Bonnie Scotland to an audience of around 300 schoolmates. A statement and a question followed: 'We are all coming to Scotland for our vacations' and 'How come you speak such good English?'

Today we have a new Scottish Tourist Board, with my friend and near neighbour Sir Hector Maclennan as Chairman. This was a fine, imaginative, courageous selection, announced by another friend of mine, Dr J. Dickson Mabon, a Minister of State. I have no doubt that the new set-up will prove itself in due course. Meanwhile, my comment is this. The new chairman with his wide experience, his handsome appearance – an asset as a representative of his country anywhere – and 'Dicky' Mabon, one of the brightest politicians in a mixed bunch, and myself, on call when the first Scottish Tourist Board was born, are all graduates in Medicine of Glasgow University. What does that prove? Precisely what you think when considering careers for the boys.

At this point the ship is approaching the Panama Canal on the homeward voyage. Down the Pacific Coast I have had another look at the Tourist angle of Civic and State activities. Risking the charge of audacity, my counsel to the new Scottish Tourist Board is: –

Do not squander your money on financing further research projects. A sensible man sitting at a desk with the evidence in front of him of what other, more alert governments – municipal and national – are doing, could produce a report in a week.

Look to your overseas publicity. Think of some new techniques with an eye on using – through British Consuls – the Scottish businessmen who are promoting their own interests overseas. Persuade them to work for Scotland's Tourist Industry as a side line.

Take a lead in keeping Scotland tidy. Pollution of rivers etc. and the menace of a litter-strewn landscape are a threat to the loveliness of our country. Until such time as education can have an effect, spend money in collaboration with local authorities in having some kind of salvage corps to follow in the wake of those who make a mockery of prospects designed to please.

The Arts Council

Another bit of history writing will have to be done on the Arts Council of Great Britain, with special reference to the first Scottish Committee. It began as the Council for the Encouragement of Music and the Arts, which was immediately shortened to CEMA. I have never been able to free myself from regrets at the change of name, especially the loss of the sound of the initials abbreviation. It has a warm, friendly, active, caressing kind of sound – *CEMA*. Arts Council is remote, dignified and very official. The original idea was a great advance in government recognition of the value of the Fine Arts. It was the beginning of something which has continued to grow and must keep on growing.

I was often critical of some of the things CEMA was doing, or was failing to do. I thought it should have, with greater enthusiasm and energy, followed the advice given by the first Chairman, Lord Keynes, who in effect said, 'Get out of the Metropolis. London can look after itself. CEMA's job is throughout the country.' And, at the time, my sympathies were with Miss Mary Glasgow, the first Director. Her pioneer efforts in getting things going were lost sight of in the course of some shabby treatment which made a number of people very uncomfortable.

O. H. Mavor became the first Chairman of the Scottish Committee. My memories of O. H. Mavor go back to our student days at Glasgow University. When I came up (in 1909), Osborne Mavor and Walter Elliot were looked upon as chief among the leaders who settled the line of action in most student adventures, from the GUM (Glasgow University Magazine) to Rectorial Elections. There were of course others identified with the Union and Student Representative Council (SRC) and Sports. To expand the record is not within the immediate purpose. Let's refer again to the GUM. Elliot, transforming his initials W.E.E. into Parvus, and Mavor (both in verse and in brilliant drawings and caricatures) developed a worthy inheritance into a production which even the present day undergraduates admit has never been equalled. I must not forget C.J.K. (initials which hid the identity of Charlie Kirk, who practised in Darlington until his death some years ago). C.J.K. supplied the GUM with slightly diluted Kipling verse, with an up-to-date topical flavour. They won, as they merited, a collected volume.

I tried, once or twice, to gain admittance to the pages of the magazine without result. My efforts, modelled I confess too closely on C.J.K., were probably too watery a solution to stand up to printer's ink. I revenged myself by inflicting some samples as a substitute for post-prandial oratory on the members of the Western Infirmary Residents Club. As a matter of fact, I was very much on the side lines of most of the exciting undergraduate rags and social activities generally. I did not have much money. It was later on before I really got to know my immediate and illustrious seniors.

Rummaging through a forgotten bundle of old University papers I came across the Menu Card and Toast List of the 2nd Annual Dinner of our year. My name is on it as down to reply to the toast 'Alma Mater'. Three things are thereby indicated. The first two allow me to reflect that I must have been well enough liked by my fellow-students and I must have acquired some kind of reputation as a speaker. The third reveals a mistake. As a recent arrival I should have been proposing 'Alma Mater' and a senior member of the University should have replied. However, I spent a lot of time on the appropriate research and prepared some wonderfully 'fresh' observations on the functions of a University and her place in the community, not to mention her effect on the hearts and minds of all her students.

I tried every known device to capture the intellect and emotions of my fellows and our masters. It was a terrific flop. I have found some compensation in more recent years by telling Glasgow Graduates in various parts of the world, that in the year 1910 I resolved that if I were ever again called upon to speak on or about 'Alma Mater' I would get down to the level of my audience and stay there!

I think I was lucky in belonging to that particular period. The claim that an unusually large proportion of my fellow-students reached eminent positions is well founded. The only fly in the ointment was that most of my contemporaries were much better endowed with pocket-money. I had to earn mine. Others who had to do the same appeared to be able to take it all in their stride and were careful not to lose sight of the main objective – passes in professional examinations and a degree.

Among my pocket-money earning efforts was the job of 'holding copy' in the *Glasgow Herald*. That is to say I was an assistant proof reader. This was a job which the management very willingly gave to students. It was interesting enough but very exhausting. From seven in the evening till sometimes well past midnight we read all kinds of scripts, and how illegible some of them were! We sniffed smelling salts to keep ourselves awake and, in my time, the pay was 3/10d a night. Three nights a week and 11/6d for our pockets were ample.

Walter Elliot became a prominent politician. As an undergraduate he was a Fabian Socialist. Legend has it that when in France in service during War 1 he received a telegram inviting him to stand as a parliamentary candidate for a Lanarkshire constituency. He replied 'Certainly. What party?' Every advance he made, and the range of his interests was remarkable in quality and variety, led most of us to the conviction that he would end up as Prime Minister. As well as possessing the plausible charm of the politician, Walter was intellectually brilliant. Generally careful in what he said, like all people with a leaning towards calculation he could make mistakes. That he gradually drifted into the phase of elder statesman without achieving leadership of the people is perhaps due to two things. He lacked political courage at the right time, and he failed to hit it off with Winston Churchill.

To judge from the various diaries and memoirs in which Elliot figures prominently this would seem to be a reasonable deduction. In the thirties we occasionally met in the Caledonian Club, then situated across St James's Square from our gallery in King Street. My partners, Reid and Macdonald, were members and our colleague from France, Etienne Bignou, loved to be taken there for a meal. There was no place in the world could beat it for smoked trout. When Tom Johnston became Secretary of State for Scotland, Walter, a predecessor in the office, thought it appropriate to have the Scottish Secretary a member of the Club. He had forgotten or dismissed the fact of Tom's authorship of *Our Noble Families*, an indictment of the Scottish aristocracy. This had rankled in many an old family bosom long after it had been sold out, and the Secretary of State for Scotland did not become a member of the Caledonian Club.

During the thirties when Elliot was Secretary we were very friendly with the permanent under-secretary, Jack Highton by name. Following a meteoric career in the civil service he had less than a year in the highest post open to him. Actually he became ill one night on the train from Edinburgh to London. O. H. Mavor was on board and rendered first aid. It was of no avail. Highton died three days later. His successor, Sir Horace Hamilton, inherited a list of personal friends to be invited to the Trooping of the Colour. The two balconies at Dover House (the Scottish Office in London) gave a superb view of this colourful ceremony. Sir Horace allowed Jack's list to stand and we were included. Unfortunately we were shown up to the wrong room and out to Walter Elliot's balcony. I sensed there was something wrong, for with all their grace and charm

Walter and his lovely wife could scarcely conceal the unspoken query, 'What the devil are you doing here?' We were rescued in time and transferred to the right balcony. It was the only time we have ever given the appearance of gate-crashing a political occasion. Bridie must have been told of it. For a spell he addressed me as Romeo, but the spelling was Roameo. Years later when Walter was High Commissioner to the Church of Scotland we were honoured guests at one of the Banquets at Holyrood. There were no balconies and we did not get lost. What a splendid couple the Elliots were as representatives of the monarchial establishment.

I had an extra-mural link with O. H. Mavor. His mother and mine had common interests and membership on some social welfare committees and they held each other in high regard and respect. Unfortunately they would compare the scholastic records and progress of their offspring to the discomfiture of the latter. Each of us knew that the embarrassment of a student when he is ploughed in an exam is as nothing to the embarrassment of a parent. For a time, and because of his absorption in the GUM and other undergraduate interests, O.H. failed with laudable persistence and I was kept in countenance. I was able to point to the plea he addressed to the new Professor of Anatomy. It has become a classic.

> *Oh, Dr Bryce, oh Dr Bryce!*
> *Your predecessor ploughed me twice.*
> *Oh Bryce,*
> *Let twice*
> *Suffice!*

Then O.H. became afflicted with the idea that life was real and earnest and began to sail through the curriculum. And, perforce, for the sake of domestic peace I had to follow suit.

Privileged and proud to continue to follow him, under his pen name which was to achieve international repute, James Bridie led me on to the board of the Scottish National Theatre Society where, with John Brandane and others, many a battle was fought in the interests of Scottish drama. Whatever may be due to Sir Barry Jackson and the Birmingham Repertory for making Bridie's work and name known to the English-speaking theatre, his roots were planted among the Scottish National Players, and John Brandane was the man who nurtured the promising plant. Brandane, from the West country, was also a medical practitioner. His best known play is *The Glen is Mine*.

By the time I reached the West End (speaking of Glasgow's geography), O. H. Mavor was a near neighbour – in Woodlands Terrace. He was now on the visiting staff of the Victoria Infirmary. In appearance he had not changed a bit. A large head, broad brow and bright eyes which, with his round glasses, could help him to assume an owlish expression. He has caricatured himself in innumerable Christmas greeting cards. His smile was expansive – more of a grin – and his voice was something he never quite knew how to use. His brilliantly witty remarks when speaking in public were often lost, because he addressed them to his waistcoat. The front rows would titter when there ought to have been a loud roar of laughter. He seemed to want to leave it all to his players.

We saw a lot of each other and it was no uncommon experience to barge into his home to find him busily engaged writing a play, pad on his knee, while across the fireplace would be his wife, Rona, calmly darning socks. O.H. had difficulty in deciding whether and when he should give up medicine altogether. He took a long time to make up his mind and I often wish he had taken the plunge sooner. From now on he is James Bridie – even if there were moments when I addressed him as Osborne.

Our association became closer when the Citizens' Theatre was started some years later, but when we moved to London our meetings were frequent and I know how great the pressure was to move his own home south. It would have been in his interest financially, to operate from the centre of things, theatrically speaking, but he never departed from the conviction that by staying in Glasgow he could best help to revive the theatre in Scotland.

At this time, in spite of all the pressure of professional work I devoted a lot of time and thought to the fringes of the theatre. In other words, the amateur stage. My younger brother and my only sister were enthusiasts. The former 'went' professional and the latter, now Mrs John McPherson, in spite of or because of domestic demands, has for many years taken an active part in producing the Milngavie Players. Her husband, one time Provost of Milngavie, is her greatest supporter.

Although he belongs more to another story I should explain that my younger brother is known as Murray Macdonald. He assumed his middle name when he took the plunge. The Murray part, I think he got from a well-known Glasgow railway time-table. They tell me he is quite a figure in London theatrical circles. In a review of the

Contemporary Theatre, Kenneth Tynan once said of him, 'Murray Macdonald, a solid craftsman aiming slightly higher; guilty of no false moves, errors of judgment or memorable fancies, he remains the safest producer of recent years, with his surprising flair for squeezing drops of quality out of bad plays.' (In *He that Plays the King*.)

Murray certainly had a reputation in his Glasgow days for squeezing quality out of bad old plays and out of very bad old and young actors. I think his greatest talent is his calculating logic. He started as a juvenile lead in Repertory and touring companies. Having no flair for playing character, he knew his days as a juvenile were numbered. Therefore, into stage direction and then up to Producer (nowadays they are called directors). Along come some young and brilliant young men and new fashions in plays, players and direction, so he is wise to get into management. One can stay there until the sweet or bitter end, unless catastrophe overwhelms us all.

When he was Walter Macdonald Honeyman my brother founded the Albany Players. He made me its President and, when struck by the sudden withdrawal of a member of the cast, would push me into a part. It was often impossible to memorise the lines in the time available and I had to have chunks of script concealed here and there on the set.

When he departed we continued, under demand from medical charities, with what was to all intents and purposes a family concern. Talking of family – my wife rather deplored these excursions into the theatre, on two counts. She thought it was a lamentable waste of my time and because, to save costs, we rehearsed in our dining-room. She very properly deplored this unwarrantable encroachment on our domestic life. Very cleverly we persuaded her, in association with the wife of a medical colleague, to displace our rather feeble trio – violin, 'cello and piano – and play duets for two pianos as the interval music. The result was not what we expected. Mrs Nell Wallace Anderson and Mrs V. C. Honeyman were so good that the audience remained in their seats at the intervals and were restless throughout the rest of the evening. Incidentally, as far as Glasgow was concerned, it was a piece of pioneering in a new form of interlude music.

When we pushed on to London I continued with an interest in the theatre. As the chairman of small syndicates under the name *T. J. Mellish* I made two attempts in presenting, at the Arts Theatre, plays

which the West End managements had rejected. One was a Bridie,
Colonel Wotherspoon. It wasn't very good and has never had a long life.
The other, *The Lake*, was by Dorothy Massingham and Murray
Macdonald (he had got the idea from observing the antics of a
Glasgow family). It was produced by Tony Guthrie with Marie Ney
in the leading part. It was successful and Anmer Hall bought it for
his new Westminster Theatre, where it ran for three months. It was
sold to America and was produced in Boston, I think, with Katherine
Hepburn in the lead. We began to build castles in the air. They fell
back to earth with a bump. Dorothy Parker in reporting on *The Lake*
compressed her criticism to 'Miss Hepburn covered the gamut of
emotions from A to B.' Goodbye to a long run and, maybe, a packet
from film rights.

We have indulged in a far cry from Bridie and the Arts Council,
not without making the point, I hope, that my interests in the Arts
were not detached. There has to be something subjective in any
approach to this kind of public service. No one can view the
activities of bodies like the Arts Council and take part in the
administration, solely from an objective view. Somehow or other
we must get actively involved.

Bridie, then, started the CEMA enterprise in Scotland and I was
included in his team. The others were Dr (now Sir) Ernest Bullock –
Professor of Music at Glasgow; Sir William McKechnie – HM
Inspector of Schools; Dr J. R. Peddie, CBE – Carnegie Trusts; and
Sir George Pirie – President of the RSA – an elegant cross-section
of top people in Art and Education. This time I did not seek official
permission to accept this invitation. Convener Alex Burnett considered it unnecessary. In his opinion the importance of the Glasgow
Art Gallery made it essential for the Director to be a member of
anything to do with Art in Scotland.

Most of us soon became restless under what we felt was too
much London domination. I was to have similar reactions on other
national bodies as a representative from Scotland. They listened to
the voice of Scotland with sober attention and great courtesy, and
then passed on to the next business, as if the gentle interruption was
an unfortunate waste of time. Nevertheless Bridie kept on fighting
for a greater autonomy for the Scottish Committee and eventually
got it. As far as Art was concerned, and with Glasgow in mind, it
did not operate to our advantage. Now and then we could get a
chance of having the big exhibitions, e.g. Van Gogh and Picasso,

which were organised and opened in the South. When Scotland got its degree of independence it lost the big exhibitions.

Later, when the Edinburgh Festival came along, the Arts Council at the London end resumed co-operation. Edinburgh then got the exciting exhibitions and Glasgow – the centre of population by the way – had to languish in the back water.

The allocation of Arts Council funds to Scotland at the beginning was around £9,000 per annum to cover all the Arts. It is now over £700,000. Sounds like a lot of money, but quite inadequate for what the Council is supposed to be doing. All our governments are good at paying lip service to the Arts. Their spokesmen, when elections are imminent, bring tears to the eyes and raise lumps in the throat; but how slow they are to take action.

The city state of Hamburg supports the Fine Arts with an annual amount in excess of what the UK does for the whole of Britain. I reported this after a visit to Germany and was criticised for having made a 'bitter attack on the Arts Council'. It is the Government I am 'agin'. Sometimes I think the Arts Council might be more enterprising and less sensitive over constructive criticism. Nevertheless the Arts in Scotland would be in a worse shape if it were not there. The present Director is Ronald Mavor, who, like his father, qualified in Medicine. He came to his important job via Drama Criticism on the *Scotsman*. I think his is a splendid appointment, and the future under his guidance should be less exasperating than it was in his father's time. It will be more appropriate to expand on the function and performances of the Arts Council when I reach the point of prophecy in a concluding chapter.

Meanwhile Ronald Mavor has recaptured his freedom and gone back to writing, as a free-lance operator. I wish he had carried on for another five years at least.

The Citizens' Theatre

When Bridie got some of us together to examine the possibility of restarting a Repertory Theatre in Glasgow, we hummed and ha-ed for a long time. The appearance of CEMA reduced our fears almost to the vanishing point and encouraged him to say, 'Now is the time'. The Citizens' Theatre story has already been told, in great part, in a book on Bridie by Winifred Bannister. In it there is a good summary of the early days. The inaccuracies are negligible – the overall picture is composed with great understanding, sympathy and enthusiasm.

We thought of it as Bridie's Theatre, but CEMA's earlier support was invaluable. At the same time we were often up against remote officialdom. The entertainments tax was one of our chief problems. We thought, as a non-profit making institution, we ought to be exempt. That was too simple for HM Treasury. They appointed three assessors whose duty it was to determine whether a play was entertaining or educational. If the former, tax had to be paid. If the latter, exemption from tax was the order of the day. In Bridie's view the three assessors knew little or nothing from reading a script, especially if it were in a Scots dialect. He described them as 'The Three Blind Mice'. Nevertheless, what they decided had to be accepted. Some of their decisions were comic. The standards seemed simple enough. If the play was bright and likely to produce laughter it was entertainment. If it was dull and dreary it was educational. We were puzzled on one occasion to discover a play by J. B. Priestley was marked entertainment (tax due) when done by the Glasgow Citizens', and educational (tax free) when done in his native Bradford.

When Lord Keynes died his successor as Chairman of the Arts Council was one of 'The Three Blind Mice . This was too much for O.H. He resigned. Perhaps it was the James Bridie side of him which felt aggrieved, or maybe he thought this was the best way to register a protest. My reasons for going with him were less significant. I was becoming too much involved in affairs which were continuous and likely to become more demanding. Moreover, as an executive myself it seemed a bit unseemly to be a Committee member liable to discuss recommendations by other executives in the same line of business. Dr James Welsh, Lord Provost of Glasgow, who succeeded Bridie thought there was substance in my viewpoint.

Coming off the Committee did not prevent the continuation of our close contacts with the Arts Council in a number of exhibitions. Indeed, with Dr Welsh who had been, before my time, the Convener of the Glasgow Gallery Committee, an even closer association was developed. His enthusiastic devotion to the Arts was his chief delight and was probably responsible for a great contribution in shaping the future of the Arts Council work in Scotland. I think he had an influence on his political comrades.

Still on the subject of extra-mural interests, I must refer again to

the Glasgow Citizens' Theatre as it affected myself. A great deal of
my leisure time was spent in trying to solve problems concerning
policy, plays and publicity. Although we had differences of opinion
the Chairman had the unswerving loyalty of his friends, official and
unofficial.

Whatever criticism may be directed against it – and it has never
been short of critics – one notable achievement lies to its credit. In a
period when the live theatre – outside the metropolitan area –
appears to be slowly dying, the Citizens' has remained alive. It has
lasted much longer than any previous effort to establish a repertory
theatre in Glasgow. Its record is such that its chief sponsors, the
Corporation of Glasgow and the Arts Council, are not now likely to
see it fade away. When the problems associated with civic and
national support of the Fine Arts are eventually solved, the Citizens
in my judgment will have justified the faith of its chief begetter,
James Bridie.

The week before I embarked on this voyage the outlook was
gloomy. In spite of all our hopes the rulers of the City of Glasgow
refuse to or are incapable of 'thinking big'. I had better suspend
further comment until I get back home. Wisdom may have prevailed
in the long run – a very long run.

I must take this chance to give my version of how the thing got
started. Bridie assembled a few likely people in the Glasgow Art
Club – early in 1943. Most of us could remember the exciting times
of the Repertory Theatre, and were agreed that if it had not been for
the outbreak of World War 1, Glasgow's first attempt to create a
civic theatre might not have faded out. It was also agreed that we
had arrived at the opportune moment to have another try. But this
time, as soon as post-war conditions would allow it, we must get a
theatre of our own. From the very beginning a Civic Theatre,
eventually involving the Corporation, the body responsible for
running the city, was the idea in the minds of the majority. A few
were for independence.

In an article I had written some time previously I had tried to
concentrate on a simple question. If a city can spend less than a 1d
on the rates to support an Art Gallery, why can't it make the rate
$1\frac{1}{2}$d and be able also to support music and drama? Bridie allowed
this bee to buzz a little longer, but was clearly of the opinion that it
would be hopeless to rely on immediate help from the city. If we
made a success of it we could approach the town council with a

proposition, but in the first place a few private citizens could be persuaded to put up a little money and the Arts Council would do the rest.

What Bridie thought was enough money was soon forthcoming. Enough, that is to say, to let a start be made in the small Athenaeum Theatre, the only place available. It may be assumed that minor and major errors of judgment were committed. The first major error was in thinking there is ever enough money. We had started off with great goodwill. The timing was perfect, but we ought to have launched a general appeal for larger funds to get this new and overdue enterprise off to the right kind of beginning with greater resources. I think the result would have been strikingly satisfactory and would have led us to be more courageous. As proof of this and as evidence of failure to cash in on Bridie's influence and personal popularity there are at least two subsequent events.

When we had to leave the Athenaeum, the Princess Theatre was made available by Harry McKelvie on a ten years' lease at the very moderate rent of £1,000 per annum. Harry, a great character in Glasgow theatrical circles, was getting on in years. His lean and hungry look belied the warmth of his heart. He did not want his beloved theatre to fall into the hands of Messrs Muck and Mick (as he described a particular form of entertainment). For years he had admired Bridie and he wished the 'Citizens' well. So, if we would guarantee ten years' rental – and he would pay the first year himself – the theatre was ours. It could not be sold because, according to a Trust Deed, the property would pass eventually to the Victoria Infirmary. Without any fuss or bother the £10,000 came along from the late Sir Fred Stewart, not as a guarantee, but in actual cash.

Some people had thought it a mistake to start operating in the Athenaeum. This neat little theatre, with totally inadequate backstage facilities had always been associated with amateur productions. It was said that the public would never be got to realise the professional character of the Citizens'. Even the name was wrong. That name gave us a lot of trouble. Bridie spent days and nights thinking out a name for the new adventure. Rejecting all the suggestions, most of them hackneyed, we decided as a temporary measure only on The Glasgow Citizens' Theatre and we got stuck with it. It seems now to wear well enough. Probably the most amateurish thing about us was the Board of Directors. A theatre, we were told, cannot be run by a Committee. True enough, but the man or men to run it must be chosen by someone, and it is not a bad thing when responsibilities have to be shared.

I am supposed to be recollecting, not writing a history of the Citizens' Theatre, but the excitements of the early days are apt to be lost in the factual record. Besides, when, in memory, I cast my eye round our boardroom table I think it worth while to detain you with a comment on who were in at the start. They made the climate. It was fun. We felt important when we were not glum. Bridie's first team in addition to myself was: R. W. Greig, a prominent Glasgow wool merchant, he spent most of his time furthering the interests of the Scottish Orchestra. With the memories of many financial anxieties affecting music organisations in the city, his outlook was cautious. Yet, when he thought we ought to go slow, he would also agree that nothing is achieved without some kind of risk. When he decided to spend the rest of his life with his ain folks who had made their home in Kenya, we missed the benediction of his smile and admired his courage in transplanting his roots from safe ground to a very uncertain prospect. Norman Duthie, a leading Glasgow accountant, had varied interests ranging from the University Court through church and benevolent institutions to Government enquiries or commissions at home and overseas. His office was the obvious place for Board Meetings, but the intense palavers where personal opinions could be expressed without restraint took place in his home. There Peggy Duthie, the perfect hostess, took us in hand. Her wonderful dinners and drinks to suit all tastes invariably left us with the conviction that in this colourful world not a single problem remained to be solved! Paul Vincent Carroll, who first made his name as a playwright with *Shadow and Substance* in New York, and who began his adult life as a schoolmaster. He was mostly responsible for meetings lasting longer than they should. How entertaining he was and how shrewd in his judgments! That is, when not applied to his own way of living. With my supposed bias towards publicity I once suggested having a competition for new plays. Paul was vehement in opposition. 'You'll never find any play worth a damn in a competition.' To and fro went the argument until Bridie, having had enough, remitted the issue to Paul and myself as a special committee 'to consider and report'. We arranged a lunch meeting a few days later. I developed an acute laryngitis, which almost reduced me to speechlessness. Paul turned up with two lovely black eyes and a hangover. We decided to recommend the competition, but the result proved that he was right. I tried to find solace in persuading myself that if it did us no good it did us no harm, and the publicity was good. George Singleton knew more about show business than any of us. Although his experience was chiefly concerned with the cinema the last thing he would permit himself to do was to stay in a narrow groove. Before the war he started the Cosmo Cinema – with quality films, mostly continental, in mind – and in defiance of all the head shaking and gloomy forecasts from his associates. It was a huge success from the beginning. Enterprising, but not blindly so, George was prepared to listen to any new proposal. If it *was* new and not a re-hash of something that had been tried and found wanting, his support was assured. Many worthwhile efforts on behalf of charitable objects owe a lot to George Singleton and his family. Even some less than worth while, for his tendencies were all towards encouragement. He took chances with the doubts. We had no doubts about our affection for George, not to mention his lovely wife Jean. The Cinema Exhibitors Association also looked his way in the same way, for they made him their President.

John Boyd, later Sir John Boyd, Professor of Mercantile Law was with us in the two-fold capacity of legal adviser and John Boyd himself. He belonged to the Mavor-Elliot vintage period at Glasgow University. Very slightly my senior, I envied him the great gift of imperturbability. His calmness at Board Meetings had a steadying influence until we discovered he was asleep. John Boyd often made me think of our meetings as reproductions of the Mad Hatter's tea-party, with him as the dormouse. Yet he had the amazing capacity of waking up at the right moment to enter the discussion as if he had heard every word spoken in the course of his quiet snooze. He may have been kidding us. I don't think so. It may have been a brilliant technique. I could never work up enough courage to ask John's wife. Cathie Boyd is a qualified legal authority in her own right. Probably she would have brushed my query aside and changed the subject with a disarming smile. Our first Managing Director was Guy McCrone, who became very well known as a novelist. A cousin of Bridie's, he had been persuaded to suspend his writing for a spell to help us get the Citizens' Theatre started. Guy in turn persuaded his wife, Sylvia, to help him. These two, operating from a tiny room somewhere behind and above the Athenaeum, had to deal with a series of crises which, from time to time, threatened to bring the house down, in more ways than one. They survived but failed to receive due thanks for all they did. For that matter none of us did. None of us wanted thanks. Bridie made by far the greatest sacrifices in time and money.

It will have been noticed that wherever I could I have squeezed in a reference to the ladies. Apart from being their constant and devoted admirer I know now how much we owed to them. We all had to do our bit in various war-time committees. In Glasgow, from the day the Poles poured in each of us found plenty to do in helping to make things easy for any and all of the allied troops. Our homes were open and when we were not to be found in them it was because we were occupied either on official business or in advancing some cause calculated to keep up 'the spirit of the people'. If we did not grow weary in well-doing the credit is due to our women-folk who tolerated our tantrums and suppressed their urge to laugh at our moods of smug self-satisfaction.

Regarding my own particular contribution at the launching of the Citizens' Theatre, I have been described as the father of the Citizens' Theatre Society. There was quite a series of arguments before this baby was permitted to come into being. Bridie was, at first, un-favourable. He thought it would certainly stamp us as amateurs. It was absolutely necessary to register in the public mind as a profes-sional outfit, able to compete with the commercial theatre. Against him I proffered the differences already existing. Unlike our friends the opposition, chiefly the Howard & Wyndham organisation, we had no proper theatre and we were a non-profit making concern. I thought too, that inasmuch as we would have to build up our own audience, the creation of some kind of supporters' club might function as a nucleus. Even if a society did little more than exist as a mailing list it would be a help in the period of propaganda.

There was nothing original in the idea. It had been done elsewhere and I undertook to find out how it worked. I consulted Tyrone Guthrie and Lewis Casson. Each of them had knowledge of the Glasgow theatre situation. I have already referred to Sir Tyrone. He had practically started his brilliant career with the Scottish National Players and had taken a prominent part in introducing Bridie's plays to the South. Lewis (later to become Sir Lewis and an LL.D. of Glasgow) was then Director of Drama with CEMA. Both were strongly in favour and advised us to go ahead. We then called a meeting of those likely to be interested in the new proposal.

A packed audience, bubbling over with enthusiasm, was the result. Bridie promptly changed his mind, became the President of the Citizens' Theatre Society with myself as its first Chairman. Gordon Laing, another prominent Glasgow Accountant, with a long experience in the Community Drama Movement was the obvious man for Secretary. We had to press him – a very busy man – to take on the job. If it had not been for him we might easily have been overwhelmed by the rush of applicants for membership. In a short time a large number of people, three thousand or thereby, joined up, but at no time was their interest big enough or sustained enough to lead any of us to believe the faithful constant audience was going to be easy to win.

There was plenty of excitement and action. Large and interested groups of members turned up to hear Dame Sybil Thorndike, Ivor Brown, J. B. Priestley and others who wished us well, and proved it by generous expenditure of time and thought. Alas! When it came to supporting the theatre, in the important practical way of buying seats, the society behaved in the same manner as the general public. If the plays were too 'experimental', too 'heavy', too 'classical' they would not come. If they were light, with special emphasis on the Christmas Show, we could expect and got capacity business. There were several exceptional occasions, when we thought 'at long last we are established' and then back we were plunged into periods of persistent losses.

It would be wrong to allow the sense of unfulfilled hopes to make one forget the benefits the Theatre Society brought to the Citizens'. Indeed it might be a fair enough comment to say it performed some very notable services. From time to time, when reconstruction expenses assumed formidable proportions, a timely contribution from the Society funds saw us through the difficulties.

Towards the Citizens' Theatre the Corporation was friendly from the beginning. By the time the lease of the Princess Theatre was due to run out – and for a time it looked as if we might be without a home – the Theatre had established itself as the chief representation of dramatic art in the city. The councillors and magistrates appeared to think so. The City bought the theatre, spent a bit of money in improvements and guaranteed continuity. The Lord Provost and the City Treasurer became ex officio members of the Board. This was the logical follow-up on what Bridie had said twenty-five years before. 'It is our intention that the Citizens' Theatre should become the Glasgow Civic Theatre, as permanent and as much a public concern as the Art Galleries.'

My successor as Chairman of the Board, Michael Goldberg, brought his remarkable talents and devotion to the theatre to furthering this desirable project. A warm-hearted man, always sympathetic and generous towards individuals having a miserable time even if he did not see any immediate cure for the miseries of the world, Michael's enthusiasms were infectious. When he spoke he looked and sounded like a leader, a man who could take hold and build things up. There is plenty of evidence to support the notion. With his brother Ephraim the celebrated Departmental Stores in Glasgow and Edinburgh (with others opening up in other towns) have become a feature of Scottish commercial undertakings. A number of people think of them as gold mines.

Michael Goldberg started the Close Theatre, a complement to the Citizens', where experimental plays could be tried out and where the support might be found in a club atmosphere. He thought that in this kind of thing lay the hope of the future, if the live theatre was to be kept alive. He poured time and money into the effort, and it would be deplorable if, in the light of successful similar activities elsewhere, his vision became overclouded by a bunch of timid reactionaries or irresponsible theorists.

George Singleton succeeded Michael Goldberg. The difficulties confronting him were formidable, but the problems are not insoluble. It looks as if the main barrier is at corporation level. If only they could convert 'agreed in principle' to 'direct and immediate action'.

A week before I left home Lord Taylor, the deputy chairman, had a well-informed and penetrating article on the present situation. In discussions thereafter I was left with the conviction that the further outlook is very unsettled, not to say depressing. And I do not hesitate to blame the City Council for the lamentable state of affairs. It is not a new problem. It has been with them for years. What to do with the Gorbals is an old, old story. The urgent need to rescue the Citizens' from the handicap of its situation has been evident all along.

There is a story of a poor man who proposed to Sir Isaac Wolfson that in exchange for £1,000 he would confide in him the secret of eternal life. Sir Isaac, amused, asked for the secret 'Just you come back and live in the Gorbals. In all history no rich man has ever died there.' (The same story has been told with Baron Rothschild as the benevolent and wealthy philanthropist and a ghetto in Poland as the eternal city.) The image of the Gorbals is part of civic history. It cannot be changed. It might be replaced.

Not so long ago Michael Goldberg had an excellent article in the *Scotsman* 'What kind of Theatre for Glasgow'. It made me wish the City would listen to him. As the result of being a well-travelled man with a passion for the theatre, he knows, more than anybody I know, what is the right solution. His article concludes with this:

'Good theatre is a vital part of the cultural life of a community. The Citizens' Theatre has made its contribution with many notable productions over twenty-seven years. It has acquired an honourable tradition and an enviable reputation. Will these, too, disappear under the rubble of the Gorbals?'

Whatever happens, nobody can wipe out the memory of some wonderful people I met during my twenty-one years on the Citizens' Theatre Board. Playwrights, actors, directors, designers and all the rest of them – back-stage and front of the house. What a mixture of vanity, conceit, modesty, laziness and energy. We cultivated men and women who had genius in them, even if we didn't know it at the time. It is a joy to see and hear some who crept to the top when they appear on the West End stage or on television.

Others, especially hopeful dramatists, regarded us – the board – as worse than 'cut-throat bandits in the paths of fame'.

Out of the friendships which have endured are those formed with Patricia and John Casson and their family. Of course we knew all about them before they arrived. His parents, Dame Sybil and Sir Lewis Casson, were famous as the leading pair of troupers in the Theatre. John had five rewarding – for us – seasons at the Citizens', and brought back to my mind the original Scottish Repertory Theatre where in 1914 his distinguished father directed a number of plays and I, as a student from a seat in the pit at 9d, saw him play John Tanner in *Man and Superman*. We had a memorable visit to Melbourne in 1963, and through Patricia and John met everybody who was anybody in and out of the Theatre from which they had contrived to escape.

From a beautifully converted farm cottage in Somerset, when they are not on television, Liz and Richard Mathews in the course of wonderful hospitality to various old colleagues, radiate reminiscences of their days acting and directing in our active years.

I must not linger with a list of men and women who were, to us, much more than merely players, but for different reasons two are firmly fixed in our memories. I had a fellow-feeling for Duncan Macrae. When we opened the venture with Bridie's *Holy Isle* (a beautiful play) Duncan threw his bonnet over the windmill – abandoned school teaching to become a whole-time professional actor. And, through many a notable creation, achieved a leading position in the Scottish Theatre, to which he and his wife Peggy were slavishly devoted. James Gibson (Gibby) had his roots firmly planted in the old Scottish National Players. A wonderful trouper, his influence on the company was soothing and sensible in many a crisis. We often bumped into each other in unusual places. I recall meetings in Toronto, New York and elsewhere, when he spent a year in America touring as John Brown with Helen Hayes in *Victoria Regina*. Our children, when young, loved Gibby as the funniest man they had ever known. We old stagers can never forget his partnership with Duncan Macrae in the 'hing-ower' scene in the celebrated and record-breaking *Tintock Cup*.

Now, following a period of hot and cold controversy, Bailie William Taylor has become Chairman. A past leader of the Labour group in the Corporation, ex City Treasurer and for several years a member of the Board, it would now appear that Bridie's concept of a Civic Theatre is near to fulfilment. But the last thing Bridie wanted to see was the Citizens' run by a committee of the Corporation. This was also the unanimous view of the board, and in accordance with the conditions of Arts Council support. Some of us were a bit emphatic on the point, for we remembered the Corporation's museum-mindedness – its lamentable mismanagement of the Burrell Collection and inefficiency in handling the great gift of Pollok House, its contents and surrounding park. In the view of many informed citizens Bill Taylor was outstanding as Convener of Glasgow Planning Committee. (At the end of his term the general criticism was that the standing orders or whatever you call them prevented him carrying on.) He is now called upon to plan the future of the Citizens'. May I remind him that in the good old days the Theatre was run by a team with Bridie the Chairman, not the director, as the Captain. More power to him.

Partly due to my interest in the Citizens' Theatre, partly due to brother Murray's introductions, and partly due to our own involvement in multiple affairs, we were, from time to time, favoured in our home by visits from a number of celebrities. We prefer our

guests to have breakfast in bed, and I appointed myself butler to
Dame Sybil Thorndike, Dame Edith Evans, Dame Flora Robson and
Dame Rebecca West. My services were exclusive for, as the family
put it, 'he only "buttles" for Dames'. This is not quite accurate as
one of our most charming and vivacious of guests was Joyce
Grenfell. And there are others who should be Dames.

How kind they all were and how sweetly they allowed us to use
them to open sales of work and other charitable enterprises, art
exhibitions, school visits and the like. Indeed, each of them was the
highlight of many an occasion and we, forsooth, basked in a
background of glory.

12

Over the Border

The Middle East

In December 1944 the central Advisory Council for Education in HM Forces 'sent' me by telephone and letter an invitation to spend a month in the Middle East to lecture to the troops. The Committee agreed – one member dissenting – to grant leave of absence. I never discovered the reason for the dissent. Someone thought it might be anxiety over my personal safety. The war was not yet over, but the end was within sight.

Air transport to Cairo could not be described as luxurious, but the whole experience was unique and very, very interesting. Cairo seemed to be full of Scots, chiefly from Glasgow. I was a bit lost until I met James Fergusson (later Sir James Fergusson of Kilkerran and Keeper of Records). He knew his way around and was kindness itself in guiding me. Off and on we talked of many things, especially the likely changes in a post-war Scotland. I remember listening with pleasure to a poem he had written. It had something to do with 'I got my love a loofah where the broad Euphrates flows'. It sounded to me a very good poem, even if it made both of us home-sick.

The reason for these tours of 'civilian lecturers' (that was the label) was to help to do something to interest the troops who were said to be 'browned off'. The fighting in the desert was over and time hung heavy on them. Moreover the shining hour was to be used to prepare the boys for their return to civil life. My role was to inject a 'shot of culture' by way of talks on trends in Art (painting, sculpture and drama). In Cairo with good accommodation and projector it wasn't so bad and one's audiences always included a few who knew something about the subject. On some occasions it became evident in the discussion subsequent to the lecture that my place was at the receiving end of the channel of communication. I was reassured later by Esmond Wright, Glasgow's Professor of

Modern History and a TV personality, later to become an MP, that I held my end up to his satisfaction on at least one occasion. He was there.

On turning over a heap of memoranda I came across a letter I was sure I had lost. It is from a Major Ryan who is a complete stranger, and I have for long regarded it as chief among my collected testimonials. He writes from HQ 17th Area, MEF on 17th February 1945.

'Many thanks indeed for the privilege of listening to your stimulating talk last night. Quite apart from the brilliance of your exposition and your masterly introduction to artistic controversy, you should know how even your mere presence in these parts is appreciated by "home starved" troops who happen to be your fellow citizens. After many years in the sandy ruts of the Middle East it is mentally refreshing to be reminded that Kelvingrove is not a distant mirage.

Could you, when you get back home, tell "them" to send out more people to talk to us – people like Bridie, Linklater, Compton Mackenzie, Grieve and some of the younger men. We would like to know what has been happening in Scotland since 1939. Like sleepers in the fairy tale we will have to wake when Peace comes, to recoup as best we can the lost years.

Till then, and may it be soon, my very best wishes for your lecture tour in the Middle East.'

Away from the centres like Cairo, Alexandria, Benghazi and Tripoli talks on Art and Drama were out. I became a one-man Brains Trust, with the emphasis on the Trust. Flying over or motoring across the desert, noting the scars made on the landscape – very fierce some of them – halting overnight in camps, villages and towns, the names of which not so long before made headline news, all added up to a wonderful adventure. I got home, physically weary, but otherwise fine and grateful. I had seen a lot, learned a lot and met a lot of very worthwhile people. The only fright I got was on the way home.

We left Cairo after tea on a Saturday, in a Dakota, very inadequately adapted for passengers. Through the night the cold was terrific, and the flying height made breathing difficult. It was a relief to cross the French coast in the bright sunshine early on Sunday morning, making for an aerodrome near Marseilles. Round and round that aerodrome we circled. The first sight of it had made me think of a wash and breakfast. Most of my fellow-passengers – all service men – were sound asleep and unconcerned about anything. Round and round. My appetite disappeared and I found myself having a quiet whisper to Saint Peter, apologising for daring to appear at the gates of heaven in such a filthy state. I was sure the pilot was using up petrol in preparation for a crash landing: the landing gear was jammed or the Germans had swept back south again and we had no place to go. Eventually we flew down and in with the greatest of ease. Of course I had to know what all the trouble had been. Our *wonderful* pilot, while we enjoyed a *wonderful* breakfast, told me the trip through the night had been *wonderful*. The delay in coming in was due to the fact that a following wind had brought him in sooner than expected. It was a Sunday morning. Apart from control no one was around. They had been celebrating another successful advance by our *wonderful* troops. The regulations prohibited any plane coming in to land unless the fire-engines and ambulance were standing by. The delay was entirely due to the fact that the necessary crews had somehow got mislaid.

I like flying. I have flown a great deal, and that is the only time I have been really scared. And, although it has now become commonplace, I am still impressed by the recollection of having tea in Cairo on a Saturday evening and lunch in Bournemouth on the Sunday.

The British Council

Although my sympathies have been, off and on, with the Scottish National movement I do not think I qualify for inclusion in the 'Lunatic Tartan Fringe' type of propaganda for Home Rule. One of the curses of Scotland, in addition to the quarrelsome tendencies of men and women who could be our leaders, is the concentration of far too many interests in London. This applies to Industry, Commerce and the Arts. I am, of course, thinking of direction and decision making.

For a time I was the sole Scottish member of the Art Panel of the British Council. When I arrived at my first meeting the welcome could not be described as cordial. Sir Eric MacLagan, Director of the V and A was in the chair. Strongly addicted to snuff, he was pleasant in his aloofness. The others, some of whom I had known slightly in my London days, seemed to be puzzled by my presence.

What, in heaven's name, was I supposed to be doing in their company? The climate warmed up considerably when Clive Bell came in. He had evidently had a good lunch and was still enjoying a half-smoked cigar. He literally gave me a hug of welcome and began a series of questions going back to my Lefevre Gallery days and the occasions when we argued about young Scots artists. The Chairman had to call both of us to order.

The Arts Departments of the British Council were active, well run and, in the face of much adverse criticism from academic quarters, did a great service for Britain overseas. I should have written ENGLAND. That was, more or less, my constant grouse. Following repeated suggestions the panel had one meeting in Scotland. It happened at the time we had on view a very large selection from the Burrell Collection. Our distinguished visitors appeared to be more interested in the doubtful attributions of some of the items. The discussions were illuminating and fruitful. An outstanding recollection of the occasion was a remark by the Duke of Wellington, a member of the visiting panel. Following some general observations on the Civic Art Collection he said, 'I regard the Giorgione painting "The Woman Taken in Adultery" as the finest example of Italian Art in this country.'

At my last meeting – Sir Philip Hendy was now the chairman – I bowed myself out by saying 'You are doing a great work for Art, but I think you ought to change your name. You are really the English Council'. We will spare you the details and the chapters and verses produced to support the indictment. I had one supporter who was vocal. Professor Ellis Waterhouse, who had been for a short spell Director of the National Gallery in Edinburgh, thought there was substance in my complaint.

I have met and admired a number of well qualified and devoted men and women who were engaged, at home and abroad, in advancing the British way of life and in welcoming overseas students to our Universities and Colleges. In Glasgow I played a small part in the early days of the latter activity. I was not favoured, as were some of my opposite numbers in England, with invitations to go abroad as an 'official' spokesman on Scotland's part in the realm of the Arts. There was one notable exception which was, I think, unofficial. I was invited to Paris by Harvey Wood who was then the British Council representative in France. The sponsors were, I believe, some Franco-Scottish societies. At any rate I was the guest of the

Harvey Woods and no one could wish for a more kindly or more hospitable couple.

I cannot recall any Scotsman who has devoted so much time and energy to furthering the interests of his country in literature and the Arts generally who has received so little in the way of recognition. For example, it is not as well known as it ought to be that the Edinburgh Festival would not have started when it did but for Harry Wood's persistence. He did not take 'No' for an answer in the preliminary investigation. Others collected the credit due to him. In Edinburgh, Paris, Rome and London he was, for me, the ideal British Council representative. I have met others – in the Middle East for instance – who were neither so bright nor so reliable. I forgive them.

Among the parties and receptions in Paris I was greatly honoured in being introduced to several distinguished people. I remember M. Gabriel Marcel who spread himself, to my delight, on the subject of James Bridie's contribution to the contemporary British Theatre. The highlight of this particular visit was the occasion of a lecture in the Amphitheatre Richelieu at the Sorbonne on the subject of 'French Masterpieces in Scottish Collections'. It was a near disaster.

I had assembled a fine collection of coloured slides by way of illustration. Just before we were due to start the projectionist tumbled the lot out of the carrier and replaced them in any old sort of order. My inadequate French could not cope with his special accent and discomfiture. We had to face a makeshift 'talk' using the illustrations as and when they appeared, to emphasise the interest Scotland had always taken in French Painting. In a very sympathetic audience were some friends including Louis Carré from my Lefevre Gallery days. We continue to be friends.

A few weeks later a sequel reached me in the form of some verses by a lady unknown to me but later identified as a Franco-Scot, ex Edinburgh. In the land of MacGonagall they merit quoting if for no other reason than their main function – to serve as a remembrance of a very unique and happy occasion, and as a salute to Catherine Lhombreaud.

> That seat o Lear, the great Sorbonne,
> Was honoured here last Friday:
> There cam a cultured gentleman,
> Weel buskit, crouse an tidy;

A cantie lad, an fu o crack,
A sonsie chiel, no cheeky,
He sang the Ert o Glesca toun.
(He wisna frae Auld Reekie.)

Some fowks were wearing spectacles
An some were wearing posies;
Nae man was tentless or asleep
As though on beds o rosies.
Wi mous agape, they hist the tale
O Scotia's braw collections
Begot by famous Frenchmen syne
(Waesucks! There were corrections!).

Some slides were showed us back tae front,
An inside-oot some ithers,
An some were even upside-doun,
Till we had a the dithers.
Bit that gran Dr Honeyman
He didna bother ony;
Ilk pictur was his bosom-freen
An well-beloved crony.
The colours cried, alive an true
In splendour an in glory.
(Except, o course, for Edinbro,
Plain black an white THAT *story).*

The evenin flew on fleetin wing;
The Rector seemed tae worry,
Aye keekin doun intil his watch
Gin he were in a hurry.
Owre sin the last ward he pronounced,
Owre sin the fowks were leavin
An croodin roun tae tak his haun
(Their compliments were deivin).

Ye maun come back an tell aboot
Thae picturs owre the Channel.
It's ye maun dae't; Nae ither man
Tae ye can haud a canle.

In 1952 there was published a Report of a Committee on 'The Export of Works of Art etc.' It is a first-class survey of a very important problem concerned with the machinery of Export control and a number of related issues. There is a three-page list of 'Evidence Received' and I find my name included. I do not remember what my evidence amounted to, but I suspect it was critical of some aspects of the procedures then in operation. I note now that the Committee summarised the 'Defects of the Existing System' thus:

(1) That it was uncertain, unfair and apparently arbitrary.

(2) That it has a prejudicial effect on trade and relations with other countries and tended to encourage fraud and evasion.

(3) That it was over-centralised and failed to take account of the needs and wishes of local institutions.

(4) That it caused a large amount of work to little purpose.

(5) That it was, on the whole, ineffective as a means of conserving national treasures.

Some time after this report I was honoured by an invitation from the Chancellor of the Exchequer to become a member of the Advisory Council. I have never ceased to wonder why. Probably it was another case of 'better have someone from Scotland and Wales or there will be an outcry'. Anyhow, in the capacity of a complete passenger I was able to get a good view through the window. The view was not impressive.

We were, it seems, not the only country to institute a system of control for the purpose of safeguarding national treasures. Italy, for example, has had something of the kind since 1802. Yet in the 1890's two superb works by Salvator Rosa were acquired by a Scottish collector and later given to the Glasgow Art Gallery.

Since I find something inherently illogical in this particular activity (should we, for example, retain the Italian and Dutch masterpieces in our galleries?) and since I favour international free trade in works of Art, my comments are of no great significance. Moreover, as I am not well informed on up-to-date practices an analytical survey is out of the question. But I think it is relevant to remark that one result of 'rules of export' is the acquisition of notable items at ridiculously high prices. I have already said that a work of Art does not come to life until somebody looks at it. The artist is at one end of a line of communication. The spectator is at the other. Would it not be a good thing if more money was switched away from adding masterpieces to our collections towards the encouragement of the different enterprises devoted to the Appreciation of Art? The government could continue to make it easy for the wealthy, public-spirited collectors to add to our Art Treasures – without cost to the Nation. We could then leave it to the Universities, Colleges, Schools, Art Councils and Art Galleries to teach us all how to enjoy them.

Sir Philip Hendy was Director of the National Gallery from 1946 to 1967. The Trustees have published a List of Acquisitions during this period. It is a great tribute to one of the great directors of the Gallery. Nothing in the way of criticism can prevail against this grand record of service, and it may sound like sheer audacity to ask a question. What were the purchase prices? I am sure there were some bargains: but I don't know. Am I entitled to know? Are we not in danger of paying too much in our efforts to make good the grievous sins of omission committed by past Trustees, Committees and Directors? In Glasgow everybody knew (or could know if they were interested enough) what we paid for our acquisitions. The Art Market, reflected by auctioneers, dealers and private negotiators, is part of the field of enquiry open to every public gallery. What advantages are there in secrecy? It comes out in the long run.

On another trip 'over the border' I found this in a leading article on 'The Future of our Museums' in *The Times Literary Supplement* (25th August 1950). '*But if culture is not to perish utterly within a measurable time the museums and art galleries must learn how to draw the public to them as willingly and regularly as it now flocks to cinemas and fun-fairs.*'

I commented on this in *Museum* (published by UNESCO 1951) saying:

'There are still quite a number of museum authorities who think this is going much too far. They would argue that in such a hypothesis there is confusion of thought and a more or less complete misapprehension concerning the function of galleries and museums. It is not part of our business, we have been told, to provide light entertainment, or if it is, the part is relatively unimportant and must not be looked upon as more than a gesture to critics who are, on any count, interfering nuisances.

In Glasgow, through observation and experience, we reached the same conclusions as many of our colleagues, viz. that a civic enterprise which professes to serve a public need must adopt every reasonable and effective method to make the public aware of its possessions and to persuade that public to take the proper steps towards a full measure of enjoyment. As we began to examine and operate various ideas and schemes – mostly adapted if not blatantly purloined from energetic and capable gallery directors at home and abroad – we found that the apparent results fell short of expectations. It then became clear that in the matter of public relations we were relying too much on spasmodic efforts and unimaginative forms of publicity. In showmanship we were amateurs, and, excluding the benefits of experience, we still remain amateurs.'

We have not departed from the conviction that public response is as important as the collecting, conservation and presentation of art treasures. If, as was asserted by a speaker at the last Museum Conference I was able to attend, museums are attracting only about six per cent of the citizenry, the problem is real enough. One step towards a solution might be to open our door in the evenings for organised 'performances'. That means a switch in the direction of spending national and local government funds.

13

American Roundabout

On 8th September 1949 I sent this letter to the Town Clerk:

Dear Sir,

Application by Director for leave of absence
to visit USA and Canada

For some time past, I have been receiving invitations to visit certain galleries and museums in USA and Canada. At the same time I have long thought that an inspection of recent developments, particularly with regard to education, display and publicity in gallery work, would be of incalculable value.

Conversations with representatives of the Rockefeller Foundation have resulted in the offer of a generous grant towards the expenses of such a visit of investigation. Lecture fees, etc., would augment the amount of such a grant, but I am anxious to keep such engagements to a minimum so as to be able to concentrate on the study of new methods.

I am of the opinion that with the 1951 Festival and the architectural aspects of the Burrell Collection in view, a knowledge of American enterprises is of importance.

I am prepared to meet any expenses in excess of the amount covered by the Rockefeller Foundation grant and any fees.

On my return I would submit to the Corporation a complete report with appropriate comments and recommendations.

I therefore apply to the Corporation for the necessary leave of absence, and I calculate, with the tentative itinerary in mind that a period of not less than two months is necessary.

I was never able to discover who had recommended me to the Rockefeller Foundation, but I had some grounds for suspecting my friends at the University, notably the Principal.

Trenchard Cox, then at Birmingham, later in command at the

Victoria and Albert Museum, with a knighthood, was at the time
planning a visit to the USA. We exchanged notes. The Birmingham
Corporation had agreed to pay all his expenses, less the amount of
any fees he might earn. My worthy masters made rather heavy
weather over my application. Was this not the kind of visit to be
undertaken by a Councillor? There appeared to be some difficulty
in understanding why the Rockefeller Foundation should want to
spend money on me. Eventually, on the motion of Councillor Robert
Gray, the prominent Scottish Nationalist, friend and supporter of
John MacCormack (King John) whom I later succeeded as Rector of
Glasgow University, I was officially granted three months' leave. For
economic reasons I adhered to the two months.

It was altogether a most varied and unusual kind of tour. I think
I got from it all that was possible. I brought back a full report, with
a great bunch of photographs and an abundance of literature. We
arranged an evening in the Gallery to which the Council and
interested officials were invited to have a cup of tea, to inspect the
display and to ask any questions. It was not a success. Very few
turned up. It looked as if I had committed a grave error of judgment.

I think it was at this time I sensed that my star, corporation-wise,
was in the descendent. My journalist friends must have been over-
doing the personal build up and I was beginning to topple.

I have read a great number of books by English and Scottish
travellers and writers who have visited America. Something seems
to have gone wrong with the contact lenses and auditory aids of
most of them. My favourite is Sir Denis Brogan. As a Glasgow man
he is an authority on the Irish anywhere. He has been to the places
I know or have seen, from the Players Club in New York's Gramercy
Park to what is left of the Barbary Coast in San Francisco – and many
more of these kind of places. He knows how to extract their essence.
Besides, I am a Glasgow man myself.

Among the mass of notes, cuttings and 'raw material' I have
brought aboard with me is a review, by Sir Denis, of the second
volume of the Autobiography of Bertrand Russell. He drags me in.

'Not all is sex, marriage, politics. . . . His academic career in
America was chequered. He quarrelled with the famous or
notorious Dr Barnes, a quarrel on which Dr T. J. Honeyman
could comment usefully, especially on the real merits of Argyrol.
Appointed to a chair in one of the New York city colleges he was

driven out of it by one of these excessively virtuous Irish-American legal politicians who disagree with the dictum of the new Prime Minister of Canada that government should stay out of the bedrooms of the nation.'

It was in New York in the early thirties that I first became interested in Art Gallery and Museum administration. I began to meet the Directors and Curators of Art Museums. From them and their publications, and the journals of their professional associations I was made aware of a different approach to the function and purpose of Art Galleries, Institutes, Associations and the like.

In some cases the reliance on private endowments and the apparent ready availability of funds for various activities – acquisitions, education and administration – were to me, a revelation. For the first time I heard of 'public relations' in museum work. There appeared to be a much greater recognition of the desirability of an 'informed public' among the people who were interested enough to want to visit museums. There was nothing new or remarkable in the practice, but there seemed to be something new in its application. Especially did it seem that the rising generation was given much more consideration than they received in Britain. Some people advised me to take it all *cum grano salis* but I was curious. Something was happening and I ought to look into it, even if I did no more than collect the facts, before reaching a judgment on impressions. In every respect I was a novice.

A well-known London and Paris art dealer, Percy Moore Turner, in 1921 wrote a book *Appreciation of Painting*. As a small introduction to a large theme I found it very helpful. Turner has been acknowledged – somewhat grudgingly I think – as the man who, as adviser to Samuel Courtauld, played a big part in the growth and development of that famous collection. I got to know him very well. He was the source of some very valuable information in my earlier days in Glasgow. His was the first donation when we created the Glasgow Art Gallery and Museums Association. I remember him for two things. The last sentence of his book, when speaking of those who buy for public collections, 'It is useless to look for any improvement till the men who control these galleries recognise that the appreciation of art is at least as highly specialized a matter as the conduct of their own businesses.' And it was from him that I first heard of Dr Barnes of Philadelphia. He quoted Barnes who had said, 'Barring the few congenitally great aesthetes it is more laborious to learn to recognise quality in a painting than to write a popular novel.' It was written in 1915. It struck me as an odd comment.

Then I paid my first visit to the Barnes Foundation and met Dr Albert C. Barnes. His phenomenal collection of paintings and his experiments in art and education were conversational currency. I also knew that throughout the twenties he was a regular visitor to Europe and seldom returned home without having added two or three more important pictures to the collection. It was made clear to us that we should think ourselves very fortunate in being invited to visit the place at all. We have never ceased to be grateful for many pleasant hours and for the gracious hospitality extended to us by Dr and Mrs Barnes on several occasions.

I admit that I looked forward to the first visit with a considerable amount of apprehension. Bignou, our French colleague, had created such a fantastic picture of the formidable Dr Barnes that I thought, maybe, I should enter the portals on tiptoe. There he was – Dr Barnes – a distinguished looking middle-aged man but probably looking younger than his years, balancing himself on two legs of a chair with his back to a window beyond which was an extensive garden. On the wall in front of him was the most amazing group of first-class examples of Cézanne, Renoir and others of the French School. He was smoking a cigar. After formal introductions I produced a cigarette case with the intention of lighting up, but a signal from Bignou made me hurriedly restore it to my pocket. A whisper indicated that only the Doctor smoked. I wandered around by myself for a while to give Bignou a chance to discuss some business relevant to pictures. In the interval the background of my career had obviously been discussed, for when the Doctor joined me he seemed more interested in my medical associations with Glasgow. He had recollections of his one and only visit to the city and his account of it was very entertaining. Some years later he sent me a detailed memorandum on his Glasgow experience. As a comment on the Scottish Sabbath, the Salvation Army and the solace of whisky, it reached the heights of super-realism.

Dr Barnes was a distinguished pharmacologist and his considerable fortune was the outcome of his discovery, or invention, of the antiseptic Argyrol – a silver nitrate preparation with multiple uses and universally distributed. In his earlier student days he had come into contact with and formed a great regard for one of my teachers,

Professor Ralph Stockman, who was for many years a well-beloved figure in the Medical Faculty of Glasgow University.

I have often thought that Dr Barnes's friendliness to myself in particular, was due more to our common bond in medicine than to our common interest in paintings. Nevertheless, I am rather proud of his inscription on the fly leaf of the presentation copy of his book *The Art in Painting*. It runs thus: 'To my friend, T. J. Honeyman, in recognition of his efficient ambassadorship for good pictures in Great Britain'.

On this, my very first visit to the Foundation, I had the good fortune to find Dr Barnes in a most communicative mood. For over two hours he sustained a running commentary on the collection of pictures which amazed me more and more as we went from one gallery to another. At this time his observations struck me as being the most original I had ever heard. The history, and the incidents associated with the acquisition of some of the most notable exhibits were told in a forthright, positive manner, lightened up every now and then by an entertaining anecdote. Obviously, he was proud of his achievement. Probably the most gracious act of the afternoon was his refusal to put me to any test. This I had dreaded because of what had been allowed to grow up in my mind – a picture of an irascible man, incapable of suffering fools gladly, and known to have shown people to the door if they dropped the slightest pebble, not to mention a brick.

As we walked round the galleries I became very much aware of a longing for a cigarette. I said to myself, 'Well, the least you can do is ask permission.' This I did, by saying to the doctor, 'Do you mind if I smoke?' 'Not at all,' he said, 'Have a cigar.' Until then my cigar smoking had been very, very occasional and it may be the merest of coincidences, but from that day I became rather addicted to the habit.

From time to time I give up smoking – chiefly as an exercise in self-discipline. I have not smoked cigarettes for nearly thirty years and I stopped the pipe when, once in Switzerland, I failed to get a tobacco I could enjoy. In America I acquired a taste for the cheaper brand of cigars, the aroma of which disgusted my friends. 'Put away that "toofor" and have a real smoke,' they would say, handing me a choice Havana. It was quite a time before I discovered that 'toofor' was an abbreviation of 'two for a dime'. With cigars in Britain priced beyond the range of 'it doesn't matter', we have been able to create another family wisecrack. 'Dad enjoys indulging in the vice of smoking a good cigar but he does not commit the sin of buying them.' Blessings on my friends who, on their visits to America, remember my drug store cigar-counter weakness and act accordingly.

As the afternoon wore on we were joined by Cath and some others who had been entertained by Mrs Barnes. At 5.30 sharp we all adjourned to the house where the conventions of high-balls and soda were faithfully carried through. An abundance of soft drinks was there for those who preferred it. With great deliberation whisky and soda were measured out with care; but as the evening proceeded it was obvious that the measuring business was beginning to fade out into an unnecessary interruption. Repetitions were done with the eye or the fingers as the standard for assessing quantities.

Conversation at the Foundation was always stimulating. For me particularly it was a valuable education to hear of the inner workings of picture exchanges, purchases, gifts etc. From time to time I have met a number of people who have envied me the chances which came my way, especially the visits to the Barnes Foundation. I know of quite a number who have tried very hard to gain admission. They had failed to discover the right way to go about it. Dr Barnes was often criticised for his refusal to open his door to visitors who were obviously interested and held positions which might reasonably be accepted as proof. Some, who assumed that it was just a matter of routine to arrive at the door expecting to be shown round the gallery were handed a ticket. On this it was clearly stated that the Barnes Foundation was not a public gallery. It was an Educational Institution, with a programme for systematic work organised into classes which are held every day and conducted by a staff of experienced teachers. And then it concluded 'Admission to the Gallery is restricted to students enrolled in the classes.'

Dr Barnes had for many years insisted that his collection was for educational purposes. He had tried, in the earlier days, to leave it open and indeed to welcome a great number of students with their teachers. On listening in to the type of instruction being given to these students, he had reached the conclusion that it was all a lamentable waste of time. He did not hesitate to say, no matter how celebrated the professor or lecturer might be, 'You appear to know all about Art, but you do not know the thing itself when you see it.'

Professors and Directors of Art Galleries don't like to be told that they do not know what they are talking about.

Arising out of these excursions and incidents Dr Barnes thought the time was ripe to establish something entirely new in the way of teaching the appreciation of art. Unquestionably, from the moment of my first meeting I was led to become very much more concerned in the questions so often asked, but never completely answered, 'What is Art?' and 'How does one look at pictures?'

I also admit that my interest, once aroused, was increased for reasons that can only be defined as sentimental. First, Dr Barnes's account of his student days and early struggles and his regard for Professor Stockman, as already mentioned. Second, Professor John Dewey, whose portrait by Epstein I remembered. I also remembered his name as the Gifford Lecturer at Edinburgh University in 1929. His subject was quite beyond me – 'The Quest for Certainty'. In a journey between New York and Philadelphia, Dewey told me about Francis Hutcheson of Glasgow University. Until then I had never heard of him. I know a lot about him now, chiefly for his authorship of the first book on aesthetics to appear in Britain. Third, George Santayana – whose philosophical writings, to a lesser extent than those of Dewey, had influenced the Barnes school of thought – had a link with Glasgow. His mother was born there (the explanation is given in an autobiographical volume).

My enthusiasm for the Barnes approach was not shared by a number of people – writers, critics and teachers – I was to meet on subsequent visits to America. Generally I discovered most of them had made valiant, but unavailing, efforts to get into the Foundation. Obviously this had coloured their conclusions and their views had to be somewhat discounted.

I had already been trying to keep abreast of contemporary English writings on aesthetics and like most of my generation, whose loyalties wavered between Roger Fry and Clive Bell, I thought I had uncovered the clay feet of the great John Ruskin. Maybe, as a Glasgow man, I had to be pro-Whistler, as I was never allowed to forget that 'we' had been the first public body to buy a Whistler painting.

Then I thought, the Courtauld Institute is the place. The start of this great idea had been a bit sticky. W. G. Constable had gone to Boston, where I was to meet him later and enjoy a delightful evening. The Courtauld had announced a series of lectures and I thought these are sure to be up to date. I attended one and found myself sitting beside Herbert Read. We were both very disappointed, feeling as if we had slipped into the history class of a boys' school. Then, in the course of reviewing a book *The Works of Man* by Leslie March Phillips, I came across the passage in the Introduction by Herbert Read:

'Good Art Criticism is rare in England. We have had Reynolds and Ruskin and today we have Mr Berenson and Mr Roger Fry. But there has been no real tradition in the criticism of Art at once well informed and vigorous and restricted to its proper sphere. The result has been disastrous for the general reputation of English art, especially abroad. . . . The weakness of English Art Criticism has been due to two causes: to the low place which the visual arts have occupied in a puritanical scale of values, and to an innate English inability to philosophise about an abstract quality like beauty.'

Whether all this new-found interest in 'Art and Education' was of any use to me in my job of selling works of art is open to question. I had to regard it as a side-line. It was by way of being my hobby: but as it turned out, my efforts to find out what was happening in universities and colleges was going to save me a lot of trouble some years later.

One thing was clear, the training technique evolved in the Barnes Foundation was not yet sufficiently known or appreciated in Britain. It may be that Dr Barnes had so surrounded himself with controversy that the value of his methodical approach had been overlooked, or written off as negligible. His argument, in a nutshell, was this:

'What has made the study of science valuable and fruitful is *method* and without a corresponding method of learning to see and hear, the study of painting and music can lead only to futility. In the realm of the arts, seeing and hearing are activities which must be learned; they are not things which we all do naturally as we breathe. Similarly, the development of taste in the arts must not be regarded as something left to chance.'

The question I kept posing, without finding the answer, was 'Where do we get the teaching?'

During the war, when I sustained contact with Dr Barnes through the exchange of letters, he elaborated a little on the aims and methods of his educational programme. This was at the time when Bertrand Russell had, according to Dr Barnes, failed to fulfil the letter and spirit of a contract accepted by him. This was apparently a Barnes rescue operation when Professor Russell's appointment as Professor of Philosophy in New York had been unjustly terminated. The conflict was said to be between Bertrand Russell's autocratic and authoritarian attitude towards life and the democratic and scientific attitude on which the Foundation's programme had always been based. The match which set the fire alight appears to have been the fiery-headed Lady Russell. She attended the lectures and sat in a back seat, and improved the shining hour by knitting some ill-defined garment. The noise of her knitting needles disturbed the class. Barnes insisted that her presence was not part of the contract. The affair went to court and Lord Russell won. The doctor may have got some satisfaction from the further proof of the uncertainties of law and justice. There was more to it than that but, while it would be very interesting to give a full account of the clash between two powerful personalities, it belongs to another time and place.

It was again emphasised by Dr Barnes that his aim was to apply the fundamentals of the philosophy of John Dewey to Education. This implied that the prevailing academic methods of instruction are misdirected from the very beginning. 'What the student needs to know is not how men of genius produced immortal masterpieces long ago, but how in the world that his own eyes show him, he can discover more and more of what lends colour and zest to what he does from day to day. The masterpieces have their indispensable function, but it is this function of guiding and training the student's own perception, not of standing in remote isolation as objects of worship or occasion for gush.'

It seems now that I ought to have been more on my guard against this all-embracing conception of art. Susanne K. Langer, another American critic-philosopher, whose *Philosophy in a New Key* was presented to me in California (1950), a few years ago published ten lectures on the *Problems of Art*. In one of them she asserts that it was not Barnes who was influenced by Dewey. It was the other way round 'since in fact he (Dewey) was influenced – enlightened, but also deeply confused – by Barnes.' I beg leave to doubt it!!

Often, when I began to talk about Barnes and his work I was dismissed as a crank. This did not worry me very much for it soon dawned on me that I knew more about Albert C. Barnes and the Foundation than anybody else in this country. Oddly enough, I got to know the man as distinct from the controversialist in the course of an amazing day in London. Following an exhausting round of galleries I took him to see Ralph Richardson in *The Amazing Dr Clitterhouse*. He did not enjoy it. 'Why does a good actor squander his time and talent on mediocre material?' From there he went on to entertain me with his views on the rogues and vagabonds in medicine and art he had known and admired. A never-to-be-forgotten day with 'The Amazing Dr Barnes'.

The outbreak of war, in September 1939, did not stop everything and after I had got settled down in Glasgow I again got in touch with him. There was, of course, an ulterior motive. I had been told that the Civic authorities in their new outlook on art had arranged a closer link between Town and Gown. In point of fact, I was misled, but the discovery came later. Here are some extracts from Dr Barnes's correspondence, which reflect better than anything I could write something of the man and his views.

31st July 1940

'I am delighted to hear from you and to learn that your new job is not only interesting but promising of good results for the future. Your possible tie-up with the university is particularly interesting because it will probably be more productive of real progress than the usual approaches to the general public.

It goes without saying that any service I can be to you will be cheerfully rendered. Of course you may use the questionnaire in the first edition of *The Art of Painting*. It was devised by a former assistant, Dr Thomas Munro, for use in his particular classes. We did not continue to use it because I thought its tendency would be to mechanise the principles expounded in the book instead of applying each principle in particular instances. It may be, however, that it would be useful in your case, especially since you do not have around you so many modern paintings as we have at the Foundation.'

Due to the war, letters became fewer but we exchanged greetings and publications regularly. The following long letter is by way of being a reply to a request for information. The University had begun to examine the possibility of creating a History of Fine Art department. The Court did me the honour of co-opting me as a member of a Committee of Investigation. In addition to the obvious course of finding out the procedure and practice in other British universities, I suggested that German and American universities were ahead of us

in the matter, and that it might be worth while looking into it.
It was hinted by someone who knew the American scene, that the
Barnes Foundation methods and its publications were not highly
esteemed. So! The date is 17th June 1948.

'It was good to hear from you again and to learn that you are on
the way to doing something worthwhile for the University.

Your letter asks for "a list of the academies and universities
which use your publications" but I think it would be easier to give
you a list of those that do *not* use them. Fourteen years ago we had
a fight with the fossils in the art world and the case was taken into
court. At that time, as a witness, I produced original orders and
documents which showed that my book *The Art in Painting* was
used in 110 universities and colleges. Since that time the number
has probably doubled, but since they order from book-stores, we
have no way of checking it.

It is safe to say that in every worthwhile American university
and college our books are used as texts. In the universities of
California and of the State of Washington, for example, young
people who were trained by us not only carry out our methods of
teaching but control the whole situation, which was formerly in
the hands of people trained either in the German universities or
in those of America where they mistake photographs or book
statements as adequate to teach understanding and appreciation
of art.

If your university is really seriously interested in putting our
method into practice, I have a suggestion to make that will not
only enable you to accomplish it, but to do something that no
university in Great Britain or on the Continent does. My suggestion is simply for you to send a young man in the late twenties and
let him take our courses for two years. If he had not been spoiled
by what has been taught him in art schools, has a naturally good
mind and is diligent, he could bring about a revolution in Glasgow,
providing he has sufficient old and modern masters to use in
the demonstration of the ideas and methods. We have been doing
this now for many years, and scattered all over America men
and women trained by us have brought about a change for the
better.

I want to add a note about your Scottish Art Review, which we
read with interest every time it arrives. I can truthfully say that

it is much better than most art journals and appears to me to be a step in the right direction.'

Sincerely yours,
Albert C. Barnes

Dr Barnes never got to Glasgow again, as he had hoped, to repeat the experiences of his first visit. He was killed in a motor smash in 1951, the same violent end met by Vollard a few years before.

I have been in Philadelphia twice since then. The collection of paintings struck me as more remarkable than ever, but the atmosphere of the place was different without the extraordinary mixture, the man who made it. As with an artist, his creation has been given a separate life. The doors are not now so rigidly closed. One day, the true and complete account of a unique enterprise will be written. We are supposed to believe in taking a man as we find him. Barnes was, for me, original and worth listening to, with some qualities one could hardly define as admirable.

I must quote Sir Kenneth Clark from his introduction to 'Great Private Collections'.

'Dr Barnes and Sir William Burrell, two of the greatest collectors whom I have ever known would tell with relish hair-raising stories of how they had watched at the bedside of dying widows or paid monthly calls on poor clergymen, in order to get their teeth into some delicate morsel.'

This is contrary to my experience and I also knew both collectors very well. They were eccentric, each in his own peculiar way, and in their 'off' moments they could be entertaining and always informative. I never sensed anything Frankenstein about them although I do not think either of them knew much about the art of living. I met Sir Kenneth a few weeks before I left home on this voyage. He had become Lord Clark. Somehow or other the subject of Barnes and Burrell crept into our conversation. He had not changed his mind. Of both these illustrious collectors of art he insisted 'They were monsters'.

When I arrived in New York on my 1950 tour of art galleries, museums and universities in the USA I had, in addition to the Rockefeller Foundation welcome, the pleasure of meeting some very helpful people. They were in the British Information Service and the British Travel Association. As an active member of the Scottish Tourist Board and its representative on the BTA it was easy to make use of the facilities and the guidance so freely offered. I got to know James Turbayne, a Scot who continues to be chief leader in the 'Come to Britain' campaign throughout the USA. Like the old advertising wheeze he was as British as the weather but reliable.

The British Information Service seemed to suffer from a variety of ills and frustrations. They received me most kindly and it is perhaps a poor return for their courtesy to have to say that I got more misinformation out of their office than from any other source. I may have struck a bad patch in time. But for years, subsequent to my visit, others, in and out of parliament, have been more critical. I found the British Consular Offices much more useful.

I was on a fact-finding tour but willing at the same time to be of service in explaining and publicising the commendable features in our way of living. Later I became aware of the disturbing fact that some institutions were fed up with the English lecturers thrust on them. The BIS had been landed with the wrong people.

They put me off the English Speaking Union. It was only when my tour was half completed I discovered the ESU was brilliant in supplying me with the best occasions to meet and talk with really informed citizens. I had been briefed by the BIS to present Britain as suffering from post-war malaise, going through a tough time but by no means down and out.

The lighter aspects of this American visit have been recorded in a series of articles which appeared in the *Glasgow Evening News*. The lamented demise of this popular daily was deplored by many who delighted in its up-to-date comments on the Arts. I did not include an account of a radio broadcast in San Francisco. It came back to mind as we sailed out of Oakland three nights ago, when the lights of the Bay and the gloomy darkness of Alcatraz revived more memories.

I had flown south from Seattle with a stop at Portland to be met by a beautiful member of the British Consulate staff. I saw her again not so long ago. Following a distinguished career in diplomacy she is now Executive Director of the English Speaking Union – Miss Kathleen Graham, CBE. They had arranged for my inclusion in *Mrs Trumbell's Lunch Hour Talk* a kind of *In Town Tonight* programme, a feature of the early BBC days. We were given lunch at the Top of The Mark with its panoramic view of San Francisco and then 'on the air'. I remember some of my fellow-guests: The Medical Officer of Health 'selling' a Red Cross week; Mr Thomas, a distinguished politician, perpetual Socialist Candidate for the Presidency; Miss Mindy Carson whom I was to see playing the lead in *Mary* years later in New York and the magnetic 'Carmen', due to sing in that night's Opera. Mrs Trumbell started with me by saying, after a most flattering introduction, something like this: 'My name, before I was married, was Macdonald, but I have never been to Scotland. You are a member of the Scottish Tourist Board. What would be the first thing you would show me?' Now Mrs T. was a very attractive blonde, full of charm and with a lovely voice. The radio audience must have appreciated all this and I was getting a whiff of it across the table. It flashed into my mind to reply, 'Well, for the sake of domestic peace the first thing I would show you would be my wife.' It won a laugh all round and the nervousness disappeared from all of us.

When reporting this at home no one would believe I had the nerve to perpetrate a wisecrack like this on the radio. Weeks later, out of the blue, came a recording of the programme. It is still used as evidence against me – particularly the tail-piece. In reply to a final question, 'Have you enjoyed your visit to the US?' I replied, 'It has been a wonderful experience. Everything I have seen and heard has been of *inestimable value.*' It seems I say the last two words with some sort of peculiar emphasis. The phrase is now a family legend and I no longer bring it into use except by way of defiance.

One other sequel to this celebrated broadcast was more immediate and was a fine demonstration of the value of the radio as an advertising medium. I had been engaged to speak at an English Speaking Union tea-party. I forget the name of the hostess but I remember it was the first time I had seen on a card of invitation 'Mrs So-and-so will pour'. When we reached a lovely home in a fashionable part of the town there was an unusually large crowd – much to the surprise, but not the discomfiture, of the hostess. She had been inundated by telephone calls all afternoon. Evidently my broadcasting effort had been listened to by a number of exiled Scots and their families or other curious people. Anyhow, I addressed a large audience, inside and outside the house, from a stance at the corner of a large french window. My theme was Glasgow's Art Collection, the Burrell Gift, and the present state of affairs in Britain. Afterwards a tall, fine-looking gentleman, who told me he was the husband of a niece of Dr Leonard Gow the well-known Glasgow ship-owner, paid me a fine compliment in a sentence.

'My dear sir, you have done your country a great service this day –
much more than you are ever likely to know.'

The details of visits to universities, art galleries and museums –
inspecting the outsides and the insides – with Glasgow's future
planning in mind, have been recorded elsewhere. I retain the
photographs. Many of them would now be regarded as out of date
by American standards: but, alas, still up to date by ours.

Towards the end of the tour I came to Cincinatti. At a dinner
party I sat beside an elegant sun-bronzed young lady. Her first comment, on discovering where I belong, was, 'Goodness! Not more
Glasgow.' She explained, 'I have just come from Miami. Last night
we were entertained by Danny Kaye. His entire act was about
Glasgow – the greatest city on earth! How wonderful was his
reception! There was a Sir somebody (I filled that gap – Sir Alex. B.
King). Oh yes, and there was the great Sir Harry Lauder. He
finished by singing Lauder songs – one with a peculiar title.'
I suggested 'A Wee Deoch an Dorus' and I was right.

I have been back in the USA several times since. I think I have
made good use of every opportunity to 'tell the world' about
Scotland, Glasgow, the University and the Art Collections which
we have the good fortune to possess. I can never forget the occasions
in Chicago, Detroit and New York when I was the favoured guest of
the St Andrew's Societies. The New York banquet stands out for
several reasons. The Reverend Doctor George Docherty, Minister
of the New York Avenue Church in Washington, DC and myself,
two Glasgow men 'doing the honours' of an amazing evening. The
Master in command of the affair was Col John MacGregor. His
passionate aim was to create exchange scholarships for young Scots
graduates to spend a year at an American university and vice-versa.
Apart from the distinction of being elected an honorary member, an
additional reward for my contribution to the Society's history was
the privilege of nominating several Scottish charities to receive
donations from the President's Fund. – A great chap, this kind,
energetic and generous member of the Clan MacGregor.

An attempt was made several years ago to form an association of
overseas Scottish societies, clubs and associations. It was fostered by
the Tourist Board. A man in Portland, Oregon, asked me, 'What
happened to it? Has it petered out?' I did not know the answers.

14

The Dali Story

The acquisition of the painting 'Christ of St John of the Cross' by Salvador Dali has given rise to a very considerable amount of discussion – relevant and irrelevant, reverent and irreverent. In making this a special Salvador Dali number we are attempting to put on record the facts. These may or may not present sufficient justification for the unanimous decision arrived at by the City Council. Probably the best and ultimately the most coherent judges are still in the nursery.

This was the opening paragraph of our editorial in the *Scottish Art Review* (Summer 1952). The particular issue has long been out of print, and the excitement of having to run three editions of the magazine is fading in the light of sustained controversy.

It all started one day in December 1951 when, as was my custom on visits to London, I looked in to see my friends in the Lefevre Gallery. The place was crowded. The chief interest was centred on Dali's large painting of Christ on the Cross. I was strangely moved by it and began immediately to suspect my reactions. To be taken in by a trick is an affront and there is little enough reassurance in observing that others are being fooled at the same time. Thus heading for the detached attitude of the 'experienced observer' I was pulled up by the effect the painting appeared to have on the steady stream of spectators. I got out to try and find some place for a spell of quiet thinking.

The general colour scheme of the painting was faintly reminiscent. An hour later, in the National Gallery, the vague memory was refreshed. *The Virgin of the Rocks* by Leonardo da Vinci must surely have been in Dali's mind. (Later Dali replied to my query on the point with this: 'The analogy to the "Virgin of the Rocks" by Leonardo is very interesting, for it is one of the masterpieces which has stirred me deeply. Nevertheless when I painted my Christ I did not consciously think of Leonardo but of Zurburan.')

The link with Leonardo has been noted by many critics – e.g. James Thrall Soby: 'Dali's recent works also testify that his admiration for Leonardo has not been merely ideological. . . . Leonardo's technical influence on Dali's craftsmanship is in certain cases unmistakable.'

Still puzzled, I returned to the painting and the crowd. My chief difficulty was how to reconcile the theme with Dali's philosophy of art and public utterances as I remembered them. It became clear that I had been out of touch with recent developments and that there was less reason for surprise or doubt concerning Dali's motives or integrity. The painting seemed out of period; a piece of unashamed romanticism in an age of eclectic classicism.

This started an argument with a friend who had pushed his way out of the crowd in my direction. My line of thinking was related to the effect of the association of ideas which was being set up in the mind of the spectator.

What was the purpose, if any, behind Dali's painting? Was it propaganda such as I had observed in the USA and in Italy? Was it satirical? Was the peaceful setting and placidity of the Lake (? Lake of Galilee) a pointer to the 'Prince of Peace' or was it plain sermonising as in the early days of church patronage of the arts, e.g. 'I, If I be lifted up. . . .'?

Somebody afterwards reminded me of Beethoven's letter to Hans Nageli concerning the Mass in B. 'My chief object in the composition of this Grand Mass was to awaken, and deeply impress, religious feelings both in the singers and the hearers.'

Two more questions emerged. May not the content of a picture have an aesthetic value in its own right, apart from the added values given it by the artist in pictorial or formal language? And do we need to bother ourselves with the man concealed behind the artist?

Dali's 'Christ' was an art event, but Glasgow cannot afford to purchase events at fantastic prices. So what about the reasonably priced drawing?

When I got back to Glasgow I telephoned the Convener, my friend Jack Kelly, who was also at this time City Treasurer. Evidently in talking about the drawing my enthusiasm for the painting impressed him. He thought something might be done and this could be the occasion for the City to risk a courageous act, if it were financially possible. There was no harm in having it sent up for inspection. Up till then, over a number of years I had been informed by the Town Clerk that only the interest of the 1901 Exhibition Art Fund was available for art purchases. Bailie Kelly confirmed with the City Chamberlain 'that the Art Fund capital could be drawn upon'.

When the picture was rushed to Glasgow the response of a fair cross-section of the public was much more remarkable than I had seen in London. We had neither time nor the inclination to sort them out into extroverts or introverts. Indeed the range of personal opinions was so extraordinary that I thought, all things considered, we had here an abundance of material for our aestheticians, psychologists and art critics.

To the Sub-Committee appointed to examine and report on the possibility of acquiring this work I proffered all I knew about the artist and his place in contemporary art, especially the so-called advanced school. I had known him and his work for twenty-five years. Recently he had started to concern himself with religious themes. If we got the painting, strong opposition was not unlikely; but with the memory of the Whistler Carlyle episode maybe this was again the time to make a heroic purchase.

To the parent committee I repeated this plus the information that the purchase price would include the copyright. The importance of this was an unknown quantity, but I thought it might well turn out to be a very valuable property. Perhaps the most significant fact in this whole transaction was the unanimity with which the purchase of the picture was recommended, step by step, to the final decision by the Corporation. At no stage was it found necessary to put it to the vote.

It would be a grave omission not to mention three people, without whose aid we might have failed to acquire the painting. A. J. McNeill Reid, head of the Lefevre Gallery, is one. He has in many ways demonstrated his goodwill to Glasgow, especially through important gifts to the Art Collection. Throughout a long friendship, surviving the period when we were partners in business, McNeill has sustained the great tradition established by his father. It was easy to discuss with him Glasgow's interest in the Dali and he went out of his way to co-operate, to the extent among other favours of being satisfied with a very nominal commission for his firm's services.

Georges Keller, Dali's agent in New York, where they both were at the time, was most helpful. He built up for the artist the importance of Glasgow's collection and persuaded Dali to conclude the negotiations before the painting was shown in Madrid and Basle in fulfilment of a previous arrangement. If this had not been done it is more than likely Glasgow would have been confronted with strong competition. We had evidence of widespread increasing interest in the face of growing public reaction, favourable and otherwise.

My first meeting with Georges Keller was in Paris in the spring of 1929. My second meeting was in Glasgow in 1930. It was his first visit to Scotland. Throughout the following years we have often met in Paris, Switzerland and New York. One meeting was in London when I sat beside him at the record-breaking sale at Sotheby's (October 1958). Georges made history, for it was his bids, on behalf of Mr Paul Mellon, which raised the price of paintings by Cézanne and Manet to phenomenal heights. He may not like it, but most of his friends regard him as a three-part mixture: one third the charm of Charles Boyer; one third the wit and perpetual youth of Jack Benny; and the other third his indefinable self. His descriptions of fierce discussions, recollected in tranquillity are poetic – 'I looked him blank in the face'.

The 1930 visit to Scotland was in the nature of an overdue vacation. Georges had two friends with him, and inasmuch as McNeill Reid, Macdonald, Bignou and myself had affairs of business to attend to, I arranged a short motoring trip round the west of Scotland. In a hired car, with a chauffeur, armed with instructions to show our visitors from France the outstanding scenic attractions of Scotland, they set off. They stopped at Helensburgh for lunch, and decided that the appropriate drink must be the wine of the country. It was their first experience of whisky. When the waiter brought them the usual portion they were indignant and pointing to another table, where they were probably drinking beer, by emphatic signs they indicated that they were adults and expected to be treated as such. The waiter saw no reason to offer any guidance and gave them what they wanted. They were certainly impressed by the potency of the 'wine' and concluded that the Scots were a hardy race. They remembered being assisted back into the car, which was so very comfortable. They fell asleep. The day was completed according to schedule, but none of them has yet seen the famous lochs, which are chief among the features of the west coast.

The third person whose assistance one must acknowledge is Margaret Sharkey. She was regarded in the Bignou New York

Gallery as a 'treasure'. We know her as Zue and have many family reasons to be grateful to her and her lovely sister Anne, for an abundance of help and hospitality over a number of years. A honey-haired neatly built young woman, with bright eyes and lips, which, when pursed, promised a sympathetic purr or a devastating explosion of comment on art and artists, Zue Sharkey is now engaged roaming the world in pursuit of artists willing to be persuaded to help in the making of those remarkable Christmas Cards produced by UNICEF. From headquarters at the United Nations she spreads grace and competence in the handling of people and affairs. She knew how to handle friend Salvador Dali. From him she extracted the biographical information and up-to-date material which was of immense help when we had to prepare our special Dali issue of the *Scottish Art Review*.

There is more to it than all that, but these three are part of the 'Dali Story' and I think justify the digression. They are also very much a part of my pre-Glasgow and post-Glasgow Art Gallery activities.

Of course we expected criticism, but not quite the concentrated bitterness or irresponsibility on the matter of purchase price, £8,200. The decision reached by the Corporation was not lightly taken. Glasgow wanted the picture and Glasgow had to pay the price, which, after considerable negotiation, was fixed at the lowest figure acceptable to the artist – the catalogue price had been £12,000. I remember that about the same time a small picture – in an imperfect state – *Christ and the Woman taken in Adultery* by Peter Brueghel was sold in auction for £11,025. Commenting on this Denys Sutton, then art critic of the *Financial Times* and now editor of *The Apollo* magazine, said 'Its price, though high, bears greater relation to its value than the £8,200 paid by Glasgow for a painting by Salvador Dali.' I still wonder who and what determines that. His and similar criticism led me to retort:

'Some years ago a leading gallery in this country paid something like £12,000 for a "genuine" Old Master. It has now been discovered that the "Old Master" is still alive, and the picture now reposes in a basement as a "curio". At least we *know* who painted Dali's picture. Recently a collector paid an even larger sum for another "Old Master" which is a triumph of the art of the restorer. The "hand" of the master is buried in the velvet glove of contemporary pigments. Paint and canvas begin to undergo the perishing processes within a short time after the completion of a painting. By that token we should be able to enjoy "pure" Dali for a much longer time than some other expensive works.'

We also reproduced in the *Art Review* the pre-Raphaelite picture *Christ in the House of His Parents* or *The Carpenter's Shop* by Sir John Millais which, not so many years previously, was bought for £10,500. It is in the Tate Gallery. The vicious contemporary criticism, including a piece by Charles Dickens, was also reprinted with a final comment from William Armstrong.

'Not the faintest attempt is made to discuss the artist's standpoint and to look at the theme from his side.'

The Annual Report of the National Arts Collection Fund (1921) contains a list of subscribers to the appeal for the acquisition of the Millais painting. It includes some well-known Scottish names such as The Earl of Crawford, Mr & Mrs Alex Maitland, D. Y. Cameron, William Burrell, Leonard Gow, J. L. Caw and Arthur Kay.

To the artists, including Augustus John, who deprecated this 'wilful extravagance' and deplored such a 'mad price' for a work by a living painter, we said something like this:

'Extraordinary! Why do they not rejoice that, for once, the artist rather than the collector or dealer or their descendants reaps the benefits from his labour? Salvador Dali is a man with an international reputation. His "news value" is at least as great as that of Picasso and Matisse and he considers this painting of Christ to be his masterpiece.'

A few months later it was reported that an English actor was to receive £40,000 for playing a part in a film.

The events of the art market of the last ten years, related to living painters, make it seem to appear that we had created a precedent.

Stephen Bone of the *Manchester Guardian* in reporting the distribution of works commissioned by the Arts Council said:

'Will any of them reach Glasgow, a city that has just spent many thousand pounds on a surrealist Crucifixion by Salvador Dali that no art critic could take seriously? After this sensational extravagance it may possibly be felt that Glasgow Corporation is a little ill-placed for receiving gifts from the taxpayer, but this would be a short-sighted view. Glasgow may soon feel the need of good modern paintings in its galleries.'

His was more than a short-sighted view, for no gallery in the country had acquired through its own limited purchase funds more modern works than Glasgow. True, like most of the others, we didn't rise very high in sculpture. In recalling some very ill-informed criticism I am provoked into a bit of boasting to support our defence: or is it defiance? In my time and on my recommendation Glasgow acquired, by purchase, *Blackfriars* by Derain for £150 and a Utrillo for £450. Other French paintings by artists such as Cassat, Courbet, Gauguin, Marquet, Monet, Pissarro, Signac and Sisley came through the Hamilton Trust. They do not reveal the purchase price but I know all were between £1,000 and £4,000 at the most. We bought excellent examples of L. S. Lowry (in 1943 for £42, and in 1944 for £135). The works of a number of English and Scottish artists, when they were at the beginning of their careers, were acquired for very little expenditure. We like to think that to the ridiculously small sums might be added the value of an official gesture of support. From the Contemporary Art Society we received some good works, but as we were more distant than our English colleagues the first choices seldom came our way. The Arts Council never favoured us by adding works to the collection.

The Art School, staff and students, were with very few exceptions, particularly against the purchase of the Dali. Some of my University friends were convinced we had made a grievous blunder. 'It will be down in the basement in three years' was the prophecy of one of them. A few had no objections to the acquisition of a work by Dali. After all, he was a leader of a particular movement which was part of art history; but why did we not get a typical surrealist painting instead of this 'non-characteristic' example? One exasperated critic was certain we knew very little or nothing about surrealism. This drew from us the defence of personal recollections.

I was closely associated with Dali's large scale London Exhibition in 1936 (the very first London Show was at the Zwemmer Gallery in 1934). I have Dali's original sketch for the invitation card. This intrigued me. It was a variation of the theme that the mind and body can be analysed into compartments. Here was the mind pictorially represented as a drawer in the cabinet of the brain. And, for the purpose of the exhibition, it was being suggested to the spectator to keep an open mind. That's what I thought. Dali shrugged his shoulders and grinned when I asked him if that was in *his* mind.

There were 29 paintings and 18 drawings in the exhibition. We were introduced to what the philistines described as a rigmarole.

'Snapshots in colour, prompted by Dreams, Phantoms, Images in Half-sleep, Morphological spectres, Lilliputian uneasiness, Paranoiac associations, Caprices within the womb, Malleable watches, Images of concrete irrationally, etc. etc.' For over a month I was able to study these productions daily. We all had a smattering of Freudian psychology, and some of us could almost recite André Breton's preface and Herbert Read's introduction to the New Burlington Exhibition which was on at the same time. This was the exhibition where Dali, speaking from the depths clad in a diver's dress, narrowly escaped asphyxiation.

There is not the slightest doubt that the significance of the 'paranoiac associations' escaped the majority of the visitors to the Lefevre Gallery show. The phallic symbols and hints of abnormal sex preoccupations eluded the understanding of Dali admirers. This is no longer surprising when one recalls how the Lawrence 'experts' had similarly missed the 'hidden' significances in *Lady Chatterley's Lover*.

When surrealism was at its height, in the mid-thirties, it seemed to me, retaining some knowledge of psycho-analysis, that quite a number of the practitioners in surrealism were bogus. Their efforts were little more than pictorial illustrations of mental case histories borrowed from medical literature. It might be argued that Picasso in his 'morphological' period did much the same thing, inspired by text books in Anatomy.

Dali was a detached phenomenon; so detached that his change of front, political as well as pictorial, lost him the friends of the early days. The Christ brought down, on his head and on ours, a mighty volume of rage and indignation.

Although the final purchase of the painting was completed in February (1952), it was not put on show in the Art Gallery until June. (This in accordance with arrangements previously made for exhibiting in Basle and Madrid.) The storm broke out again. Some idea of the extent of it can be gathered from press notices, reports, letters to the editor. The BBC featured a programme in Arts Review, 27th June 1952, in which all the participants, with the exception of Edwin Muir who reserved judgment, damned the painting in the finest collection of sneers ever to come over the air in so short a space of time. An appeal to give a chance for the other side to be presented was made in vain.

When the dust had settled the BBC allowed several references to the painting and I was permitted in the course of a series of broadcasts, 'Look At This', to discuss the Dali at some length. Last year I was invited to take part in a Sunday evening programme to include a dialogue with the Rev. Campbell MacLean. I readily agreed. Then I received this (dated 17th January 1969),

'The proposed interview between yourself and Campbell MacLean has had to be cancelled. The Director is unwilling to let us use the gallery on the double score of blocking off the Dali section and that it ought to be one of his staff who does the talking. We may involve you in a studio discussion but we are not at that stage of the planning yet. Thank you for all your help.'

In January the gallery is usually at its quietest! It is more than likely the present regime has had enough of the Dali and would now like the public to turn its attention to other features. On the other hand I would have seized every chance to put the gallery and its possessions on any publicity medium. And when Guyana produced two stamps (25 cents and 5 cents) to celebrate Easter 1968, featuring Glasgow's painting, I think I would have made a splash on a unique event. It just shows the difference between two schools of thought.

From among the abundance of letters to the editor of the *Glasgow Herald* we enjoyed this one most:

'No one can speak for the majority of the Citizens of Glasgow on the subject of Art, for the majority is not interested. But any sensible man must conclude that those responsible for the purchase of the Dali painting have made a grievous mistake – to say they have been gullible is putting it much too mildly. Dali has done more than exploit a sacred episode. He has shown that he has no regard for the feelings of Art Lovers. Anyone can tell from looking at this painting that the artist must be insincere. To sum up and to prove that I am not biased, let me tell you that until now I never heard of Salvador Dali nor have I seen the picture.'

It occurred to us that one way to meet the charge of wilful and indefensible extravagance was to get busy in testing the public reaction by presenting opportunities for those who were on our side to contribute to the Art Fund. The net receipts for the first six months totalled £3,200.

Up-to-date information can be summarised thus: Over £33,000 has been received by the Corporation in various ways, donations, royalties, sales of reproductions, postcards etc. A great variety of popular and church magazines have published it. In the Spanish, Italian, English and American editions of Bishop Sheen's *Life of Christ* the Dali painting is featured on the cover over the caption 'The most popular Religious Picture of 1960, it illustrates the Fine Art Trade Guild brochure "Pictures & Prints" (1961)'.

Miniature reproductions are sold to religious seminaries all over the world to be used on diplomas, etc. It is often used by churches of different denominations in a variety of charity appeals. The 'Pirates' are legion.

I recollect a great number of sermons with the Dali painting as the text. Among them was one by Father Matthias Bodkin of Dublin. I showed a reprint of it to his brother, Professor Thomas Bodkin. He approved of the sermon, but pretended to be critical of his brother's decision to serve the Church instead of creating a family. There was nobody to continue the family name since Thomas had succeeded only in fathering a bunch of girls. One of them, Mrs Mary Vaughan, settled in Scotland to delight us all with a sweet Irish brogue and all too infrequent journalistic comments on current affairs.

Having acquired the copyright with the original – and Dali was delighted to let us have it, principally because of the over-riding control we would be able to exercise – our problem was to find out an interested maker of prints. To our surprise and delight the Ganymed Press were keen to take on the job. They had already made excellent reproductions of the Matisse, Utrillo and Braque in our collection; but we had imagined a 'popular' religious subject as something unlikely to appeal to them.

Everybody knew the Ganymed Press to be part of the *New Statesman* organisation. In the course of negotiations Managing Director John Roberts invited me one day to the weekly lunch meeting of the celebrated journal. Unaware of my new friend John's sense of humour, I soon found myself acting the role of Daniel. I kept a list of the lions. Chief of the pride was Kingsley Martin, who introduced the subject of the Dali painting with 'I thought it was an odd way to view the Lake District'. Janet Adam Smith welcomed me, for old times' sake, with a reminder of her first art purchase, a Francis Hodgkins drawing made available by me at a bargain price. John Raymond, T. C. Worsley, Benedict Nicolson, were pleasantly and smilingly detached. John Berger, vocally vague, terribly intense, courteously registered unqualified disapproval of Glasgow's recent acquisition. By way of defence I accepted full responsibility. An 'Art Event' was surely part of the process of running an art gallery. Besides, why should we regard our emotional reaction to a work of art as genuine and seemly, and deny the authenticity of the plain man's response? I did not get away with that, but I expressed some surprise that the critics were unconcerned about the amazing effect of the painting on the emotions of the great majority of spectators.

Before we could develop an argument in what I thought were two failings of current art criticism, i.e. having become too political and too strongly partisan, Kingsley Martin intervened with a change of subject. He talked about America and President Truman. A delightful party from which I collected at least one story. The wife of an Australian aborigine had presented her husband with a new boomerang. This confronted him with a dilemma – he couldn't throw the old one away. It kept coming back.

Among the books my wife persuaded me to take as a relief from the main purpose of this voyage is the second volume of Kingsley Martin's autobiography. I have greatly enjoyed it, chiefly because it revives memories of a number of people I encountered when living in the South. Like myself, Kingsley Martin had come to London in 1930 to seek his fortune. He nearly became a professor, and he blames himself for failing to be elected to a Fellowship at one of the Cambridge colleges. 'I had been tactless, conceited, doctrinaire and opinionated'. From our one and only meeting I was left with the conviction that he was still the same. He couldn't help it.

Maynard Keynes, the power behind the throne, figures largely in this volume. His name recalls some early impressions of my London spell. I met several sensitive people, informed buyers of pictures, forming collections of works by the Masters, or for that matter collecting other things – books, illuminated manuscripts, or porcelain. They were most approachable and helpful if asked to interest themselves in young painters who were finding things a bit difficult. Lord Keynes, as he became, and Mr Hindley Smith (one of the first buyers of Renoir) created a fund out of which regular monthly payments were made to three young artists, to allow them to devote all their time to their painting. This was done, anonymously, through Reid & Lefevre. I know because the administration was my special concern. The benefactors are dead but the artists are still living – two of them quite well known.

Dali continued to paint religious subjects. The most notable of

Portrait of Alex Reid by Vincent Van Gogh
Pasteboard 16″× 13″ Signed lower right
Van Gogh painted at least two portraits of Reid. This one probably dates from the
late summer of 1887.

Christ of St John of the Cross by Salvador Dali 1951
Oil on canvas 80⅝″× 45⅝″
When first published in the *Scottish Art Review* in an attempt to counter adverse
criticism we printed two quotations:
Let us not make random judgements on the greatest things – Heraclitus
The true work of Art is but a shadow of the divine perfection – Michelangelo

these, *The Last Supper*, hangs in the National Gallery at Washington. Another is in the New York Metropolitan Museum. None of them appears to have achieved the same popular appeal as *Christ of St John of the Cross*. Distinguished visitors to the Glasgow Gallery, when asked to give their views, are now much more hesitant. They prefer not to take sides in an issue which is not yet dead. For example, when pressed to give an opinion, John Betjeman said 'Let's leave it at "a shrewd buy" shall we?' One friendly enough observer thought a church rather than the Art Gallery was the right place for a picture of this character. He may be right, for the wrong reasons. Carried to the conclusions of his logic, Rembrandt's painting *The Slaughter House* should be hung in the cattle market.

If I were ever asked what I would do with the Dali, I think I would reply on these lines: Put it into circulation as much and as frequently as possible. It was once loaned to an exhibition in Rome, and Dali was not very pleased when Glasgow refused to let it go on to Venice. If any responsible institution wants to organise a retrospective Dali exhibition, especially in America (North and South), let them have it. Eventually, why not make its permanent home in the Cathedral Church of Glasgow? The Minister at the time we got it, the Very Rev. Dr Nevile Davidson, once said 'Glasgow Corporation has made a venture of faith in purchasing a picture. . . . I believe posterity will judge that faith to have been justified.'

I do not regard the Dali painting as the greatest work of art in the Civic Collection. It is a masterpiece of its kind. There are others, in all the schools of painting we are fortunate to possess, which are greater masterpieces, within the pure aim and purpose of pictorial art. Its acquisition stirred up a variety of emotions covering all aspects of love and hatred. It is now becoming an old story, but the end of it is by no means in sight. If Glasgow ever wants to get rid of it I am freely at their service. I know several places where they would like to have it. It might not be immediately feasible, for I note in one of Glasgow's brochures prepared for visitors, the Dali is featured to represent the Art Gallery contents. It has become a tourist attraction.

I have no regrets. Why should I have? I retain the friendship of all concerned in the production and the purchase, notably that of the artist. He continued to address me in scribbled notes and catalogues with sketches depicting me as the Don Quixote of the Museum world tilting a lance at the Establishments.

In the case of Georges Keller the legend of St George and the Dragon is the theme of his sketches.

On several occasions subsequent to Glasgow's acquisition of *Christ of St John of the Cross* I did my utmost to persuade Dali to pay us a visit. It was impossible to nail him to a date, although he never doubted the warmth of the welcome awaiting him. He dislikes travelling, refuses to fly, and Glasgow was too much off his beaten track. Eventually, and this was a few years ago in New York, he said, 'You come to see me in Spain, and I'll come to Glasgow.' The onus was then on me but, as the victim of changing circumstances, I found it difficult to fix a mutually convenient time. Out of the blue, a few years ago came a telegram from Georges Keller 'Can you meet me in Barcelona and we'll go together to visit Dali?'

Our host was in top form. Discussion ranged from the pictures in course of preparation for a New York exhibition, to the problems confronting Art and Science in present international winds of change. It all sounded to me like something very much 'off stage'. There was no audience, excepting G.K. and myself, and therefore no need to put on an act. It was very illuminating and rewarding. One does not often meet a man so well informed on a wide range of subjects. There came back to mind a sentence which seemed to sum up Dali's attitude on the art of painting. 'Art is the Imagination having fun with the Understanding'. When I said something of the kind, Dali responded with 'There is much more to it than that' and, with what was intended as a sigh, he added 'They criticise my interest in religious subjects. I stated my views thirty years ago and I have not changed them.' I checked this later and found that in 1941 in *The Secret Life of Salvador Dali* he wrote:

'Since 1929 I have ceaselessly studied the processes, the discoveries of the special sciences of the last hundred years. It has not been possible to explore all corners of these because of their monstrous specialisation. I have understood their meaning as well as the best – one thing is certain: nothing, absolutely nothing, in the philosophic, aesthetic, morphological, biological or moral discoveries of our epoch denies religion. On the contrary, the architecture of the temple of the special sciences has all its windows open to heaven.'

He was busy on a large canvas to which he gave the sub-title *Homage to Crick & Watson*, and from his conversation one gathered he was up to date in the knowledge of recent drug discoveries on the phenomena of perception.

One thing was clear. Dali is not bothered by the 'Two Cultures'. He insists that Art and Science are not separate human activities. They are always converging towards each other. Each of them is concerned with Truth, and Truth is another name for Beauty. As we were conducted here and there through this rambling house, with its nooks and crannies, and extraordinary objects, each with a history or a purpose – and were to see some of them better in the light of the next day – I began to grasp a little more of Dali's philosophy of art. He may yet pay the promised visit to Glasgow. If and when he does it will be another art event.

15

Memoranda Galore

The best bit of a salmon they say is the middle cut. My second five years at Kelvingrove were not better than the head or tail-piece, but I think they were busier. Although at times I have dashed away from the main course of this narrative, with accounts of other activities, I was never far away or for long from the job I was engaged to do.

It might appear as if I did not have very much spare time. As with others, family life had undergone profound changes. Two of ours were in the forces and the youngest on the point of graduating in Medicine. Our home, although some distance away, was in some respects an annexe to the Gallery. My wife with her church background knew all about having to act as an unpaid assistant. Throughout the war years, hospitality was often on the pot-luck basis, but she worked marvels on short notice.

Many of our visitors were in Glasgow in charge of the numerous touring exhibitions which continued to be among our attractions. Both they and we found many advantages and more comfort in talking about interesting things and people round a fireside. We got to know each other better and as a result I think we helped to make the exhibitions more successful.

In 1945, of the twelve special exhibitions we were hosts to nine. The others, such as the Victor Cumming Collection of Silver, the McInnes Collection, and Art in the Day School, originated with us. 'American Architecture', 'Meet Canada', 'Modern Brazilian Paint-int', 'Soviet Graphic Art', 'French Book Illustrations' helped us all to think internationally. Through these shows we were also fortunate in meeting some very delightful and informed people, many of whom continued, through correspondence and literature, to keep us up to date with developments in other countries. The publications received from other galleries were often of great service. Some we blatantly imitated or adapted in an effort to improve the appearance and character of our own catalogues, invitation cards, etc. Sometimes we tried to be original, later to be flattered with the evidence of reciprocal action.

From an attendance and general excitement viewpoint the two most notable exhibitions were 'Picasso-Matisse', early in 1946, and the 'Van Gogh' in 1948. Both of these were sponsored by the Arts Council. They gave rise to the unusual sight of queues round the building lined up for admission.

We had benefited greatly in the way of advance publicity from the reports of public response when shown at the Tate Gallery. The Glasgow press was, as always, most helpful and took from us articles or inspired gossip paragraphs. The results went well beyond our expectations. The Glasgow public is not usually prone to purchasing art exhibition catalogues. On both occasions we were constantly telephoning or telegraphing Philip James of the Art Council, 'More catalogues. Situation is desperate. More catalogues.' During the Picasso-Matisse Show we ran out completely. In a great hurry, and to bridge the gap, we cyclostyled a list of the pictures on view, with as much data as could be squeezed in. It went against the grain to give the sheets away for nothing. This is said to be a Scottish characteristic, but I know it is universal. We charged 2d. The customers raised no objection. They seemed to be sympathetic over our dilemma and grateful for the makeshift. We were rather pleased with ourselves on this indirect contribution to the expenses.

Alas! We had not gone about it the right way. This was a transaction involving finance, not to mention policy. The City Chamberlain's department also took a dim view over our failure to check the number of cyclostyled sheets before entrusting them to the staff for sale. I could only plead an emergency and preoccupation with affairs, which left no time to entertain doubts about the honesty of reliable members of the staff with long and faithful service. Was it not apparent to authority, I argued, that we had got in some money instead of paying it out? At the time I thought the storm in a teacup was fantastic, not to say pathetic. I still think so.

From all the exciting, amusing and rewarding incidents surrounding the Picasso-Matisse Show I select two. Deliberately, and with slight malice aforethought, we had arranged the exhibition so that the visitor had to pass from Matisse to Picasso and then finish up in a gallery containing a selection of our old masters, now safely returned from their war-time hide-outs. It was very interesting to hear a great number of people, when they had reached the end of their tour, say something like this, 'Ah, now, this is what I call art. That modern stuff is just a passing phase. These are the paintings (Dutch, Italian and British) I have always loved and will continue to admire.' We asked many of them, 'When were you last here to see your favourites?' and not infrequently the reply was, 'To be quite honest I haven't been in the Art Gallery for years.' The irrelevancies surrounding Picasso and Matisse could bring people in to see other things. A valuable lesson in showmanship from which we were to profit some time later.

I spent a lot of time – and I think it was well spent – listening to the comments of sincerely curious and interested visitors. Some would say, 'This is very much beyond me, but I feel it is all very vital and I have become more aware of the significance of colour and of – would it be movement?' The classic summing up appeared in the *Glasgow Herald*. I think it came through Alistair Phillips, most enchanting of commentators. In a short paragraph he reported the incident of a man seen running down the steps of the Art Gallery escaping from Picasso and Matisse, muttering 'For God's sake let me out of here. I am beginning to like them.'

The Van Gogh Exhibition was equally memorable but for different reasons. The bulk of our visitors knew what to expect and the surprises were more related to pleasant discoveries. From reproductions and publications Van Gogh was well known. Although I had talked and written plenty about it, very few knew or perhaps cared very much about the link the artist had with Glasgow through Alex Reid. We tried our best in an article in the *Scottish Art Review*. In my case the outstanding value of this particular exhibition which, from the spectator's point of view was more effective than the Picasso Show, lay in its retrospective character. One got the whole range of Van Gogh from his roots upwards. Picasso was too startling a discovery. The sincere and searching art lover, when he comes to an exhibition, like this particular one of Van Gogh drawings and paintings, prefers to do his own thinking. He brings some understanding with him and is probably aware of the profound truth: when one follows another, one is always behind.

Apart from the pleasure of moving around watching and listening to appreciative comments and sensing the excitements generated in large crowds, our visitors from Holland made the occasion memorable. We had Engineer Van Gogh, son of Vincent's brother Theo; Dr Sandberg of the Stedelijk Museum, Amsterdam; Dr Hammacher of the Kröller Müller Collection, at one time situated at the Hague, now at Harskamp, Otterlo, Holland. Incidentally it was in the Kröller Müller in the Hague where (in 1928) I had my first introduction to a collection, as distinct from an isolated painting, of Van Gogh's work.

Some of our Dutch visitors had their ladies with them and we made it our business to show them how hospitable Glasgow could be. Of course, we were delighted when they told us that in this respect we had far excelled London and Birmingham. One thing helped us. Princess Margaret was on a quick visit to Glasgow. In her honour the Lord Provost gave an evening reception and we were permitted to 'gate-crash' our visitors. They were thrilled to note HRH dancing, apparently unconcerned by the terrific crush which seemed likely to engulf her. The Arts Council arranged a lunch party. The Chairman of the Scottish Committee, Dr James Welsh, made it a very happy party. In the course of some kind remarks Dr Sandberg, not very fluent in English, seemed anxious to acknowledge the warmth of their reception at the Art Gallery. Perhaps with the sweetness of my name in mind all he was able to say, pointing at me, was 'He is a lofely man'. Dr Welsh, whose laughter can most appropriately be described as infectious, for many a day teased me with this embarrassing description. The friendship with the Van Goghs and their colleagues has continued throughout the years. We don't see or write to each other so often, but every now and then, out of the blue, comes a greeting or a remembrance of our time together in Glasgow.

Exhibitions apart, the general routine and administration made the days fly. The Art Gallery and Museums Association was progressing satisfactorily. Our forecast that it would ensure good audiences for opening ceremonies, lectures and other kinds of gatherings had proved correct. The *Review* had caught on, in spite of some disastrous experiments towards finding the right kind of cover. Visitors to the city or at the University on other business, were either directed or wanted to come to see what we were doing. References in the Press, south of the border, were often flattering and stimulating. We were especially encouraged by a very generous account of what we were trying to do by Harold Nicolson (later Sir Harold) in the *Spectator*. I must quote him.

'I spent two hours last week in the Glasgow Art Gallery and Museum, and was much impressed by the ingenuity and enterprise devoted to rendering this superb collection part of the community. The present Director is not the type of specialist who believes that pictures can only be appreciated by the expert . . . and the citizens of Glasgow are thus encouraged to regard the Gallery as a proud personal possession and as a source of enlightenment and pleasure.'

He went on to say:

'Perhaps the most striking merit of the Glasgow Art Gallery is that it contains one of the most comprehensive and illuminating collections of French Pictures from Delacroix to Matisse that I have ever seen. . . . Any person wishing to understand the development of nineteenth century French Painting would find in this gallery a succinct summary of the whole movement.'

Naturally, I purred with pleasure when I read this. To me Sir Harold was the first person, outside my own circle of biased friends, to see and understand the two chief points in what I have been bold enough to describe as my mission. I wonder if he remembered the occasion when we scliffed past each other in a London restaurant. I stopped him to say thanks for the friendly boost he had given me. He replied, 'Yes! I got a row over that article. I was told not to forget that we had good galleries in London.'

Talking of the *Spectator* recalls to mind quite the best in the way of a personal boost to come my way. It appeared in the *Daily Record* over the signature of Iain Hamilton. A full column headed 'Glasgow Art Gallery Transformed – He brought it to Life' was generous to the point of embarrassment. Iain Hamilton went on to London to make his mark and to survive the most miserable raw deal ever to be handed out in erratic Fleet Street, when he was Editor of the *Spectator*.

The goodwill and support of the Press were my constant companions. Without them it would have been tough going. Sydney Harrison, then editing the *Scottish Field*, engaged me to do a number of articles on Scottish Artists and complementary themes. He was a tolerant and stimulating 'boss' and helped me greatly to establish a kind of authority on art matters. This was of value in contacts I was keen to develop among our overseas friends.

The late William Power, doyen of Glasgow journalists and an essayist of some distinction, seemed to regard the Art Gallery and what we were doing there as his special concern. Jack House, BBC quiz expert, with a devotion to Glasgow and its citizens which scarcely stops this side of idolatry, was always willing to lend a hand. We differ in some minor public issues – he is an authority on pubs and I lean to coffee-houses – but we are united in our concern for making known the true image of Glasgow and the quality of its people.

The ladies of the Press found a happy hunting ground in the Art Gallery, and how greatly obliged we were for the feature articles or gossip paragraphs. Every time I see or hear Magnus Magnusson on the air I remember this Viking from Iceland taking for himself as his wife the vivacious Mamie Baird with the devastating smile and flair for newsworthy events.

The cartoonists were also on our side, notably Emilio Coia. By way of being an all-rounder, critic, broadcaster and penetrating, kindly recorder of human frailties, he has become a near permanent president of the Art Club. Neither of us is likely to forget his struggling days in the London of the thirties. He once had a show of celebrities in the Lefevre Gallery. At the time he was free-lancing for one of the weekly journals with some original caricatures of prominent personalities. When he later expanded the idea into something like lecture recitals, he demonstrated a remarkable memory for the peculiarities of the features of well-known faces. At the Edinburgh Festival he is one of the annual events, given to the expensive practice of 'spoiling' good tablecloths with brilliant cameos of casual visitors.

I suppose our deliberate efforts at showmanship laid us open to the charge of window-dressing. However, we knew that behind the scenes a solid structure was in process of development. Other things, less reassuring, were also happening behind the scenes. Always ready to acknowledge our debt to others, when the memory is active and reliable, I have frequently confessed to being Scotland's leading plagiarist. I am known to covet the flowers in other people's gardens. In any case, I find comfort in the advice given to my father by a well-beloved schoolmaster, who told him 'When a man says or writes anything he makes it public property. Within the limits of courtesy, help yourself. Besides to copy from one book is plagiarism: to copy from more than one book is research!' (I do not know where this wisecrack may have originated. Recently I saw it credited to the Incredible Mitzners in the USA.) It is, at least, ninety years old. I appear to have put it in circulation again following the first lecture in 1940.

If anyone has prepared more memoranda on a greater number of subjects, I would like to meet and commiserate with him. In course of time, like others, we became weary of the phrase 'post-war planning'. One of the first things to be tackled – it was not peculiar to our department – was the question of official salaries. It appeared that Glasgow was in the unenviable position of paying much less than other comparable cities. The National Association of Local Government officials – N A L G O for short – was very active and persistent on the subject. I think I did something on behalf of my junior colleagues and advanced their interests when I could. In conversation with colleagues in other Corporation Departments I became aware of much exasperation over what they thought were unnecessary delays.   At one time the Town Clerk's Department came under heavy criticism. It could be summed up in a catch-phrase of the period, 'I'm all right Jack'. I remember that the substantial advances there were concluded without any of the irksome – not to say humiliating – publicity which applied to the rest of us. At this time, when very confidential discussions were said to be taking place, relations among the top officials became 'somewhat tense'. To have the responsibility of advising the Conditions of Service Committee could not have been easy going.

The Convener of the Art Galleries Committee at the time was Mrs Helen Gault. At one time a school teacher, she was an ardent member of the Independent Labour Party (I L P) – strongly inclined towards the left. She was one of the few who seemed to enjoy being on the Galleries Committee and when she occupied the chair became very interested in all we were doing. A good speaker who, appearing to be casual about it, made certain she was well briefed. On visits to London – generally once a year to view the Royal Academy and other exhibitions – Bailie Gault enjoyed herself greatly, if somewhat alarmingly to others in the deputation. Suffering from a degree of deafness she was apt to choose the silences in a hotel lounge or in a theatre to ask awkward questions and make penetrating comments on the appearance of passers-by. The pitch and accent, decidedly Scottish, enabled her voice to reach everywhere, and the only person undisturbed by the reactions to them was herself. No convener ever gave me or members of the staff greater support or encouragement. In her efforts to keep up to date or to have ammunition to fight our battles in the secret conclaves of her party, she would generally conclude a cross-examination with 'Give me a

Note of That.' The note had to be a very full memorandum, which often led to another one by way of amplification.

When the senior officials' salaries came under review early in 1946 I was instructed (a) to find out what was the scale in other cities, and (b) to state a reasoned case for a fair remuneration for my job. I tried to make out a case for a 'satisfactory arrangement regarding the repayment of expenses incurred on Corporation business'.

No satisfactory arrangement was ever arrived at. I got some childish, if deplorable satisfaction in sending in claims for 'reimbursement of outlays' in entertaining distinguished visitors, by couching the 'reasons for entertaining' in facetious terms such as 'We tossed to decide who should pay and the Corporation lost'; 'The inadequacy of the Sunday joint at home'. These amused some of the junior members of staff in both departments. One day Jack Kelly, who had become City Treasurer, took me to task on the subject, saying that the City Chamberlain's Department was not amused. In a petulant outburst I asserted that I was finding some consolation in registering my opinion of a body who could insult its senior officials through their petty decisions. I would keep on with it as long as I could think up any more funny accounts and when I had collected enough I might send them to the Press. I never did, and eventually got tired of the game. I know that some of my colleagues shared my views and told me they preferred to forget their expenses rather than suffer the indignity of submitting the kind of claim required by the new regulations. They were probably wiser. I was, it appeared, suffering from a peculiar type of audacity, unbecoming in a corporation official.

There seemed to be a lot of secret meetings. Those of us who were not regular frequenters of the Corridors at the City Chambers were out of touch with the current gossip. Along the main corridor were the doors to a number of Committee Rooms and on the opposite side the Corporation buffet. In and out of these doors came and went councillors and officials. When there was anything exciting or newsworthy in the wind the gentlemen of the Press were there or thereabouts. And they were gentlemen. I do not remember a single occasion when a confidence of mine was ever betrayed. Often I was grateful for an interesting hint, or piece of news which they passed on. Indeed more often from the newspaper representatives than from official sources was I kept informed.

One evening Convener Mrs Gault telephoned me to ask 'Were

your ears burning today? Some very nice things were said about you and the Committee has agreed to raise your salary by £150.' She added that this would have to be confirmed by the Conditions of Service Committee, but she seemed to regard that as more or less a formality. Naturally one was very pleased at this unsolicited gesture of appreciation. And that was that. A fortnight or so later on an early morning train to Oban to inspect some pictures on offer to the Gallery, I opened the morning newspaper to be staggered by a prominent paragraph indicating that an application for an increase of salary from the Art Gallery Director had been refused. The remainder of the journey could not be described as restful or refreshing.

I got home to an atmosphere of depression and impatience. The depression due to some very kind people who did not appreciate that their sympathy failed to banish a sense of humiliation; the impatience due to wondering how I would take it. I didn't take it at all well, and not even the philosophic observations of less disturbed colleagues, 'It's just one of those things!' succeeded in cooling me down. I wondered if the Town Clerk might be persuaded to inform the Press that I had not asked for any increase. His only reaction was to say he was not responsible for how the Press interpreted the Corporation decision, and that I ought to forget about it. I found it impossible to do so, and with unqualified family support I sent in my resignation.

It seemed, at this time, the best way to avoid further disagreements and all round unhappiness. A couple of nights later, and partly to escape the telephone, daughter Margaret and I went to the cinema – the Cosmo. The film was *The Grapes of Wrath*. Nothing more suitable, but the tragedy of it turned into rather unbecoming hilarity. The hero's name was Tommy. He addressed his indomitable mother as 'Ma'. I was now unemployed and Margaret and I decided, if the worst came to the worst, we would go fruit-picking in California.

The resignation, to our discomfort, created a bit of surprise and a spate of sympathetic letters. A leader in the *Glasgow Herald* read like an Obituary Notice. Of the letters some will long be remembered. For example, Stanley Cursiter in writing, not to me, but to the Lord Provost, paid tribute to his opposite number, so to speak, in very cordial appreciation of the kind of thing I was doing for art in Scotland.

From the National Gallery in Edinburgh to the Art Gallery in Glasgow the distance often seems to exceed the distance between the two cities. In my time Stanley Cursiter narrowed it down almost to the point of disappearance. The friendship formed in the course of mutual efforts on behalf of art and artists has persisted. Perhaps one bond which unites us is the awareness of occasions when each of us has been shabbily treated. We separate in our responses. He takes it in his stride and suffers in silence. I make a song and dance about it and want to tell the whole world. Incidentally, it is a pleasure to report that, in my time, the relationship between the National Galleries in Scotland and England were more cordial than they had ever been previously. This is very important if mutual help and understanding are to be sustained.

Sir William Burrell, at length to the Convener, brief to me: 'My advice is meet them half-way or more'; 'Now is the time to put right the 814 pin-pricks.' (I never have discovered what he meant by the 814.)

Dr James McCallum, the donor of the unique Print Collection to the University, begged me to pipe down on the 'artistic temperament' and was sure nobody wanted me to go.

When Sir Hector McNeill, the Lord Provost, came to the Gallery following up what he had written, 'to see if something could be done to avoid your leaving the Corporation service' I was very greatly, and I hope humbly impressed. I was even more so when he brought Dr Welsh with him. As the preceding Lord Provost, James Welsh was highly respected as the elder statesman of the Labour group in the Corporation. I had good reason to believe that in joining Sir Hector he was acting in defiance of the group's attitude towards my rebellious 'publicity stunt'. What could one do in the face of such a friendly and sympathetic gesture by two of our leading citizens. It may be remembered that Sir Hector was sometimes spoken of as big Hector to distinguish him from the MP Hector McNeill, whose brilliant career was prematurely cut short by his untimely death in New York. He was on his way to the United Nations Assembly, where he had earlier made his mark in dialectic combat with the Russians.

When Sir Hector quizzed me on what was behind this particular antic I took the chance to clear the misconceptions which had been aired in letters to the Press. My resignation had nothing whatever to do with the refusal of my Committee's recommendation regarding salary. I had written the reasons on a scrap of paper, which I read and gave to him. They were:

1) A protest against the Corporation's method in dealing with adverse announcements regarding officials' salaries, i.e. the apparent disregard of the individual's feelings and that of his family in the resultant publicity.

2) A protest against the methods by which the present decision was arrived at.

3) My failure to succeed in convincing the Corporation that the Art Galleries job is or should be the biggest job of its kind outside of London. I have succeeded apparently in convincing the Art Galleries Committee but the Corporation and some of my senior colleagues evidently do not regard this municipal enterprise as of any great importance.

Sir Hector allowed me to quote chapter and verse. He then expressed agreement with much of what I had to say, and he concluded by asking me to withdraw my letter of resignation. My irritations were not of the incurable sort and he was sure happier times and greater successes lay ahead. He would put his request in writing that very day. This he did a few hours later. Following a family palaver and a decision to try again I withdrew my resignation.

It would be pleasing to be able to record that from then on everything in the garden was lovely and that thereafter we all lived happily together. But it would not be true.

It gave Hugh McDiarmid a chance to have a smack at Bridie and me. His comment was 'The two most recent disasters to afflict Scotland have been the withdrawal of Honeyman's resignation and the return of James Bridie from America.' (Bridie had set out for a spell of writing for films in Hollywood but returned after one week in New York.)

The incident left me with a mixture of regrets balanced by the knowledge of an abundance of goodwill. It taught me a number of things. As a local government official one must never on any account take a stand for a principle – only City Councillors and Magistrates are supposed to do that. The correct behaviour is to show an easy tolerance for all things and never, never demonstrate enthusiasm for anything. If you can't help feeling it, you must do your utmost to suppress it. Above all, why should an official expect to understand the peculiar procedures of central authority? Isn't he paid not to understand it? And if he tries to be independent he will only succeed in becoming unbearable. I had another go at this kind of reasoning a month after I had *finally* reached the point of departure. The occasion was my installation as Rector of the University, when in the course of a Rectorial Address *The Clear Horizon* I said:

'A city or nation which ignores or silences or intimidates men who have something fresh and original to contribute will become second-rate. It will be unimaginative in its social legislation and administration. It will waste emotion and throw enthusiasm away.'

I tried to balance all this by adding:

'It is conceivable that some of you are toying with the idea of political service. May I counsel you to give some thought to the service of the city. Whatever you may have been led to think to the contrary, those who have taken upon themselves the government of our cities have a respect for men who have had the privilege of a University education. If I am wrong, it is certain that the fault lies in ourselves.'

The resignation interlude was over, but the further outlook continued to be unsettled. I got back to the job, interrupted every now and then to pursue the pastime of preparing more memoranda. In many of these repetition seemed to be the soul of business. One of them got me into more trouble.

When A. B. Mackay became Convener we had a look together at the past and the present situation in Glasgow's efforts to make the citizens interested in the Arts – all of them. A.B., retired from long and notable service in The Glasgow Savings Bank, was an idealist. An admirable chairman at lectures and public occasions in the Gallery, he was well informed and keenly interested in art and artists. He approached every issue methodically, and although not always agreeing, once persuaded a certain course was the right one to follow he was unwavering in his efforts to persuade the party leaders to lend support – without, as it invariably turned out, much success. The chief reason why he eventually retired from the Town Council was, I am sure, because of a sense of incompatibility. He found it more congenial to advance the cause of the United Nations Association in the West of Scotland.

At this time both parties in the Council were very much concerned with propaganda. They followed the current fashion by defining every project as 'post-war planning'. They had to re-state the party programme and present to the voters a design for future living and prosperity. Stemming from this Bailie Mackay asked me to provide information and suggestions on a number of points. My first effort took this form —

MEMORANDUM ON FUTURE DEVELOPMENTS OF
ART ACTIVITIES IN GLASGOW

General. Following government lead, and increased powers conferred on local authorities, I suggest consideration of the following:

a) The present Art Galleries and Museums Committee to be renamed the 'Arts Committee' to administer civic enterprises in the three Fine Arts – Music, Drama and Painting (including sculpture).

b) The Arts Committee to operate through three sub-committees, Music, Drama and Art, with co-opted members selected by the Corporation or recommended by representative associations, or both.

The cost would not amount to more than 2d–2½d on the rates.

If some such scheme were evolved Glasgow would gain much credit for giving a lead to other cities.

This must have leaked out. It may only have been a coincidence, but in the course of a very friendly recorded interview in the *Scottish Field* the brilliant and disarming Peggy Phillips said I wanted to abolish the Art Gallery Committee. Explanations followed quickly and I continued to live.

In more memoranda I had this:

a) For a long time it has been recognised that a new art gallery is essential for proper and complete development. The present building to be adapted as a museum with modern display methods.

b) A Museum devoted to Shipbuilding and Engineering is long overdue and should be included in any future programmes.

c) The City should acquire the historic Royal Exchange Building to be used as a Museum devoted to the History of Glasgow (I had mentioned this before, adding that provision should be made for down-town exhibitions and lunch-hour music or tours).

d) The development of methods in Further Education cannot be disassociated from this department. We have the material – all that is necessary is to make the best use of it, not forgetting broadcasting.

On another occasion I advocated the taking over by the Gallery and Museum Department of (a) the care and maintenance of sculpture throughout the City, and (b) the care and maintenance of historic churchyards, e.g. Ramshorn Church with particular reference to tombstones of celebrated citizens such as the Foulis brothers.

On more general lines I spread myself thus:

I think attention should be paid to the inadequacy of opportunities for recreation and refreshment in the evening for many of our young people. The Art Gallery is full every Sunday afternoon and could be the same in the evening – but the tearoom facilities are non-existent. I hope it will be possible to find a solution for this very real problem, but as it perhaps touches upon the interest of the Parks Committee, joint conferences would be advisable. For example, Kelvingrove Park. I would advocate the erection of a building which could be made chiefly of glass on the banks of the Kelvin with a promenade terrace, good cafeteria arrangements and a hall which could be used either for dancing or concerts. This cafeteria would serve as an evening tearoom for the Art Galleries where, owing to difficulties such as smoking, it would be impossible to organise much in the way of facilities for light refreshment.

Encouraged to continue with these 'day-dreams', I began to have visions of a Glasgow which would show the rest of the world what could be done in giving prominence to the 'place of the Arts in the life of the Community'. I was brought down to earth to discuss practical issues and had to point out the importance of the right kind of staff. We were lacking in qualified people. At the time we had two vacancies but the salary scale was not high enough to attract first-class men of experience and maybe too high for trainees (the National Galleries and Museums invariably got the pick).

Against my own interests, as subsequent events were to prove, I advocated the desirability of dividing my post into two – a Museum Director and an Art Gallery Director. I put it this way. This is common to all large cities, but with this difference – that generally there are separate buildings. Separate buildings must be a part of future planning, but even today a greater degree of efficiency, especially on the Museum side, might flow from an adjustment in senior positions. It seemed a good time to consider the question, for John Fleming the Depute Director was on the point of retiral.

There was no doubt about the encouragement to expand one's views. If hope is a habit-forming drug I was one of the sure victims. In the subsequent malaise when so little was realised one was tempted to search for those who were to blame for the failure. In the long run I suppose it had to come back on myself.

In addition to the Convener, quite a few, on both sides of the House, were prepared to listen to the short and long term policies I thought would be in the public interest. Sensing some doubt on the Museum Director idea I argued that now was the time to begin something which might not be concluded for quite a long time. The Burrell Collection was one big future undertaking. Here was another one. I visualised that one of the chief tasks of a new Director of Museum would be to create interest among industrialists, engineers and shipbuilders leading to the founding of a museum devoted to shipbuilding and engineering, a serious omission in the Glasgow museum service. I had seen in Stockholm and Detroit similar schemes in full and successful operation. And Clydeside was internationally known in this field. Perhaps a preliminary step would be to convene a conference and to try and get things going. A reference to civic history produced ample evidence of private citizens as the first promoters of services which later became public property. Well, that one has not yet been started.

I then returned to an old story. Frequently, letters in the press or questions following lectures would ventilate again the hours of admission to art galleries. This applied throughout the country. It would be said, 'How can the average citizen get a chance to enjoy the things he is supposed to enjoy when he has to be at work all day?' Most galleries close at five in the evening. On Sundays the 'rabble' makes it impossible for one to enjoy art, or the works of man in other directions, in comfort and silence. In staff conferences, beginning shortly after my arrival, I raised the issue over and over again. 'Why should pictorial art close the door when music and drama go on till all hours?' I asked. I was told that evening openings had been tried often without any response from the public. We tried again and it was a flop. It then occurred to me that music and drama don't merely open the door, they put on a performance. Our performance was to organise group visits in the evenings. The experiment proved a success and fully justified development in a big way.

I commented on it in the course of a farewell memorandum in this way:

'I am convinced that the future of Art Gallery and Museum activities must include regular evening work. Staff must be prepared to adapt themselves to the idea (as in libraries, theatres, concerts, etc).'

Although the committee approved and encouraged the idea, the Corporation did not see its way to lend support to it.

We had been ticking over with the group visit scheme, and the potential was great if an adequate trained staff were provided, and it did not mean a large staff. The special evening group visits were conducted by the curators with help from attendants all on a voluntary basis. Attendants were paid overtime. I suggested to the various departmental heads the option of equivalent time off or a fee. Arguing that the evenings were in the nature of a conducted tour with no preparation involved, as in lectures, I might persuade the Committee to allow £2.2.0 for this evening work. (Generally in the Education Department's 'Further Education' series of classes the fee then was £3.10.0 for work by people with similar qualifications.) My Committee agreed, but as the proposal involved money it had to go to the Finance Committee. They reduced it to £1.11.6d! I remember being in the corridor as the members poured out of the Finance Meeting on their way to the buffet. One of them said, 'Sorry, Doc, but you know we have to protect the ratepayers, and you guys make enough anyway.' The treatment, not the money, nearly wrecked the scheme at the outset. However we got it going, and I know most of us enjoyed our evenings and did not grudge a moment of the time spent.

Another memorandum which in spite of much encouragement from Convener and Committee led to nothing was prepared in the hope of getting a new post created – a publicity officer. Once again it was not a very original idea. I had seen it elsewhere and it altogether conformed with contemporary practice. We wanted the citizens and visitors to come in. As publicists we were amateurs – very good amateurs, but this side of the work was expanding beyond the capacity of the existing staff. To help the Convener to put it across I prepared this:

PUBLICITY OFFICER

General charge of advertising – press releases (communicating to press and public) news items on significant acquisitions and special features of our work.

Preparation and layout of catalogues, posters, etc. associated with exhibitions and special events.

Organising group visits for tours and evening visits.

Preparation of material for broadcasting, and especially planning television programmes in the future.

Charge of Art Gallery and Museum Association membership drive – arranging meetings, publicising lectures and educational courses.

Generally improve quality of all publications and develop same along popular lines.

Create and maintain contacts with all manner of societies, associations, clubs and the general public in order to make the work of the department more effective.

Demonstrate initiative and supply ideas which will make the citizens of Glasgow and visitors to the City more fully aware of the Art Gallery and Museum and the opportunities provided for the enjoyment of works of art and museum objects.

This was cordially received and remitted to a sub-committee for study and report. Unanimously approved and later confirmed by the full committee, but killed stone dead by the party bosses, who were not interested in examining the pros and cons of the issue. Just another 'one of those things'.

There were more memoranda after this. Most of them on demand, I once had a dream about them. I saw them being pulled out of pigeon-holes, torn up into small confetti-like pieces to be scattered over my head as I rushed down the gallery steps like the fellow escaping from the Picasso Show.

A postscript is needed to pull one down to earth again. I have had a short correspondence with the present City Treasurer (December 1970). It began in what I thought was a good-natured criticism of the Corporation's ineptitude in dealing with a Charles Rennie Mackintosh tea-room. I must have upset the man. In the course of his reply he says, '*God knows you have left us plenty of problems to solve. You gave plenty of advice for which we paid pretty heavily.*'

Repeated efforts to have this explained have failed to bring any result. A prominent city councillor, friendly to us both, well informed on my fifteen years' service, proffers the view 'He can only be thinking of the Burrell Collection.' It was certainly my pleasure and privilege to advise its acceptance; but the subsequent problems are entirely the creation of the Corporation.

From Hippocrates, the Father of Medicine, we got 'Life is short, Art is long.' It was Walt Whitman who reminded us that 'Audacity is never-ending.'

16

Failure of a Mission

Whatever may be the cumulative effect of the complaints registered in the foregoing pages, nothing must hinder me from the final attempt to make one thing clear. I enjoyed the fifteen years at the head of affairs in the Glasgow Art Gallery. I consider myself fortunate in having been given the chance to show that a Municipal Art Gallery and Museum, when allowed to function fully, can play an important part in the general life of the city. The possibilities are by no means exhausted and if those with power and authority could become so inclined, they will find an abundance of successful efforts elsewhere to prove the case.

I like living in Glasgow. I know it has squandered much of its great inheritance. It is, at present, badly governed, and it is the worst publicised city in the kingdom. But in no other place have I found more love, more tolerance, more wit, more brilliance, more mediocrity, more encouragement, more frustration, more sympathy, more envy, more big men in small jobs and more small men in big jobs. There may be places where the women are more lovely, but none where beauty and charm are found so often together. Whatever its present shortcomings as a city, Glasgow has always been hospitable. Many a stranger within its gates has put the virtue on record.

It may well be that our sense of humour, in taking on a national bias towards the macabre, gets mixed up with our feeble sense of publicity. How else can one explain the apparent reluctance to forget the sordid patches in our history – 'The Massacre of Glencoe' and 'Murder in the Gorbals'?

I suppose I must have been taught to count my blessings. Chief among these was the extent of the support I was able to win from the Gallery and Museum staff. I liked them and most of them liked me. Sometimes they exercised their privilege in concluding occasionally that I was a bit off the beam. Some of our innovations led a few to think I could get away with anything. This mostly applied to the old timers who pretended to be aghast at innovations which ran contrary to Corporation procedure or practice. I am certain that, on the whole, and over the fifteen years, we were a happy group of people. Our spasms of discontent were more the result of conditions beyond our control.

Why then am I left with this sense of failure? This grew out of the circumstances surrounding my departure and the changes thereafter made by the Corporation in the conduct of the department.

I had no doubts about the mission idea: 'To put Glasgow back on the map of the Art World.' The shortcomings and incoherencies of a missionary do not invalidate the importance of the mission. Before my appointment the attitude was clearly 'Let's find someone who will shake this place up – the Art Collection is said to be famous and a prominent attraction for our visitors. So, let's make it an "Art Man".' As already noted, the search, via the usual forms of advertisement, attracted some very highly capable men. I was lucky. Unfortunately I also appear to have been responsible for the change in outlook fifteen years later. In an effort to raise the status of the Museum side – and how I fought for it – I took the wrong turning.

Every now and then the public is treated by the Press to reports of the stupidity of city councillors, aldermen and magistrates in matters appertaining to the Arts – how they have refused masterpieces and obstructed progressive ideas and so on. I have often been in at the end of discussions to hear the summing up 'It would have been a fine purchase – it was a good idea but we couldn't get it through the committee.'

 I go back to 1939 again, because I have just come across a letter from O. H. Mavor (James Bridie). He wrote me in reply to a very tentative question 'What would you think if I applied for the Art Gallery job in Glasgow?' 'I am rather anti. A good curator is very desirable and I know you would be that. The things you have to fight amount up to a fair sum. There is the COMMITTEE. You have been a sort of freelance all your life and I don't think you know what it is to serve a public body.' He went on, 'If you see a straight road for God's sake pay no attention to advice.'

Bridie was often upset by the lack of critical support his plays received in Glasgow, his native city, compared to London. (This was particularly evident when *Daphne Laureola*, after a year's run in London, had a very bad press in Glasgow.) I tried to comfort him.

'I thought you would know. In Edinburgh critical assessment stems from the basic principle "If you are on my side I am on yours." In Glasgow it is "Him? He can't be any good. I knew his father".'

In 1937, in the foreword to my first attempt to write a book on art, I indulged in a gentle criticism of some of the leading London art critics. This led to several happy conversations with Mr Frank Rutter, who was then critic for *The Sunday Times*. He told me of his five years as Curator of the Leeds City Art Gallery and directed me to read what he had to say about it in his autobiographical book *Since I was Twenty-five*. It was written in 1927.

> 'Of the Leeds City Council I find it most difficult to speak in parliamentary language. Never before had I come into contact with the kind of men who became councillors and aldermen, and – with remarkably few exceptions – I was appalled by their grossness, their ignorance and general lack of manners.'

My experience was quite contrary to Rutter's and Bridie's. The committee bogey never showed itself. The system of appointing conveners and members of the Art Gallery Committee seems to be the same in most city councils. The heads of the leading group confer together and select the man or woman who is to be Convener for a three year period. Often he or she may have had a spell as deputy. Each of the groups then puts up the members according to the respective strength of the parties. A few of those proposed are reluctant. They would prefer to be on more important committees. If they are new to the council they have to learn to do what they are told. If they are old hands a little bit of wangling can produce the required adjustments.

The 'Notable Exception' reference conveners was the last. He proved too much for me and my doctor. When he was appointed – mark you he did not appoint himself – he proudly informed the Council Officer, Tom Wilson, and some others, 'I am now in charge of the F * * * g Culture.' (I know we live in a permissive society but I still cling to asterisks if I have to deal in 'four letter words'.) He did his best to adhere to his brief 'Keep that "B" Honeyman in his place. He thinks he owns the Art Gallery.' A small man, he had a way of shooting his head forward when making a point. In repose he had the disconcerting habit of over-exposing his upper dentures while his tongue rolled round in search of the debris from his previous meal.

This bright specimen was not the reason why I decided to give up.

In a sense he was the last straw. He considered it his duty to interfere in the running of the department as no other convener had ever dreamed of doing. One result was the destruction of loyalties. Some of our young ladies spoke of him as 'Stinker' and I had to rebuke Bill Macaulay, Curator of Art, for daring to say to the convener 'Do it yourself – I am not your lackey'.

The only thing we appeared to have in common was a mutual dislike stretching towards contempt. He seemed to think the Art Gallery bunch were too superior, and increasingly leaned towards the Museum side.

Sir Patrick Dollan, no longer a member of the corporation, appeared to be the only one of my old friends to have an inkling on the situation. He said, 'You are a good fighter. You must stand up to this. It will pass.' It was not so easy as it sounds. There is, for example, the occasion when I put up a fine Renoir Bronze for consideration by the committee – it was my final art purchase recommendation. I had arranged a special price for the gallery of £675. The convener, whom I had previously consulted, as was the custom, offered no objections. At the meeting he described it as an expensive piece of old iron and moved that it be not purchased . . . 'Just to test the feeling of the meeting'. Let it be said that he did not find a seconder. (Another copy of the same sculpture was recently sold (July 1970) for £6,000.)

On matters of acquisition the committee had full powers within the range of available funds. The differences between men of high and low intellect, slow and quick wit, are easily spotted at a committee meeting. What is not so evident is that the real power is in the hands of a few people who are not present, the leaders of the party. I had clearly lost their support. Probably for them there were other things more important than the Art Gallery.

So it came about that on one man's initiative, the whole structure was changed. Even the name of the Committee was altered to Museums and Art Galleries, whereas it had been the other way round for years. The decision to separate the Art Gallery from Museums arrived at six years previously was rescinded. The Director of Museums became the chief official with a deputy-director, further designated as 'in charge of Art'. Both posts were filled by members of the staff, who had originally been appointed some years before I arrived in 1939. The return to the *status quo* was therefore complete. I was to hear the senior magistrate, defending the Corporation's position at a public dinner, say that the changes were made on the advice of the Town Clerk.

I had given almost a year's notice of my decision to retire and offered, several times, any assistance by way of introducing my successor. The only response was silence. Evidently they preferred to wait until I had gone. When the changes were made public I thought 'People will say it is no longer my business. But surely there is a duty to protest if one is persuaded an error is being made. So: Let them say!'

Lord Provost, Tom Kerr, sought me out and expressed views similar to my own, in conformity with what he had said fifteen years previously. He advised me to write to the secretary of the majority group (Labour) asking for a meeting at which I might be allowed to present a case for maintaining a further trial of the developments proposed by me and accepted by them some years ago. A curt refusal was the reply. Subsequently, when the new regime was under way, several councillors thought a backward step had been taken. Three of them became Members of Parliament, but no one, irrespective of party, cared enough to do anything about it.

Why were the changes made? Anybody's guess is as good as mine. Why did they not continue with an Art Director, searching for the best man they could find? One who would develop the good things started and abandon those which were ill-conceived and had failed. Even the word Museum belongs to the nineteenth century. While retaining the name Art Gallery the department is once again museum-minded – no doubt very well conducted, expanding with an excellent Transport Museum which, one day, may expand still further by including ship-building and engineering.

Following the efforts to re-establish a Museum image, the status of the Art side has been lowered. This is the view of a number of people who are confused, not to say amused, at the policy of plugging the Museum. It is difficult to make the citizens of Glasgow drop the habit of describing the Kelvingrove building as The Art Gallery. But in various forms of publicity, telephone responses, correspondence etc., it can be insisted that Museum comes first. The most recent example to come to my notice was the cover of a Penguin Modern Classic. It caught my eye on a bookstall. Recognised immediately as an old friend was the painting *Froanna* by Wyndham Lewis (the book was *Crome Yellow* by Aldous Huxley). The Art Gallery had purchased this in 1940 for £100 on my strong recommendation. On the back page the acknowledgment says the original is in the *Museum* & Art Gallery, Glasgow. What does it matter? What's in a name?

It might matter a good deal. An art gallery is not the same as a museum. In small towns, for obvious economic reasons, they have to be accommodated in one building. In the overwhelming majority of cities I have visited they are regarded as separate entities. I need not list them. Anyone who is interested enough and who has travelled, with a visit to either art galleries or museums as a must, can confirm this.

In Britain we have a Museums' Association. I became a member some years before I came back to Glasgow. It goes from strength to strength and I have watched with interest and pleasure the development of the quarterly Journal. I think it was Philip James (ex Arts Council) who gave the magazine its first new look. Given somewhat to mutual back-scratching at the top level, the Association is an essential enterprise in the Museum world, and I am honoured in having been elected a Fellow. The Annual Conferences serve a useful function in bringing together like-minded officials and delegates. They scared me stiff. I was afraid I might become conference-minded to the neglect of duties at home. In my time there seemed to be too many chiefs and not enough of the up and coming men of the future. It may well all be different now, but I still think it is primarily a museum outfit. For instance, the first recommendation of a working party on Museums in Education reads thus: 'That the museum profession recognises that museum services are fundamentally educational in function'. That is not the function of an art gallery and never has been. The difference between 'Art through Education' and 'Education through Art' is not really so subtle as might, at first glance, appear. Apart from polemics there is the evidence of a great number of art magazines throughout the world devoted to the interests of scholars, collectors and the general public – without anything comparable, known to me, covering the varied aspects of museum contents. There are, of course, special publications such as *The Museums Journal*, but not directed towards the non-specialist members of the public.

A final observation may help to avoid the risk of my being dismissed as a man with an obsession. If it is true that every serious student of French Painting, Tapestries, Medieval Glass, Arms and Armour, Oriental Pottery, Silver, Sculpture (and other sections of the Burrell Collection), Victorian Architecture and the beginning of Modern Architecture, the works of Whistler and of the Glasgow School, must spend some time in the city, then we are an Art Centre. And we have no Director of Art.

We have, at last, a Professor of Fine Art at the University where they have some notable works of art. They are on the point of building a new Art Gallery. History may be repeating itself. Two hundred years ago the University was the sole centre of art activity in this city. Later, and right up to the early part of this century the Municipality, the Art School, the Art Institute and the Art Club all exercised a stronger influence. They have lost it.

The heat generated when the winds of change blew on me has cooled off and it is possible to look back dispassionately. What I write now is not to express anger or resentment. From time to time, when I have seen some of the things done or not done I have suffered from both. But bitterness is never a good constant companion. Consequently, when I criticise what was done – and I am still convinced it was a retrograde move – I am not directing my shafts against individuals. Moreover, there are two sides to this kind of question, even if my side is the right one!

I must not conceal that there were other considerations which had led me to think it was time to go. Two spells in hospital – a plastic operation on an eyelid and a puzzling 'slipped disc' infirmity – plus the upsets engendered by frustrations were causing some domestic anxiety. Our doctor advised me to get out. To my plea that in another two years I would have to go anyhow – the age of statutory senility – but I might qualify for a small pension, I got the reply, 'Get out, or you won't be here to collect it.'

I was beginning to be anxious about our financial situation. My fifteen years had resulted in very much depleted resources. The very inadequate salary was insufficient to maintain our standards and these have always been modest. It was time for me to think about augmenting our income sufficiently to provide for retirement.

Most important of all was the conviction that fifteen years is quite long enough for anyone to be in command of a municipal enterprise devoted to the Arts. It must never be a static affair. The necessary dynamic calls for the introduction of new ideas and a fresh outlook at reasonable intervals.

Actually I was on my back in the Western Infirmary, with plenty of time to indulge in ruminations of this nature. I was, at the same

time, a candidate in the University Rectorial election. The excitement prevented me from indulging too much in morbid introspec-
tion. A group of nurses, the sweetest and most charming any infirm
patient could wish for, became my campaign managers. When the
medical students were attending their various clinics these bright
lasses invaded the cloakrooms and plastered hat-bands and the collars
of overcoats with adhesive tapes carrying a threat 'Vote for
Honeyman or I'll melt you'. To the delight and to the great surprise
of some of my friends and me, I was elected by an emphatic majority.
I continue to treasure the congratulation and good wishes of two of
my distinguished opponents, Lord Bilsland and John Bannerman (he
became Lord Bannerman and died – too soon – two years ago). For
both of these great Scotsmen I have sustained throughout the years a
high respect and affection.

I was still flat on my back when my jubilant sponsors and
supporters invaded my hospital room. Have you ever made a speech
of thanks from such a lowly position? Try it.

In a concluding attempt to arrive at a differential diagnosis of the
malaise afflicting Glasgow we must recognise that to ignore what is
happening now can be as lamentable as forgetting what has been
achieved in the past. Penetrating or awkward questions cannot be
brushed aside by smooth postponing platitudes. An Art Gallery is,
in Glasgow, only a small part of Corporation business but it is part
of running a city.

Who really runs a city? Is not the answer to this question 'The
Permanent Official'? It is becoming increasingly recognised, especially in the USA and Canada, that to manage a city's affairs has
become a highly skilled profession, demanding the same degree of
business talent as that required to conduct a big industrial or
commercial concern. Modern life is becoming more and more
urbanised. The institutions to be directed are expanding faster than
others in our time – in spending of money – in numbers employed –
and in dealing with day to day problems. Can the problems be
solved by operating in the same old ways? For instance, the relations
of the City and the State have become an increasing point of friction.

The management problem is obviously both technical and political.
And to smooth out the bureaucratic confusions is a very hard and
difficult task. We have had, in Scotland, the Wheatley report –
following thorough investigation of the present set-up in Local
Government areas – with recommendations of a heroic character.

I am not qualified, by experience or study, to comment on these. I am merely aware that somebody thought something needed looking into, and I am concerned with the evidence of bad government by inefficient people. Have we not too many holding important positions in National, Civic, Academic and Industrial spheres, whose chief qualification would seem to be an ability to conceal or ignore their own incompetence?

The year before I retired the Corporation brought in an expert on management. I understood his job was to investigate, in every department, administration methods and conditions of service. He was first of all confronted with a good deal of suspicion and resentment. At the meeting of chief officials at which the purpose and procedure were explained, I extended a welcome on behalf of my relatively small department. Indeed, I hoped he would start with us. We were always eager to improve our administration. I never saw him again. Evidently we were well down on the list. When he got to the Art Gallery I had gone; but I was still around, nursing a knowledge of gallery and museum work at home and abroad, which no one in Glasgow possessed. He may have been warned off. The expert in question is now a permanent official and yet there is now a fresh agitation directed towards bringing in a firm of business consultants to help the city become more business-like in the conduct of its affairs.

A week before I sailed a fresh 'scandal' had blown up over a £3,000,000 excess on the estimates of a housing scheme. Then in a bunch of cuttings posted to me I came across this paragraph under the heading 'Indictment':

'The investigating committee have produced a document which is a damning indictment of the slovenly procedure which is characteristic of many aspects of the city's administration in other departments as well as housing. Of the seven recommendations presented in the conclusions only two are solely concerned with the remit to the housing committee and the remainder are concerned with the general procedure of the corporation.'

I do not know whether we should have an Executive Director or a General Manager, but I do know that in all my fifteen years I was never once called to a meeting of the heads of municipal departments, where the civic problems and the welfare of the citizens might be discussed at *our level of interest and authority*. One does not conduct a big business in that fashion.

I do not know all the answers but I believe somehow, by action, not by postponement, we could get better value for the money extracted from us. Town planning, road and bridge-building are all very well, but it needs more than that to make a city into a place one chooses and enjoys to live in. A city cannot be great if it only functions during the day. It would run the risk of being dismissed as a collection of buildings and streets. The Arts, operating in and out of our homes, help to add vitality.

One other barrier should be removed. It is the passion for secrecy when important issues (so-called and by whom?) are under consideration. We ought to remind ourselves that a secret is not something unknown. It is only something not freely discussed in public. Why should we always be overawed into silence by someone, usually whispering through the corner of his mouth, 'It's confidential'. 'Take the public into your confidence' is among the best pieces of advice I have ever received.

I was reminded, not long ago, that it was the utter absence of secrecy as much as any other factor which made the first Moon-walk possible in 1969. And here is what Professor Robert Oppenheimer said when accused by Congressmen of being indiscreet about aspects of atomic power which were supposed to be secret.

'We do not believe any group of men is adequate enough or wise enough to operate without scrutiny or without criticism. We know that the only way to avoid error is to detect it and the only way to detect it is to be free to inquire. We know that in secrecy error undetected will flourish and subvert.'

In matters less important to the world, but very important to our immediate circle, we suffer too often from veils of secrecy. Behind them mediocrity, stupidity, incompetence and injustice are allowed to persist.

Might this not be one explanation of the fantastic and disgraceful delays in getting on with so many essential projects awaiting completion? Some are not even started. They tell us we are now an awakening city. We are destroying our slums and changing the face of our Victorian inheritance. If it be the case that we are getting on our feet, for Heaven's sake let's stay standing up.

This ship is again in the North Atlantic, homeward bound. A friendly whale has been keeping us company in a sea becoming a little rough. It reminds me of something. I know I bought a round-trip ticket to Vancouver, and had no intention of going to Tarshish.

I know, too, that a prophet ought to have a beard and that when it comes down to audacity he has no equals. He deals in the future and none can say he is wrong. Will you therefore listen to a bare-faced prophet tell you what is going to come about in due course?

Having got rid of its ill-informed and ill-equipped experts and busybodies and the risk of turning the Burrell Collection and other comparable gifts into a herd of white elephants, Glasgow will have, on the south side, an incomparable Art and Recreational centre sited in Pollok Estate and Rouken Glen. The responsible trustees will give effect to the spirit of Sir William Burrell's conditions and in the new gallery and in Pollok House there will be an abundance of riches for the art lover and scholar, and a magnetic attraction for Glaswegians and their visitors. In the west there will be the finest University auditorium in Britain, acoustically perfect and adapted for multiple purposes such as can be seen in places as far separate as Hamburg and Portland (Oregon). More costly mistakes will be made; but the cultural centre complex will disappear in a flood of enlightenment. It will be discovered that no progressive city puts all its culture eggs into one basket. There is yet time.

In the centre of the city there will rise a magnificent Concert Hall with all the complementary facilities for the comfort of musicians and audiences. On the banks of the Clyde – reclaimed from the hands of the philistines and vandals – a new civic theatre will be built and it shall be named the James Bridie Memorial Theatre. The Mitchell Library, having acquired the distinction of being able to be seen, will have the much needed extension and continue increasingly to play a prominent part in extra-mural research and enlightenment. All the lands west of a new Charing Cross will again be reclaimed for community purposes.

Out of the picture stores of the Art Gallery at Kelvingrove will come the hidden treasures, to see again the light of day in a new building, fit to be described as the best in modern architecture and containing all that is necessary to bring together the spectator and works of art in an atmosphere of relaxed enjoyment. The city will become internationally known as the Convention City *par excellence*, offering a way of living with a controlled design and with the full and rewarding use of leisure as an outstanding element.

It will take longer, but the day will come when the Cathedral will cease to be overwhelmed by the sick and the dead; when the Royal Infirmary will be moved out east, and the great tumulus of the

Necropolis will be reclaimed for recreation, rest and contemplation. With Glasgow's oldest surviving house (Provand's Lordship) safe on its island site, the cathedral and its precincts will help us to renew the hope reflected in St Mungo's prayer, out of which came our civic motto: '*Let Glasgow Flourish* by the preaching of Thy Word and the praising of Thy Name.' And the statue of missionary David Livingstone will remain as the token of a loud Amen.

When these things come to pass more will be added thereunto. Once again they will say, 'Look what is happening in Glasgow'. If this particular prophecy is delayed in fulfilment, it will mean that our old men have ceased to dream dreams and our young men no longer see visions.

Throughout the land, town and country planners and 'developers' will be asking themselves, 'What about the people?' Roads exist and keep on existing in an atmosphere of pollution – more or less. Living people are often already dead. In ten years' time, architecturally speaking there will be new cities imposed upon the old; but the citizens will ask themselves more often, 'Are we on the right road?' There will be direction in this; a kind of direction which will appear to flow over the edges of common sense, because a new generation will disown theoretical justification if it cannot be squared with a revived faith in democracy. Alas! There will still remain a section of the inhabitants of these islands too stupid to understand.

Every prophet knows that faith is the substance of things hoped for. One fine day the men and women coming out of our universities, decorated with cap, hood and gown, will be marked as persons of taste and of reliable judgment. Then we will have forgotten that up till now they have not been educated enough to find their way in contemporary literature, painting and music.

The Committee for Export of Works of Art will disappear and free trade in the works of man will be restored. The British Council, too, will be no more. Continuity in the functions it has tried to fulfil will be maintained by our Consular and Diplomatic services. The Government will realise that Tourism is a great competitive industry and that the best way to sell the 'British Way of Life' is to bring the customers into the shop. What does it matter if a few of them sneak in to have a look at the back shop?

The Arts Council will continue to flourish as the distributing channel for state patronage of the arts. It will have discovered the need to go out into the lesser places, leaving the larger centres to live up to their promises. And it will concentrate on the idea of quality in the spectator or auditor having an importance *nearly* comparable to quality in what is put before him to see and hear. It, or some other state organisation, will dig out the private patron without whom the creative artist cannot expand and flourish. And it will make it easy for both of them to become public spirited.

The selected few whose duty or privilege it is to break down the barriers of prejudice and ignorance on the lines of communication will have discovered that it is futile to assume a knowledge of Art History and Achievement which the audiences, whatever the media, do not possess.

Research will continue. An attempt will be made to find out why the two greatest British artists are sculptors – Henry Moore and Barbara Hepworth. They came out of Yorkshire and were trained at the Leeds School of Art. Who can explain it?

I have just remembered that this business of patronage of the arts is an old, old story. Two hundred years ago Robert Burns wrote a prologue for a benefit night in the theatre at Dumfries. Here is a bit of it:

> '. . . if a' the land
> Would take the Muses servants by the hand,
> Not only hear, but patronise, befriend them;
> And where ye justly can commend, commend them;
> And aiblins* when they winna stand the test,
> Wink hard and say the folks hae done their best!'

All that having been said, I am going ashore – down a gangway. I hope you have got some entertainment out of this weird voyage.

*maybe

L'Envoi

There is a story told of a doctor in a remote parish in the west of Scotland. He was celebrated more for his common-sense than for his academic attainments. To him came his patient, Donald. 'Doctor, can you do something for me? I am getting terribly deaf – awful hard of hearing.' 'Well, let's see now,' said the doctor. 'How old are you, Donald?' 'I'll be eighty-nine this year,' was the reply. 'Ach, my dear man, do you not think, maybe, you have heard enough?'

I have to tell you that I have not told the whole of my story. Sometimes the best way to arrive at a sound estimate of a man's worth is to find out about his grandmother, his mother, his wife and, if he has been so blessed, his daughter – that is, the prominent persons among his women-folk. I have scarcely mentioned them.

Actually this particular volume is a gift to my wife, by way of marking the 50th anniversary of our marriage – our Golden Wedding. And I think it is a very good excuse.

On the slightest evidence of anyone being interested in my adventures in Medicine, in Art Dealing and in my post-Glasgow Art Gallery way of living, back to my grandmother and forward to my lovely grandchildren, I shall embark immediately on another voyage to sea.

Index